Understanding Nonprofit Finances

Grantwriting Beyond the Basics

BOOK 2:

Understanding Nonprofit Finances

by Michael K. Wells, CFRE

Portland State University
Extended Studies
Continuing Education Press
Portland, Oregon

Michael K. Wells is a partner in Grants Northwest and has been consulting since 1987. He has worked with dozens of nonprofit organizations, health clinics, Native American tribes, and local governments and has helped them to raise over $50 million. He is a Certified Fund Raising Executive (CFRE) and teaches grantwriting at Portland State University. Michael is editor of the CharityChannel online *Grants and Foundation Review* and a board member of the Grant Professionals Certification Institute.

Grantwriting Beyond the Basics, Book 2,
Understanding Nonprofit Finances, 2006

ISBN 0-87678-119-9 (softcover)

Printed and bound in the United States of America
12 11 10 09 08 07 06   1 2 3 4 5 6 7 8

Continuing Education Press, Portland State University

Library of Congress Cataloging-in-Publication Data

Wells, Michael K., 1943-
      Grantwriting beyond the basics / by Michael K. Wells.—1st ed.
          p. cm.
      Includes index.
      ISBN 0-87678-119-9 (alk. paper)
      1. Fund raising.   2. Proposal writing for grants.   3. Nonprofit organizations—
Finance.   I. Title.
      HG177.W45 2005
      658.15'224—dc22

                                                        2004029303

Copies available from:
Portland State University
School of Extended Studies
Continuing Education Press
PO Box 1394
Portland, OR 97207-1394
P: 866-647-7377
F: 503-725-4840
www.cep.pdx.edu

Every effort has been made to provide current website information. All website URLs were current and correct at the time of publication. Due to the nature of the World Wide Web, URLs may change at any time and some pages may no longer be available. If a link no longer works, try using the basic URL address or do a web search for the agency name.

Printed on acid-free paper.

Contents

Illustrations

Foreword

When my colleague and longtime friend Michael Wells first approached me about writing the foreword for his new book on nonprofit finances for grant professionals, my first reaction, was: Thank God someone's taking this topic on—and double-thank God it's someone with Michael's vision, passion, deep experience, and good old common sense.

When many of us think about nonprofit finances and the myriad of issues, rules, regulations, pitfalls, and caveats they involve, often what pops up seems to be one of two images:

- A tangled, trackless and impenetrable jungle riddled with hidden tripwires and landmines just waiting to explode at the least little bump or misstep

or, alternately,

- One of those ancient, hand-drawn mariners' maps that depict a vast sea with all known land masses sketched in, leading (should one be foolhardy enough to venture so far) to The Edge Of The World and the stern and frightening calligraphic caution: "Traveler beware: Here there be Monsters. . . ."

I know. Because once upon a time, these were the kinds of unconfessed but very present inner images I tended to hold—of organizational finance in general and of nonprofit finances in particular. Even my B.S. in business administration, with all the attendant coursework in accounting, financial planning, etc. (*and* a 4.0 GPA and *summa cum laude* status, no less) did not dispel my queasiness about venturing into what seemed to my right-brained self the nonsensical and impossibly arcane wilderness of organizational finance. To be blunt, financial stuff made me feel stupid. I don't like things that make me feel stupid. And when I don't like something, naturally I tend to react by staring it down, running away from it, or—in this case—trying to pretend it doesn't exist.

Fast-forward 25 years. I'm now a seasoned professional in the nonprofit world. I've worked with a jillion executive directors, board members, and staffers representing a jillion grant-funded nonprofits and community agencies. I've participated in half a jillion grant proposals, many for amounts in the millions of dollars. Not only that—I'm now a business owner, *responsible for understanding and managing the finances of my own growing organization.* I can't afford to be intimidated or put off by the language and logic of effective financial management.

And neither can you.

I'm not a stupid person—numbers stuff just makes me feel that way sometimes. By necessity, I've been dragged kicking and screaming into the world of line-item budgets, indirect cost ratios, generally accepted accounting principles, and OMB Circulars. (Don't have a clue what I'm talking about? Don't worry—Michael will explain.) I may not (like some people I know) actually *enjoy* the tasks and processes good financial management involves, but I certainly respect the critical roles that competency and clarity around financial issues play in the health and well-being of any organization. I can certainly coach nonprofit leaders through their own financial fears. And I also know that, no, the ability to manage finances effectively isn't the result of some quirky genetic mutation or a shamanic spirit ceremony or the right configuration of planets and stars. It is, as is true of so many things in life, very much a matter of these three qualities:

- *Focused intention*—that is, a committed desire to understand and apply the principles and tools successfully

- *Confidence*—believing that you do have the capacity to do so

- *Common sense*—knowing that the same good-thinking skills that have helped you succeed in every other area of your life apply equally here.

There's another element to support your success in understanding and applying the principles and tools of organizational financial management— *skilled coaching*. You do need to place your faith in someone who knows the way already and can give you guidance. Michael Wells can be that someone, and this book can be your guide.

Have no fear. The waters ahead are not as murky as they may look from this side. And I know of no one better qualified to steer you through them than Michael. His straightforward language, clearly organized step-by-step guides, and real-life examples will keep you on a steady course. Michael is, to my mind, the consummate grant professional—not only successful at doing the work himself, but also exceedingly gifted at sharing what he knows in a way that invites others into their own success.

Traveler, proceed with confidence: You're in good hands.

—*Maryn Boess*

Maryn is founder and president of GrantsUSA LLC, a state-by-state network of information tools and resources for America's grants community. She can be reached via e-mail at maryn.boess@grantsusa.net.

Introduction

This book, the second in the *Grantwriting Beyond the Basics* series, is intended to provide the grant professional with a solid understanding of the financial side of grants. The purpose of the series can be summed up by a wonderful fortune cookie I got last year, which said, "Don't just learn the tricks of the trade. Learn the trade." As grantwriting becomes a profession in its own right, those of us who practice it need to get beyond the tricks to understanding all of the field's aspects in more depth.

Peter F. Drucker, considered the founding father of the study of management and management consulting, said two things about the importance of nonprofit finances. The first was, "The 21st century will be the century of the social sector organization. The more economy, money, and information become global, the more community will matter. And only the social sector nonprofit organization performs in the community, exploits its opportunities, mobilizes its local resources, solves its problems." The second was, "Accounting has become the most intellectually challenging area in the field of management, and the most turbulent one." If Drucker is right (and he usually is), we stand at the crossroads of two major trends, and we had better understand them.

Understanding Nonprofit Finances is being written in a time of enormous regulatory change and increased scrutiny of nonprofits. The IRS (Internal Revenue Service), Congress, states, and the accounting profession are all looking closely at nonprofits. Although the specifics of what will happen are unknown, it seems clear that nonprofit finances will become more detailed and will be examined more intensely. This will require changes in practices in most nonprofits. For the grant professional, it will become more important to know that the organization's financial statements are in order, its tax-exempt status is current, and its budgets are realistic and accurate.

It seems obvious that grants are about money, but for some reason many grantwriters don't make the next logical step: To understand grants you must understand money—which is to say, finances and accounting. I think one reason is that most accounting books are written for the for-profit world and are designed to help you do accounting rather than understand it. There are some good books on nonprofit financial management, but they're written for people who have to run organizations, not for those of us who find funding.

Understanding Nonprofit Finances is designed to let you understand finances and accounting as a consumer rather than a practitioner. It won't show you how to do double-entry bookkeeping, or year-end trial balances and adjustments. Instead, this book will help you to develop better grant proposals, recognize hazards in maintaining your tax-exemption, design better project budgets, and talk knowledgeably to the financial people in your organization. I've tried hard to reach the right level of information—enough, but not too much.

I first became interested in accounting in the late 1970s when I was the manager of a community radio station. I had run a couple of alternative newspapers and a crafts store, so I thought I understood basic business finances. But when the station accountant came to work on our books with me, it was as if she were speaking Greek. So I signed up for an accounting class at the local university and discovered that this arcane and scary subject was not only understandable and useful, it was interesting. Over the intervening 25-plus years, I've taken several other accounting classes and unfailingly found them useful, not only in my business, but in my personal life as well.

When nonprofits get in trouble, their problems are usually financial, generally because their management doesn't understand finances and/or isn't paying attention to them. The most common financial problems are lack of internal controls (like having the same person both handle all the finances and sign the checks) and not paying payroll taxes because of cash flow problems. Although these are not the responsibility of the grantwriter, you certainly don't want to be developing grants for an organization that is going to have serious financial issues—either before the grant is awarded or while it's being implemented. This book should give you the tools to recognize financial problems, ask the right questions, and try to get those problems addressed.

Understanding Nonprofit Finances is aimed at grant professionals, but it can also be useful to others involved with nonprofit organizations, such as executive directors, board members, and development staff. My hope is that it will be immediately useful to your work and that it will inspire you to find out more about accounting and finances.

—*Michael Wells*
Portland, Oregon

Acknowledgements

Dedicated to my sweet wife Julie for supporting me in this and many other endeavors, and for making my life complete.

Acknowledgements:

- Jason Orme, CPA at Talbot, Korvola and Warwick, for the use of his annotated Form 990 and for reading this book in draft manuscript for accuracy. (Any mistakes are my own.)

- Kay Sohl, executive director of Technical Assistance for Community Services (TACS), for use of their models for evaluating grant costs, as well as for invaluable advice over many years.

- Grantmakers for Effective Organizations (GEO) for use of their Due Diligence Tool.

- Community Action Organization and Portland Baroque Orchestra for allowing me to study their budgets and financial statements as models. (Note: I created the numbers and made some format changes for the examples in this book.)

Also, thanks to:

- Alba Scholz, publishing manager at Portland State University Continuing Education Press, for making this all happen again.

- Hilary Russell (content editor) and Cher Paul (copyeditor, indexer) for giving this book form, making it readable, and forcing me to use correct grammar.

- Denise Brem (layout) and Michael Marshall (cover design) for making the book attractive and reader friendly.

Accounting Essentials | 1

About Accounting

Finances and accounting exist in their own world, with its own rules and language. Before you enter that world, you should read this section to get some basic knowledge about its assumptions and jargon. For now, you don't have to remember all of the details; just get an overview, and remember that it's here in the front of the book so you can refer to it when you need to.

There are two basic branches of accounting, financial accounting and management accounting.

- *Financial accounting* is historically oriented, operates under rigid rules, and is designed to prepare reports for external users (people outside of an organization).

- *Management accounting* is future-oriented using historical data, can be customized to the organization, and provides more detailed information for internal users (people inside an organization, like managers) to make good decisions.

Financial accounting is the subject of this book, because as grantwriters we're providing information for funders who are outside of our organizations. Whenever you see the term *accounting* in this book, it means financial accounting.

The root of the word *finance* refers to money. The root of the word *accounting* refers to counting. So financial accounting is about keeping track of money. The reason it has strict rules is that it provides information to people who don't have inside access to the organization, but must use information provided by insiders to make financial decisions from the outside. These people include stockholders and bankers in for-profit businesses, funders and donors in nonprofits, and the IRS in both cases. To provide them with trustworthy, consistent, and understandable information, a whole industry of auditors, standard-setting boards, and accountants has grown up.

1

Nonprofit Accounting

Nonprofit financial statements are more complex than for-profit ones. Commercial businesses require only a single set of statements, the terminology is standardized, and accounting principles are more clearly defined. Nonprofits have to deal with things like restricted funds that don't exist in the commercial world.

In 1993, the Financial Accounting Standards Board (FASB), which governs generally accepted accounting principles (GAAP), released two new Statements of Financial Accounting Standards that had strong impacts on nonprofit accounting: SFAS 117, Financial Statements for Nonprofit Organizations, significantly altered the way nonprofits issue financial statements. SFAS 116, Accounting for Contributions Received and Contributions Made, significantly altered how contributions are recorded. (Appendix C compares nonprofit accounting before and after these two statements, as well as three other FASB statements that affect nonprofits.) The impact of SFAS 116 and 117 was so extensive that nonprofits are still struggling with them today, more than ten years later. Nonprofit accountants have gotten used to them, but many nonprofit managers and development departments still don't understand them—if they even know they exist.

The Rules of the Game: Basic Principles of Accounting

Before we get too far into the details of accounting, there are a few concepts, principles, and assumptions that we have to understand and accept. Some of them seem self-evident, whereas others can look unnecessarily picky, but taken together, these concepts are what make accounting work and what make people willing to trust financial statements.

- **Entity Principle:** For accounting purposes, a business, government, or nonprofit is assumed to have its own existence separate from the people involved in it. Thus it is viewed as a separate financial entity (e.g., a corporation or limited liability partnership).

- **Monetary Principle:** The accounting system records only things that can be measured in terms of money. The intangible value of your staff's commitment and skill or your board's involvement and community connections aren't recognized because they can't be measured in financial terms.

- **Conservatism Principle:** Your accounting system must use the most conservative assumptions. It must recognize losses or expenses when they are anticipated, but defer the recognition of gains or profits until after they are realized.

- **Cost Concept:** The accounting value of an asset is based on what it cost when you bought it, not what you could sell it for today.

- **Going Concern Assumption:** For accounting purposes, it is assumed that an organization will stay in operation indefinitely, or at least long enough to carry out its current plans (generally, at least a year).

- **Consistency Principle:** The same kind of transaction must always be treated the same way, so that all of the organization's financial statements can be accurately compared.

- **Materiality Principle:** Accountants and auditors recognize that some transactions are so small that they don't affect an entity's overall financial picture; they aren't *material*. For example, a $10 mistake in a multimillion-dollar organization isn't worth reconciling.

- **Periodicity Concept:** An entity must report financial statements to external readers on a regular and timely basis, even though the business cycle isn't complete. This means that you have to produce financial statements at a set period, even if you have outstanding bills or anticipate income such as grants that you can't yet show in those statements.

- **Dual Aspect Concept:** The bedrock of accounting is double-entry bookkeeping: Every transaction is broken down into equal debit and credit amounts. For example, if you buy a building for $100,000 cash, your books reduce "cash" by $100,000 but increase fixed assets by the same amount. By definition, Assets = Liabilities + Net Assets. This formula is reflected in the Balance Sheet.

- **Realization and Matching Principles:** These two principles are the basis of *accrual accounting*. If you perform a service in April, you must show the revenue as earned (realized) in April, regardless of when you get paid. Likewise, expenses associated with generating revenue must be shown in the same time period as the revenue (matched). So what? Well, if you're having a really bad year, you might be tempted to push some expenses into next year to hide a deficit. Or if you're having a really good year, you might try to sneak some income into next year to persuade donors that you really need money, even though you made a bundle. Under the realization and matching principles, these actions are forbidden.

Cash vs. Accrual Systems

To understand financial accounting, you must also understand cash accounting and accrual accounting. These are the two basic systems for keeping track of income and expenses. *Cash accounting* just keeps track of your cash in hand, and it's the way most people handle their personal finances. It's intuitive; you pay as you go. *Accrual accounting* is more detailed because in addition to cash, it also keeps track of what you owe and are owed. But it's also a familiar system; this is how we purchase things using credit cards and *accrue* vacation leave.

Cash accounting is a simple system, but it can be misleading—intentionally or unintentionally. For instance, if I want to appear to have lots of money, I can just not pay my bills so that cash piles up in my checking account. If I want to appear broke, I can prepay my bills several months ahead, emptying my checking account but dramatically decreasing my upcoming expenses. In both cases, my checking account balance isn't a true reflection of my financial situation.

Accrual accounting keeps track of income earned and expenses due, even though the related cash transaction may not happen for months in the future. Because it gives a much more accurate picture of financial position, accrual accounting is required by GAAP for audits, and by many funders.

Figure 1-1 compares the two systems.

Figure 1-1. Cash vs. Accrual Accounting.

	Cash Accounting System	Accrual Accounting System
What are these systems?	Records income only when it is received and expenses only when they are paid.	Records income when it is earned and expenses when the obligation to pay arises, regardless of when payment is made.
Personal example	*Checkbook Register:* You enter funds when you make a deposit and subtract when you write a check.	*Credit Card:* You buy a sweater with your Visa and no cash passes hands, but you owe Visa for the purchase.
Nonprofit example: JCCA provides counseling to low-income clients and bills the state mental health agency monthly.	Records client fees only when payments are made.	Records client fee income when they have given the service for which the fee is charged, regardless of when payment is received.

Advantages	• Simple to record.
	• Easy to understand
	• Requires little more training than maintaining a checkbook
		• Provides a more accurate financial picture of the program:
		  – What they are owed
		  – What they owe others
		  – What it really costs to provide services
		• A standard system easily understood by all trained bookkeepers

Disadvantages	• Can be misleading • Doesn't provide a systematic way to track when you owe and are owed	• Needs trained bookkeeper; organization may have to commit to training time • Other organization personnel need training to read and understand statements • Takes more time to maintain

Note: Many nonprofit organizations use a modified accrual system in which routine records are kept on a cash basis, but when financial statements are prepared, a system is used to convert the books to accrual, showing what is owed by and owing to the organization.

History of Accounting

Modern accounting was invented in Renaissance Italy. During the Middle Ages, finances in Europe were pretty simple. The king owned everything; he let the nobility use some of it, while the vast majority of people legally owned very little. This system was called Feudalism. The economies were basically agricultural and barter-based, wealth meant owning land, and actual hard cash was rarely used by most people. In this system, it was pretty easy to keep track of finances—count your sheep and, if you had any cash, count the coins.

Then along came the Renaissance, and large numbers of people started living in cities. Non-noble families like the Medicis became wealthy by loaning money and by buying and selling items (the birth of Capitalism). These nascent capitalists were dealing in currencies of many countries (and cities and principalities), charging interest, and making complicated financial deals at long distance. Soon the old method of counting your coins just wasn't adequate for keeping track. So the merchants of Venice invented something better.

It's not clear who came up with the idea of double-entry bookkeeping, but the man who wrote it down was a Franciscan monk named Luca Pacioli. His mathematics book, published in 1494 by Guttenberg and illustrated by Leonardo da Vinci, became a bestseller across Europe and earned him the title "The Father of Accounting." Pacioli described a system remarkably like modern accounting, with journals and ledgers, assets and liabilities, capital, receivables, and so forth. This system made it possible for businesspeople in Venice, Florence, and elsewhere to keep track of complex deals—albeit using quill pens on parchment and Roman numerals was far more work than typing numbers into QuickBooks. Things didn't change much until the 1770s, with the introduction of cost accounting.

In the United States, as public ownership in stock increased in the mid-1800s, the New York Stock Exchange began requiring companies to provide statements of shares outstanding and capital resources. The introduction of the income tax in the early 20th century created a boom in accounting, as accountants got the jump on lawyers in preparing tax returns. After the stock market crash of 1929, Congress created the Securities and Exchange Commission (SEC) and gave it the power to establish standards for financial accounting and reporting.

Other organizations came into being with varying levels of authority to set accounting standards: the American Institute of Certified Public Accountants (AICPA), which set all standards for several years and still sets audit guidelines; the FASB, in 1973, which sets GAAP for private organizations; and the Governmental Accounting Standards Board (GASB), which sets GAAP for state and local governments.

Nonprofit Accounting

Nobody paid much attention to the finances of nonprofits or charities until the late 1960s, when a Senate investigation of trusts laid the groundwork for private foundations through revisions of the Internal Revenue Code. In a backward way, the code defines "public charities" as tax-exempt nonprofit corporations that are not private foundations.

In 1964, the AICPA produced the "Black Book," *Standards of Accounting and Financial Reporting for Health and Welfare Organizations,* followed by the *Audit of Voluntary Health and Welfare Organizations* in 1966, revised in 1974.

In 1977, the FASB got into the act of rule-making for nonprofits and released various statements. The major ones are listed in Appendix C. But there was no uniform set of guidelines for all nonprofit organizations until 1993, when it issued SFAS 116 and 117. These new rules hit nonprofit accounting like a bombshell. Over the next few years, nonprofits were required to make major changes in the form and content of their financial statements, as we'll see in this book.

Talking with Your Internal Financial People

A good grantwriter often interacts with more departments, and at more levels of an organization, than most other staff. He or she talks to the executive director and development director about which grants to apply for, works with department managers on developing proposals for their departments, talks to program staff to find out what's happening on the ground, and works with the financial people on budgets and compliance issues.

It is in this last relationship—with financial staff—that this book can help you. Knowing how to read financial statements and develop budgets are themselves very useful skills, but they can be leveraged to everyone's advantage if you take this knowledge and use it to help integrate grants into the organization's financial structure. In working with financial staff, you can achieve a lot with these three steps:

- **Speak their language.** Hopefully you can now converse about financial statements, accrual accounting, cash flow, and budgeting. Let the financial staff know you want to work *with* them, rather than just dumping the budget in their laps. Don't be afraid to ask questions.

- **Use their budget categories.** Make sure that all grant proposal budgets use the same terminology as the organization's accounting office, budget, and financial statements. This practice saves having to translate and "slice and dice" items to make them fit different formats after the fact.

- **Understand their concerns.** The organization's health depends on its financial stability, and it is in these people's hands. Each member of the financial staff has slightly different needs, but you can make their jobs easier—and vice versa—by asking what you can do for them.

Working with Financial Staff in a Large Nonprofit

Here are some of the ways you can work with the financial staff in a typical large nonprofit:

Chief Financial Officer (CFO) and the grantwriter, in many organizations, work together on developing grant project budgets, so this can be a symbiotic relationship. One of her or his major concerns is immediate cash flow, so discuss timing when considering which grants to apply for.

- When writing a major proposal, give the CFO as much lead time as you can to develop the budget.

- Let the CFO know the major staffing and other items, so she or he can use them to calculate benefits, indirect costs, and other items.

- Let the CFO know if there are significant changes in the narrative that will impact the budget.

- Let the CFO know if the grant requires matching funds.

- The CFO is likely using management accounting as well as financial accounting. Take time to see if there are ways grants planning can help the organization's cash flow projections, capital budget, or other financial management issues.

Grants Manager has to work within different sets of rules and deal with your organization's management and program staff as well as the funder to keep the organization in compliance with all grant requirements.

- Provide complete documentation of how you reached your budget amounts.

- Provide a complete copy of the final proposal and the RFP (the funder's request for proposals).

- Make sure the budget categories fit with the Office of Management and Budget (OMB) circulars or other reporting guidelines.

- Let the grants manager know when any reports are due, milestones in the timeline, and so forth.

- Provide copies of any correspondence with the funder that might affect grant management.

Board Treasurer is the board's representative, overseeing its fiduciary responsibility, and the liaison with financial staff. Ask the Board treasurer these questions:

- Will grants affect our cash flow, and if so, for better or worse?

- How are we doing this year on budget vs. actual for grant income?

- Can grant funds help our existing budgeted operating expenses?

Budget Committee is likely to be focused on more long-term concerns than the rest, since they're dealing with the future. They will want to know:

- What is your best guess of total grants that will come in next year?

- What will be the impact of grants on expenses as well as income?

What Do Funders Want?

As grantwriters, we need to be able to understand organizational finances for numerous reasons: protecting our organization's tax-exempt status, deciding which grants to apply for, producing better-integrated proposals, being able to work with the finance department, among others. Perhaps the major reason, however, is to improve our grants and our chances of having our grants funded.

For this section I talked with foundation grants officers and federal grant reviewers to see what they look for in the financial sections of grant applications. I also looked for written materials produced for both grantseekers and grantmakers. I asked questions such as: Do you look at the functional expenses or cash flow ratios? What are you looking for in project sustainability? What do you look for in budgets? I found that their answers were often better than my questions, so I'm just presenting their comments, more or less verbatim.

From the Program Officer of a Medium-Sized, General-Purpose Foundation:

What we look for varies with the complexity of the organization. With a large established group, we'd expect to see audited financial statements and sophisticated budgeting; we'd want to know their organizational structure. For a small group, maybe all we'd get would be a balance sheet and statement of activities.

We were having a hard time getting year-to-date financial statements. Maybe 30 percent of the organizations didn't know what we asking for. So we started asking for the current year's operating budget instead. If their financial position is still not clear, we'd ask for their 990s.

From reading their financials, if it looks like they're struggling with heavy debt or a deficit, we might ask for more detail. Signs of struggling would be debt, their cash position, a two- or three-year trend of deficits, or spending reserves on operations.

We send the organization's basic financial statements to our board of trustees—the balance sheet, income statement, functional expenses, and any pertinent audit notes. If the organization is struggling financially, they discuss whether the organization looks stable enough to ensure the money is spent as budgeted in the proposal. If it doesn't seem stable, we might refrain from multiyear grants and instead make a one-year grant and invite future one-year proposals. We might ask for notes on their financial progress with their grant reports.

What we're looking for is a full picture of the organization; finances is just part of it. We want to know if they have the financial capacity to manage the grant project, and how it fits their purpose or mission. Sometimes people think of a grant project out of the context of the organization, but we want to see how it fits.

Since SFAS 117 was issued, it's become difficult to tell from the audited statements why they might have huge surpluses or significant drops in income. If these are related to a capital campaign, or there's some other reason, we'd like to get an explanation.

If a grant is for an enhancement of their existing programs, full disclosure is best. They should show how the enhanced program budget relates to their annual operating budget. We need to know if it's included in the operating budget or not. We can see when a "project" is an attempt to get operating funding, and they're better off just telling us. We want to know how this enhancement/project will make a difference this year, and how they paid for it last year.

We look to see if the project budget is excessive compared to their organization's budget. Last meeting a trustee said, "Boy, that's more than 10 percent of their budget."

If they're looking for operating support, we look at their other sources of funding, both institutional and individual. Are they being diligent in looking to build their support? We'd look at our history with the organization, and at whether this is an unusual year.

If they're approaching multiple funders, is their request to us proportionate to what they're asking larger funders?

I'm surprised by the number of organizations that send us a 2003 audit in late 2005, more than 20 months later. If they can't do an audit in three to six months and are sending us an old one, they should let us know why and when they'll have this year's audit done, and give us an unaudited year-end statement. It's part of full disclosure.

From the Program Officer of a Large, General-Purpose Foundation:

We look at their organizational budget. Is it balanced? Board approved? In line with other organizations in the same field? How are they doing with income and expense against the budget, year-to-date? How did they do last year against their budget?

We might ask some fiduciary questions such as, Are you involved in, or at risk of, a lawsuit?

I like to ask questions rather than just look at their audits; that way I find out how well they know their finances. If they're not audited, I ask about their assets—smaller organizations often forget to mention noncash assets. If they're not audited, why not? There are some good reasons, as long as they've thought about it.

If there is an audit, is there a management letter? It will be mentioned in the auditor's cover letter. I'd ask for it delicately, because it's a private communication from the auditor to their board.

If they have debt, who holds it? Is it a bank, or board members, or the founder? If it's an individual, is there proper paperwork? How professional are they? If they have a line of credit, do they pay it off each year? And do they do it responsibly, or borrow to do it?

If they have debt, how did they get there? Was it wise? Are they managing their debt; do they have a repayment plan?

We're never looking for a "correct" answer. We just have to ask the question, then make a judgment of whether the answer is reasonable.

How financially savvy are they; for example, do they use their non-financial assets? For instance, I just looked at a private school that rented its roof for cell phone towers. They're using a static asset to generate income.

I try to figure out the board's role in managing finances. I don't want board minutes, but I like to talk to the president. How do they handle their fiduciary responsibility? What information does the board get on a regular basis? Is there financial expertise on the board? Do they periodically look at their assets, cash flow, and overall financial position? If there have been financial problems or opportunities in the past, how did the board handle that?

I like to see the project budget embedded in the organization budget, but I've never seen a really good, generally applicable way to do it. Is the project budget in some reasonable ratio to the organization budget? I'd be nervous about an expansion of over one-third of their budget.

Does the budget make common sense? How are they handling administrative and other indirect costs? It's OK to say "administrative" or "indirect" and use a percentage, as long as they show how they got there and it's reasonable. Do they identify in-kind and other revenues? Are they putting their own money into the project, investing in themselves?

How will the program be supported after the grant period? Extend the budget out several years. It's OK not to know, but it's not OK not to think about it.

From an Experienced Federal Grant Reviewer and Former Government Program Manager:

Federal budgeting is looked at quite differently from foundation grant budgets. There are required forms and formats, allowable costs, indirect cost rates, and so forth. Unlike the rest of a federal proposal, there often aren't page limits on the budget section, so don't be afraid to provide lots of detail. Here are a few things reviewers look for and base their scores on.

- **Follow instructions.** The RFP and the forms 424 and 424A come with specific instructions, and you can lose points by not following them. Be sure to look for required budgeted items, which may be buried somewhere in the RFP; a common one is required travel to grantees meetings.

- **Maintain consistency among forms.** The numbers on the forms 424, 424A, and budget narrative should match.

- **Maintain consistency among sections.** The abstract, needs statement, program narrative, and evaluation should include the same items and activities, which in turn should be shown in the budget. It's bad to have something in the narrative that you don't list in the budget, and it's worse to have something in the budget that's not explained in the narrative.

- **Show where you got all of your budget numbers.** Document everything in the budget narrative. Salaries should be shown as FTEs (full-time equivalents) or hourly wages at a specified number of hours, which should match your staffing plan. Equipment should be price-shopped or bid. Saying "a computer for $1,500" isn't enough. Saying "a Dell 9100 desktop computer for $1,500" is better. Best is telling them that you did some price shopping, saying where, and that the best deal is a Dell Dimension 9100 for $1,508, purchased directly over the Internet, and including a printout of the webpage with the specs and price as an attachment.

- **Affirm your fiscal capacity.** Many RFPs ask for your organizational capability. At a minimum, you must make a declarative statement affirming that you have the fiscal management capacity to manage the grant.

The GEO Due Diligence Chart

Grantmakers for Effective Organizations (GEO), an organization of foundations interested in building strong and effective nonprofit organizations, publishes a Due Diligence Tool for use by funders in evaluating nonprofits and grants. Figure 1-2 is taken from the Financial Health section of the tool (with minor adaptations).[1] Many foundations use it, or adapt it to their needs. For large multiyear grants, these are the kinds of questions you need to anticipate, and your executive director or board president should be prepared to answer.

---

[1] The GEO Due Diligence Tool can be downloaded free from http://www.geofunders. org/index.cfm?fuseaction=Page.viewPage&pageId=150. This chart is on pages 14–16.

Figure 1-2. GEO Due Diligence Chart

Category of Issues	Questions to Consider	Effectiveness Indicators	Red Flags
Organizational Budget	• How do you develop your organizational budget? What is the role of the board in the process? • Has your organizational budget increased or decreased from last year? Please explain why. • What is your anticipated organizational income breakdown in the committed, identified and unknown categories?	• The executive director understands the financial aspects of the organization. • The expenses and income outlined in the budget are reasonable. • The organization appears to have appropriate income streams and a realistic budget that adequately covers core operating costs. • A comparison of the budget to actual year-to-date shows that the organization is close to meeting its budget. • There is someone in the organization who knows its financial performance and can explain any patterns.	• The executive director cannot explain the financial aspects of the organization. For example, the executive director cannot answer, off the top of his head, in round numbers, the question "What is your current annual budget size?" • The board is not involved in the budget development process. • In reviewing anticipated income (committed, identified, unknown), the unknown is too big. • Budgeted income exactly equals budgeted expense—this is a "plugged" budget. Nature is never this precise.
Project Budget	• Describe the budget for the proposed project and how it supports the plan outlined in the proposal narrative. • How much of the project funding is committed? • What will happen if you don't receive the anticipated funding from other sources (known and unknown)? • How did you arrive at your budget estimates? Explain any line items that are questionable or unclear.	• The project budget is aligned with the organizational budget. • The overall project budget seems appropriate for what is described in the proposal narrative. • There appear to be appropriate income streams and a realistic budget that adequately covers program costs.	• The project budget is unrealistic and/or not consistent with the proposal narrative. • In reviewing anticipated income (committed, identified, unknown), the unknown is too big.

Figure 1-2. *Continued*

Category of Issues	Questions to Consider	Effectiveness Indicators	Red Flags
Financial Systems and Reporting	• What financial statements do you generate? How frequently? Who prepares them? Who reviews them? • Describe the financial expertise on your board. • What role does the board play in financial oversight? • What is the process for providing the board with regular financial information?	• The organization has regular audits if its annual budget is greater than $250,000. • The board has member(s) with financial expertise, and the board performs regular financial reviews. • The board receives financial reports at least quarterly. • Management and program staff understand how to read the financial statements. • Financial reports are used to inform programmatic and other decisions.	• There are no financial reports or statements generated. • The organization has financial statements, but they are not reviewed by the board, or they are out of date (more than two months old). • The organization borrows from other programs or restricted funds. • The organization's mid-year financial statements indicate it is way off budget. • Auditor's letters to management indicate weakness in internal controls.
Financial Position and Trends	• Describe your organization's current financial state. • Has the organization borrowed money? If so, what are the terms of the loan? Was borrowing for capital expenditures such as a building or to cover an operating loss? • If debts exceed available cash, what is your plan for debt reduction? • If there was an operating loss, what are you going to do to avoid another loss this year? • What is your vision for (continued) financial health? Where do you see the organization, financially, in five years?	• The organization has a history of breaking even or operating in surplus. • The financial manager and executive director can describe the organization's current financial state. • The organization has a long-term vision of where it wants to be financially.	• The organization does not have enough cash on hand to meet demands.[1] • The organization has a growing accumulated deficit because it ended the past fiscal year with a deficit and is projecting another deficit this year. • The balance sheet shows negative net assets. • The organization has debt other than long-term debt for asset acquisition, such as for buying a building, and has no debt reduction plan. • There are unusual items in the organization's financials (e.g., loans from board members, unpaid salaries) that are not clearly accounted for. • The auditor has issued a "qualified opinion."

Figure 1-2. *Continued*

Category of Issues	Questions to Consider	Effectiveness Indicators	Red Flags
Fund Development Planning and Oversight	• Describe your fund development plan (i.e., fundraising goals and plan for reaching them). • How is the board involved in fundraising? • What role do board members play in developing strategies to maintain or grow the organization's contributed income? • How do you monitor progress against your fundraising goals? What role does the board play in this process?	• There is a plan for raising money, developed with the involvement of board members. • The board of directors is aware of or involved in the organization's fundraising goals and activities.	• The organization cannot articulate a plan for fundraising. • The board is not involved in fundraising. • The board members responsible for fundraising and development oversight don't have the skills or interest. • The budget projects a perfect breakeven, and the fundraising budget number is exactly the amount needed. Ask for last year's actual and see if the current-year fundraising goal is reasonable or is simply "plugged."
Funding Mix	• How would you describe the health and balance of your funding mix? Is it diversified enough?[2] • What areas, if any, do you seek to change or improve? How? • What are your concerns, if any, about your funding picture?	• The organization has diversified contributed income as well as earned income (if appropriate). • The fundraising goals (for the organization or the project) and overall budget are realistic based on the economy and past experience.	• The executive director and board member(s) cannot articulate their funding mix. • The organization is overly dependent on one source of funding. • The organization has had a difficult time meeting the public support test[3] and maintaining its public charity status.

Notes:

1. The *current ratio* (current assets to current liabilities) will tell you whether the organization can meet short-term cash requirements. It must be at least 1:1.
2. Determine an organization's dependence on any single source by looking at the revenue line item as a percentage of the organization's total expenses. Is any one source predominant?
3. The *public support test* is designed to ensure that a charity has a broad base of support and is, therefore, responsive to the general public rather than a few individuals. Grantees must develop and maintain support from a diversity of donors; this is determined through a formula established by the IRS and provided to the grantee. It is the grantee's responsibility to understand this issue and track its support to ensure that it is not in danger of losing its 501(c)(3) status (see section on Tipping in Chapter 5).

The Grantwriter's Responsibility in Grants Management

As a grantwriter in a development office or as an outside consultant, your work officially ends when a proposal is submitted to the funder. However, the success of your grant project and your chances of future funding often depend on the grant being well managed. If you're not involved in the project, or not even there, what can you do to improve the grants management process? In fact, there are several things you can do before finishing the project.

- **Make sure the grant budget is manageable.** This may seem obvious, but if the budget is too small for the project or isn't tied to the project's goals and objectives, or if the project involves complex evaluation or detailed oversight that isn't budgeted for, then it will needlessly absorb staff time and energy. Careful planning and budgeting during the grant development process is your best contribution to a successful project.

- **Use grant budget categories and terminology that match the organization's accounting system and budget.** This will make it easier to track compliance and generate useful reports. Talk to the finance manager and, if possible, get him or her involved in developing the budget—or at least reviewing it before submission.

- **Check the organization's commitment to sustainability.** One of the grantwriter's biggest headaches is being asked to find continuation funding for a program when its grant funding is about to run out. In many cases, the original grant proposal said that the organization would develop additional funding sources during the grant period, but the staff never took it seriously. If you're working on a proposal to launch a new program that the organization wants to continue, have a planning session to talk about future funding— where it would come from and whose responsibility it is to develop those sources. Try to get top management support for this planning; it's one of the best capacity-building tools any organization can have.

- **Make sure reporting responsibilities are clear.** Will the department manager or the fiscal office be creating the grant's financial reports? How will they work together to accomplish this with the least wasted energy? Have them talk about it and make these decisions well before the first reports are due.

- **For federal grants, make sure the organization has copies of the appropriate OMB circulars and is familiar with allowable costs.** Even though the staff may not regularly use them in budgeting, they can be invaluable when questions arise about how federal funds can be spent.

- **Make sure that both the program manager and fiscal office have copies of important papers.** These include the grant proposal and budget and any worksheets or documentation you used in putting together the budget.

- **Keep copies of everything yourself, both electronic and/or paper.** In the event that the organization loses the materials, has staff changes, or is just flustered, you'll be able to help them get back on track—and maybe even save the day.

Often neither the department program manager nor the fiscal office will want to be burdened with extra paper or planning until they know the grant is funded. This is understandable and can be planned for.

- Make extra copies of all documentation when preparing the grant for submittal. Put them in folders to be delivered to the program manager and fiscal office if the grant is funded.

- Create a worksheet of things to do when a grant is funded, and give it to them.

- Arrange to come back and meet with them after funding is awarded to see that the necessary grant management systems are put in place.

Honing Your Professional Skills

Understanding finances and budgeting is a vital set of skills for the grants professional or anyone involved with nonprofit organizations. I hope this book gives you the basic information to begin improving your grantwriting and development skills today. I also hope that it has demystified the subject and made you want to learn more about this field that is increasingly important to both our professional and personal lives. Listed below are some suggestions for gaining more depth and breadth of knowledge.

- **Take some accounting and finance classes.** It probably doesn't matter if they're at the university or community college level; the information is the same. The beginning classes will be for-profit oriented, but the concepts are all the same. These are common college course titles:

  – Financial Accounting (the first year, two semesters or three quarters)

  – Nonprofit Accounting

  – Nonprofit Financial Management

  – Government Accounting.

- **Participate in workshops.** These may be put on by the local Association of Fundraising Professionals or nonprofit technical assistance organizations.

- **Read some of the books in the bibliography.** I especially recommend:

  – *Financial Leadership for Nonprofit Executives*
    by Jeanne Bell Peters and Elizabeth Schaffer

  – *Streetsmart Financial Basics for Nonprofit Managers*
    by Thomas A. McLaughlin

  – *Not-for-Profit Budgeting and Financial Management*
    by Edward J. McMillan.

- **Read articles in the field.** The best sources are probably on the Internet.

  – *Grants & Foundation Review* at http://charitychannel.com/ enewsletters/gfr/. (Full disclosure: As of this writing, I'm the editor.)

  – The Grantsmanship Center at http://www.tgci.com/magazine/ archives.asp.

- **Download some 990s and 990-PFs** for nonprofit organizations and foundations in your area from http://www.guidestar.org/. Read them, using the sections in this book to guide you.

- **Download and read your local government financial statements** (if it's relevant to you) from http://www.gasb.org/repmodel/ implementers.html.

- **Read your organization's annual report** or those of others in your area. Request and read their audited financial statements.

- **Be involved in your organization's budget process.**

- **Be involved in (or see if you can sit in on) your organization's financial audit.**

Financial Statements | 2

Financial Statement Basics

Almost all private funders ask for three standard required attachments: Your organization's IRS tax exemption letter, a list of your board of directors, and your financial statements. The IRS letter lets them know that you're eligible to receive their grant. The board list tells them who's legally responsible and what their qualifications are for running your organization. The financial statements tell them your organization's size and financial health, so they can make judgments about your ability to carry out their grant purpose.

As a grantwriter, you need to be able to recognize financial statements (commonly referred to as "financials") and read them for basic information so that you can advise the organization about the appropriate sizes and types of grants to apply for and how their finances affect their chances of being funded. I say you need to be able to "recognize" them, because some smaller nonprofits won't know what you want when you ask for their financials. I've had clients give me bank statements, checkbook registers, and budgets. If the organization can't create financial statements on its own, you need to refer them to a good bookkeeper who can produce financials from the organization's existing books. If an organization is small enough that they don't produce regular internal financial statements, they're probably small enough that they don't need to pay accountant prices to do this work.

About Financial Statements

Nonprofit organizations create financial statements to present an accurate picture of their financial condition to interested parties, including their own boards, donors, and potential grant funders. Formal financial statements follow GAAP, which are created by the FASB. You'll need to be familiar with these four standard statements:

- Statement of Financial Position

- Statement of Activities

- Statement of Cash Flows

- Statement of Functional Expense.

Under GAAP, the first three are required of all nonprofits; the last is required for health and welfare organizations only.

Complete financial statements include notes at the end that explain accounting policies and any additional details necessary to understand the statement. All the statements must be for the same date, to reflect the financial condition of the organization on that particular date. They will also be linked through particular numbers, as we'll see. Formal financial statements show numbers for two consecutive years so the user can make comparisons.

Whereas a full set of nonprofit financial statements will have three or four standard statements, a minimum set prepared by a small nonprofit might have only the first two, the Statement of Financial Position and the Statement of Activities. These are the ones that most readers want to see, so they're sufficient for many small grant proposals. They're also the ones that will mostly concern you as a grant professional.

Let's look at the structure of each of the four statements to see how they work, what their functions are, and how they relate to each other.

Statement of Financial Position

The Statement of Financial Position shows the overall health (solvency) of an organization at a point in time. We can think of the Statement of Financial Position as a snapshot of where things stood on one day (specified at the top of the statement). It also lets us know the size of the organization, its cash position (i.e., ability to pay its bills), the amount of debt it has, and how much of its assets are restricted. This statement does *not* reflect whether the organization is making or losing money (i.e., its profitability). Figure 2-1 is a sample Statement of Financial Position.

The Statement of Financial Position may also be called the Balance Sheet or Statement of Assets, Liabilities, and Net Assets. The reason it's called a Balance Sheet is that the Total Assets always equals the combination of Liabilities and Net Assets—they balance by definition: one way we arrive at the Net Assets is by subtracting the Liabilities from the Assets. If an organization owes more than it owns, the Net Assets would be negative (not a good situation). The following are explanations of the categories in the Statement:

Figure 2-1. Sample Statement of Financial Position

[Name of Organization]
Statement of Financial Position
As of June 30, 2005

ASSETS

Current Assets

			Explanation
Cash and Cash Equivalents	$	XXX	Cash in the bank, money market funds, etc.
Short-Term Investments		XXX	CDs, stock held for sale, etc.
Accounts Receivable		XXX	Money you're owed for services
Pledges Receivable, Net of Allowances		XXX	Money promised by donors
Grants Receivable		XXX	Grants awarded but not yet paid
Prepaid Expenses		XXX	Insurance policies, prepaid rent, etc.
Total Current Assets	$	X,XXX	

Property and Equipment

Property and Equipment, Net of Depreciation . . .		XXX	Buildings, land, and equipment

Other Assets

Long-Term Pledges Receivable		XXX	Multi-year pledges
Total Assets	$XXX,XXX		Everything you own
			Equals Total Liabilities and Net Assets

LIABILITIES AND NET ASSETS

Current Liabilities

Accounts Payable	$	XXX	Money you owe, due soon
Wages Payable		XXX	Money owed to employees
Payroll Tax Payable		XXX	Taxes withheld from employee paychecks
Deferred Revenue		XXX	Money collected but not "earned"
Current Portion of Long-Term Debt		XXX	This year's portion of the mortgage
	$	X,XXX	

Long-Term Liabilities

Notes and Mortgages Payable, Net		XXX	Your mortgage, payable over several years
Total Liabilities		XXX	Everything you owe

Net Assets

Unrestricted Net Assets	$	X,XXX	Assets without any donor restrictions
Temporarily Restricted Net Assets		XXX	Assets with temporary donor restrictions
Permanently Restricted Net Assets		XXX	Assets with permanent donor restrictions
Total Net Assets	$	X,XXX	Total Assets – Total Liabilities
Total Liabilities and Net Assets	$XXX,XXX		*Equals Total Assets*

- **Assets (Current and Long-Term)** are conventionally listed in order of liquidity, or how fast they could be turned into cash. Cash is of course the most liquid, followed by money you expect to receive soon (grants announced but not paid, payment for services performed but not paid, and so forth).

- **Prepaid Expenses** are things like insurance that are paid in advance. You "own" $XXX of prepaid insurance coverage, although it doesn't help your cash position.

- **Property and Equipment**, like everything in accrual accounting, are valued at cost less depreciation[2]. Depreciation is a way of spreading the recording of costs of a "long-term physical asset" out over several years (its "useful life"). For example, land isn't depreciated, so only the building part of a property purchase is depreciated.

- **Liabilities (Current and Long-Term)** are listed in the order they have to be paid.

- **Wages** and **Payroll Taxes** are always listed right after Current Liabilities because employees and the IRS are the first ones in line if you go out of business. If a business goes bankrupt, it won't escape these two obligations.

- **Accounts Payable** are outstanding bills due in the near future (generally, the month of the statement).

- **Deferred Revenue** is cash you've been paid but have not yet earned. Common items are season ticket sales, tuition, and memberships. (Deferred Revenue used to be a common way of recording grants, but this changed with the advent of SFAS 117, which we'll discuss later).

- **Net Assets** is the difference between **Total Assets** and **Total Liabilities**. In theory it's the organization's net worth, or what would be left if it sold everything off today and paid all of its bills. In fact, however, Net Assets is not the true cash value, because many things aren't worth their "book" value if you had to dispose of them. Some investments, such as CDs (certificates of deposit), may have an early surrender penalty. Accounts Receivable can't be sold at face value. Prepaid Expenses, such as insurance, have little sale value. On the other hand, real estate may be worth many times its book value.

---

[2] This can be misleading, since over time land and buildings are often worth much more than their purchase price, but equipment like cars and computers often lose value faster than their IRS allowable depreciation rates. Also, marketable securities like stocks and bonds are listed at their current fair market value under SFAS 124.

Statement of Activities

If we think of the Statement of Financial Position as a snapshot, we can think of the Statement of Activities as a diary of all financial activities that happened during a certain time, often a year or a quarter (shown at the top of the statement). The Statement of Activities shows the organization's profitability, but does not reflect its solvency. Figure 2-2 is a sample Statement of Activities.

Figure 2-2. Sample Statement of Activities

[Name of Organization]
Statement of Activities
For the Fiscal Year Ended June 30, 2005

	Unrestricted	Temporarily Restricted	Total
SUPPORT AND REVENUE			
Government Grants and Contracts	$ XXX		$ XXX
United Way	XXX		XXX
Contributions	XXX	$ XXX	XXX
Foundation Grants.	XXX	XXX	XXX
Fees.	XXX		XXX
Net Assets Released from Restrictions:			
Satisfaction of Time Restrictions	XXX	(XXX)	
Satisfaction of Program Restrictions.	XXX	(XXX)	
Total Support and Revenue	$X,XXX	$X,XXX	$X,XXX
EXPENSES			
Program Services.	XXX		XXX
Administration	XXX		XXX
Resource Development.	XXX		XXX
Total Expenses	$ XXX		$ XXX
Change in Net Assets			
Net Assets, Beginning of Year	$XXXX	$X,XXX	$X,XXX
Net Assets, End of Year	$X,XXX	$X,XXX	$X,XXX

The Statement of Activities may also be called the Income Statement, the Profit and Loss (P&L) Statement, or the Statement of Support, Revenue and Expense, and Changes in Fund Balance. The ending date of the Statement of Activities is always the same as the date on the Statement of Financial Position, giving an accurate picture of what happened and what the results were during the time period.

The Statement of Activities includes only operating income and expenses. Other financial activities such as borrowing (financing activities) or buying property or equipment (investing activities) are shown on the Statement of Cash Flow and reflected on the Balance Sheet (discussed later). The Statement of Activities shows all increases or decreases in net assets during the year.

- Both revenues and expenses must be recorded on a gross basis, rather than offsetting expenses against revenues and reporting the net.

- Revenue is listed as Unrestricted, Temporarily Restricted, or Permanently Restricted, based on restrictions donors have put on its use. When temporary restrictions are met, the funds become unrestricted, as shown in the Net Assets Released from Restrictions.

- Expenses are divided into Program Services, Administration (management), and Resource Development (fundraising).

- The Change in Net Assets section of the statement is Total Support and Revenue minus Total Expenses.

- The Net Assets at the End of the Year ties the Statement of Activities to the Statement of Financial Position. This number is always the same on both statements, although arrived at differently.

Statement of Functional Expenses

The Statement of Functional Expenses (also called the Statement of Functional Revenues, Expenses, and Changes in Net Assets if those are included) takes the Statement of Activities and divides each line into categories by function. There are three required functions: Program Services, Administration, and Fundraising.[3] Program Services is further divided to show the operations of each major program. Although GAAP only requires this from health and welfare organizations, many larger nonprofits include them. Many nonprofits also include income to show where funding comes from. Figure 2-3 is a sample Statement of Functional Revenues, Expenses, and Changes in Net Assets..

[3] If classified by the IRS as a membership organization, then "Membership" is another required functional area.

Figure 2-3. Sample Statement of Functional Expenses

[Name of Organization]
Statement of Functional Revenues, Expenses, and Changes in Net Assets
For the Fiscal Year Ended June 30, 2005

	Program A	Program B	Total Program Services	Adminis-tration	Resource Development	2005 Total
SUPPORT AND REVENUE						
Government Grants and Contracts ..	$XXX	$XXX	$ XXX	$XXX		$ XXX
Private Revenue:						
Contributions					X,XXX	XXX
Foundation Grants.					XXX	XXX
Income:						
Fees.	XXX	XXX	XXX			XXX
Reimbursements	XXX	XXX	XXX	XXX		XXX
Transfers Between Funds	XXX	XXX	X,XXX		(X,XXX)	
Total Support and Revenue	$XXX	$XXX	$X,XXX	$XXX	$ XXX	$X,XXX
EXPENSES						
Salaries.	XXX	XXX	XXX	XXX	XXX	XXX
Benefits	XXX	XXX	XXX	XXX	XXX	XXX
Travel		XXX	XXX	XXX	XXX	XXX
Occupancy	XXX	XXX	XXX	XXX	XXX	XXX
Depreciation				XXX		XXX
Supplies	XXX	XXX	XXX	XXX	XXX	XXX
Telephone	XXX	XXX	XXX	XXX	XXX	XXX
Insurance.	XXX	XXX	XXX	XXX	XXX	X,XXX
Total Expenses	$XXX	$XXX	$X,XXX	$XXX	$ XXX	$X,XXX
Change in Net Assets	$XXX	$XXX	$X,XXX	$XXX	$ XXX	$X,XXX
Net Assets, Beginning of Year	XXX	XXX	XXX	XXX	XXX	XXX
Net Assets, End of Year	$XXX	$XXX	$X,XXX	$XXX	$ XXX	$X,XXX

The Statement of Functional Expenses gives the reader a more detailed and accurate look at the activities of the organization by assigning revenues and expenses to the specific departments responsible for them. An internal statement of functional expenses used by management might include more departments or activities (such as marketing and publications) than the formal GAAP financial statement created for external users.

- Functional basis reporting is contrasted with the "natural" basis used in the Statement of Activities, which classifies revenues and expenses by their natural category (all salaries are shown together, all supplies, and so forth).

- It is often assumed, especially among the general public, that low administrative and fundraising costs are good, leaving more for direct program services. In fact they can be too low, and an organization that neglects these areas is likely to be poorly managed and crisis prone. Unfortunately, the "lower is better" idea is perpetuated by several charity-monitoring websites. There is a temptation to try to underreport administrative and fundraising costs, hiding them in program.[4]

Statement of Cash Flows

The Statement of Activities and Statement of Financial Position are prepared on an accrual basis, giving an accurate big picture of your overall financial position. The disadvantage of accrual accounting is that it doesn't tell you about cash, and cash is important. If you don't have cash, you don't make payroll. So there's a fourth statement, the Statement of Cash Flows.

The Statement of Cash Flows converts your books from accrual to cash accounting. This helps the reader understand where your organization's cash comes from and goes to. It also shows nonoperating transactions, which don't show up on the Statement of Activities and cause discrepancies between it and the Statement of Financial Position. The Statement of Cash Flows reverses noncash transactions, such as depreciation and deferred revenue. that have no effect on the bank balance. It also shows year-to-year changes in accounts payable and accounts receivable, which respectively increase or decrease your cash on hand. Finally, the Statement of Cash Flows shows transactions that aren't included in the Statement of Activities, which

---

[4] The IRS and U.S. Department of Justice are pushing nonprofits and their auditors to show realistic fundraising expenses. A Form 990 that shows lots of grants and contributions with little or no fundraising expense will raise a red flag and perhaps prompt a letter from the IRS to the organization or the accountant who signed its 990.

is limited to operating activities. These include financing (borrowing) or investing (buying or selling stocks, equipment, or buildings). Figure 2-4 is a sample Statement of Cash Flows.

Figure 2-4. Sample Statement of Cash Flows

[Name of Organization]
Statement of Cash Flows
For the Year Ended June 30, 2005

Cash Flows from Operating Activities

Change in Net Assets	$ XXX
Adjustments to reconcile changes in net assets to net cash provided by operating activities:	
Depreciation	XXX
(Increase) Decrease in Accounts Receivable	XXX
(Increase) Decrease in Pledges Receivable	XXX
Increase (Decrease) in Accounts Payable	(XXX)
Increase (Decrease) in Accrued Vacation Payable	XXX
Increase (Decrease) in Payroll Liabilities	XXX
Increase (Decrease) in Deferred Revenue	XXX
Total Adjustments	X,XXX
Net Cash from Operating Activities	X,XXX
Cash Flows from Investing Activities	
Purchases of equipment	(XXX)
Cash Flows from Financing Activities	
Payments on Line of Credit	(XXX)
Net Cash Used by Financing Activities	(XXX)
Net Increase in Cash and Cash Equivalents	X,XXX
Cash and Cash Equivalents, Beginning of Year	X,XXX
Cash and Cash Equivalents, End of Year	$ X,XXX

In general, the Statement of Cash Flows is probably not of much interest to the grant professional. It shows *how* things happened, whereas the grant-writer and funders are much more concerned about *what* happened. However, if you're a development officer and involved in the actual operations of organizational budgeting and cash management, you should have a good understanding of this statement.

- The Statement of Cash Flows is figured using the *indirect* method[5] of presentation.

- Each line in the Statement of Cash Flows relates to a line of the Statement of Financial Position. In many cases, these are comparative changes, so we'd need to see last year's Statement of Financial Position in order to calculate all of the lines that show Increase and Decrease. In fact, a formal financial statement always shows two years, so the information is available to do the calculations.

- A note on stock sales: If a nonprofit has a policy of immediately selling any donated stocks, most accountants wouldn't consider the sale an investing activity, but would list it as a contribution.

Model Financial Statements

Now let's see what some actual financial statements look like and what information we can gather from reading them. The examples below are from our three model organizations—different types with different levels of complexity. A grant professional is likely to run across this variety, and it's important to realize that there is more than one right way of presenting financial statements.

Three Organization Models

While planning this book, I wanted to maintain consistency throughout the chapters, show different approaches and levels of complexity appropriate for different kinds of organizations, and use examples based on real life. However, I didn't want to take actual organizations and lay their finances out to the world. So I've created three models of grant-seeking nonprofits, each based on one or more actual organizations. The numbers used in these models are fictitious, and some facts have been changed to provide better examples, but they are generally representative of the types of organizations that may seek funding through grants.

Model 1: A small, one-program organization. Billy's Mother is a small organization serving runaway teens with housing, meals, counseling, and assistance with education and employment. Closely allied with the local First Methodist Church, it rents two houses from the Church at nominal

---

[5] There is also a less commonly used *direct* method of presentation that looks slightly different. But since grantwriters don't have much reason to study the Statement of Cash Flows, we won't bother with it here.

rates and depends on a dedicated volunteer corps and a part-time executive director. Billy's Mother receives no government funding. It relies on small grants, events, a few committed donors, and the church.

Model 2: A medium-sized performing arts organization. The Florentine Chamber Orchestra (FCO) was formed in 1988. It has been successful in performing high-quality music, but has struggled with organizational and financial issues. FCO operates from rented offices and receives minimal government funding. Approximately 42 percent of its income comes from program admissions, and 58 percent from contributions and grants.

Model 3: A large, multiservice social service organization. Jefferson County Community Action (JCCA) is a well-established agency in a large county that includes both suburban and rural areas. JCCA provides low-income families with information and referral services, child care, energy assistance, and housing stability assistance. JCCA operates a homeless family shelter and runs a pregnancy support and prenatal outreach program. JCCA works closely with a local health clinic and a community development corporation (a low-income housing developer). JCCA began as a community action agency in 1966 as part of the War on Poverty. It has an annual operating budget of $13.5 million, owns its own headquarters building, and rents other space for programs around Jefferson County. Most (82 percent) of its funding comes from local, state, and federal grants and contracts.

We'll get more familiar with these typical nonprofit organizations as we go through the book, comparing their budgets, financial statements, and operations.

Billy's Mother

As a small, grassroots nonprofit, Billy's Mother doesn't receive any government funding or apply for large foundation grants. Most of its operations are carried out by volunteers from the First Methodist and other local churches, and many of its supplies are in-kind donations. Its funders know and trust the organization and its longtime executive director.

Billy's Mother's finances are very simple. Because it doesn't own any significant assets and pays its bills promptly, it has no real need for accrual accounting. Its books are kept on a cash basis, using the Quicken check register program, and twice a year a volunteer accountant converts them to accrual-basis statements to use as reports to the board and the church. You'll notice that these statement titles use the terminology that nonprofit accounting used before SFAS 117 was issued in the mid-1990s.

Statement of Activities—Cash Basis

First, let's review Billy's Mother's finances for 2004, looking only at what passed through their checking account—their cash. Looking only at cash, we see a strong grassroots organization with good community support. They started the year with money in the bank and added to it, almost doubling their cash on hand. With a budget of about $75,000 and a bank balance of $15,633, they have enough money to survive for over two months. Assuming continuing support and no emergencies, Billy's Mother should have no cash flow problems. Figure 2-5 shows what their Statement of Activities, prepared as a Quicken report, would look like.

Figure 2-5. Billy's Mother—Statement of Activities (Cash Basis)

Billy's Mother
Statement of Support, Revenue and Expense, and Changes in Cash Balance
For the Year Ended December 31, 2004

SUPPORT AND REVENUE	
Contributions	$51,243
Foundation Grants	20,000
Local Business Contributions	9,600
Benefit Events, Net	4,597
Total Support and Revenue	$85,440
EXPENSES	
Executive Director (half-time)	21,000
Taxes and Benefits	3,780
Rent	2,400
Utilities	22,319
Telephone	1,200
Supplies	22,375
Transportation	2,400
Total Expenses	$75,474
Support over Revenue	$ 9,966
Cash Balance, Beginning of Year	$ 5,667
Cash Balance, End of Year	$15,633

From this report we can make several educated assumptions about Billy's Mother's finances:

- Over half of their income was from individual donors, usually a reliable source of ongoing funds.

- They have also been successful in attracting some foundation support and a good level of business contributions for a small organization.

- Their benefit events actually netted some cash. We don't know what their events cost to put on, either in expense or volunteer labor, but from what we know about the organization generally, we can assume that they were small in scale, involving their contributors and volunteers.

- They are paying their executive director $21,000 for half-time work. Assuming that the person actually limits this work to half time, the pay is not great, but it's not poverty level. A dedicated person with other interests might stay on this job for a while.

- They are paying the minimum in taxes and benefits (Social Security, Medicare, Worker's Compensation, and Unemployment Insurance). If their executive director has a spouse or partner with benefits (health insurance and retirement), this may not be a hardship.

- We know that their rent from the church is nominal. This amount on two houses reflects a deep discount on prevailing rates.

- The other expenses seem reasonable for a small organization working with a strong volunteer core.

Statement of Activities—Accrual Basis

At the end of the year, their volunteer accountant takes this report, the bills still waiting to be paid, and other records and creates a set of complete (but non-GAAP) financial statements. These are in accrual format, but still fairly informal and not audited. Figure 2-6 shows the resulting Statement of Activities (here called a Statement of Support, Revenue, and Expense, the pre-SAFS 117 name).

The new Statement of Activities still shows a healthy organization, but both the income and expenses have more than doubled.[6] Billy's Mother's Board of Directors has decided to recognize the value of the church's discounted rent, in-kind donations, and volunteered time. Including these items not only shows appreciation for these significant contributions, but also the true cost of operations. If they had to pay cash for everything, Billy's Mother would have to raise almost another $120,000!

---

[6] Billy's Mother lists all volunteer services, not just the professional services that would be allowable under GAAP.

Figure 2-6. Billy's Mother—Statement of Activities (Accrual Basis)

Billy's Mother
Statement of Support, Revenue and Expense, and Changes in Fund Balance
For the Year Ended December 31, 2004

SUPPORT AND REVENUE

Contributions	$ 51,243
Foundation Grants.	20,000
Local Business Contributions.	9,600
Benefit Events (net)	4,597
Church—in kind	*10,000*
Church—in kind rent	*19,200*
Volunteers—in kind.	*46,200*
Supplies—in kind.	*44,328*
Total Support and Revenue	205,168

EXPENSES

Executive Director (half-time)	21,000
Taxes and Benefits	3,780
Rent	
Cash	2,400
In-kind	*19,200*
Utilities	22,319
Telephone	1,200
Supplies	22,375
Transportation	2,400
Church—in kind	*10,000*
Volunteers—in kind.	*46,200*
Supplies—in kind.	*44,328*
Total Expenses	195,202
Support over Revenue	9,966
Fund Balance, Beginning of Year	11,327
Fund Balance, End of Year.	$ 21,293

We notice a few other things about this statement, in addition to the larger numbers:

- Each of the in-kind contributions under Support and Revenue is matched with an identical amount of Expense. This is vitally important, because it keeps the nonmonetary, in-kind contributions from distorting the financial reports. As a result, the Support over Revenue line is the same for both the cash and accrual formats.

- The Fund Balance is different from the Cash Balance, because the fund balance from the prior year included assets and liabilities that were not cash.

Statement of Financial Position—Accrual Basis

Billy's Mother's accrual financial documents will also include a Statement of Financial Position, which they call the Balance Sheet. This wasn't necessary on the Cash statement, because it didn't show any assets except the bank balance. Using an accrual basis, the Balance Sheet can show are several other assets and liabilities recognized and recorded that haven't passed through the checkbook yet. Figure 2-7 shows the accrual basis Statement of Financial Position (here called the Balance Sheet, the common term from for-profit accounting).

Figure 2-7. Billy's Mother—Statement of Financial Position

Billy's Mother
Balance Sheet
As of December 31, 2004

ASSETS

Cash	$15,633
Grants Receivable	10,000
Accounts Receivable	640
Prepaid Expenses	3,000
Supplies	590
Total Assets	**$29,863**

LIABILITIES AND FUND BALANCE

Wages Payable	$ 1,500
Payroll Taxes Payable	120
Accounts Payable	1,950
Deferred Revenue	5,000
Total Liabilities	**8,570**
Fund Balance	**$21,293**
Total Liabilities and Fund Balance	**$29,863**

So with all that in mind, what does this Statement tell us about Billy's Mother?

- Billy's Mother is in a good cash position. With $15,633 in cash, they can easily pay their $3,570 in wages, payroll taxes, and accounts payable. Not only that, they expect another $10,640 to arrive shortly.

- Their largest liability, deferred revenue, doesn't have to be paid in cash, but will presumably be "earned" as they perform their regular operations or some special program.

- On the other hand, even for a small organization, $21,293 isn't a huge nest egg, so they have to be careful with their funds. As we saw above, they could operate normally for over two months with their cash on hand, but a large unexpected expense could endanger the organization. (There's a large intangible "asset" that doesn't show up on the books: their relationship with the church—Billy's Mother's ace in the hole. We might assume that if they had an unexpected major expense, such as a new roof, they could call on the church for support.)

Florentine Chamber Orchestra

Our second organization, the Florentine Chamber Orchestra (FCO), has more complex finances than Billy's Mother. FCO is a $500,000 organization that depends on contributions and grants for over half of its income. It receives a very small amount of government grant funding, which is probably more important as a stamp of approval for its public image than as an income source. Earned revenues are 45 percent of its income.

FCO is large and established enough that it maintains its books on an accrual basis and has an annual audit done by an outside accounting firm. FCO also needs specialized fundraising software to track both season ticket sales and contributors, although we won't go into these other than to say that they need to be coordinated with the computerized bookkeeping system.

Statement of Activities

Figure 2-8 shows the Florentine Chamber Orchestra's Statement of Activities.

This statement follows GAAP, which requires showing restricted income separately from unrestricted income, and all grants as restricted income. The restrictions are released when grant conditions are met, as shown in the Net Assets Released from Restrictions line.

FCO's Statement of Activities separates income into Support (contributed income including grants) and Revenue (earned income such as ticket sales), making it easier to understand how they operate.

What can we learn from FCO's Statement of Activities?

- FCO's earned revenues are 45 percent of total income, the industry average for classical music organizations.

- Although FCO didn't make a large profit, less than 3 percent of total income, it actually had positive cash flow the last two years. This is very good for an orchestra in a field where deficits and debt are common.

Figure 2-8. FCO—Statement of Activities

Florentine Chamber Orchestra
Statement of Activities
For the year ended 6/30/2005

SUPPORT AND REVENUE	Unrestricted	Temporarily Restricted	2005 Total	2004 Total
Support				
Contributions	$185,382		$185,382	$182,926
Foundation and Government Grants.	48,000	$ 15,000	63,000	88,231
In-Kind Contributions	3,900		3,900	11,297
Fundraising Events, Net of Expenses	28,711		28,711	26,554
Total Support	265,993	15,000	280,993	309,008
Revenue				
Ticket Sales	214,870		214,870	221,783
Contract Service Fees	4,000		4,000	10,000
Other Income.	12,094		12,094	23,491
Total Revenues	230,964	—	230,964	255,274
Net Assets Released from Restrictions	48,200	(48,200)		
Total Support and Revenue	$545,157	$(33,200)	$511,957	$564,282
EXPENSES				
Salaries and Benefits	175,746		175,746	185,297
Audio Production and Broadcasting	9,712		9,712	9,264
Marketing	25,083		25,083	24,811
Contract Services.	128,733		128,733	145,971
Meetings and Conferences	1,075		1,075	1,088
Insurance.	6,781		6,781	5,043
Professional Fees	43,591		43,591	11,876
Supplies	8,499		8,499	3,461
Telecommunications.	3,842		3,842	4,831
Postage	18,766		18,766	20,577
Office Expense	1,648		1,648	3,045
Occupancy and Hall Rental	22,946		22,946	26,491
Printing	3,849		3,849	3,822
Equipment Rental	1,540		1,540	1,946
Equipment Maintenance	11,298		11,298	8,264
Dues and Subscriptions	684		684	344
Bank Fees.	5,892		5,892	7,164
Travel	18,466		18,466	16,423
Interest.	1,541		1,541	2,945
Miscellaneous.	4,613		4,613	1,050
Depreciation.	3,012		3,012	1,362
Total Expenses	$497,317	—	$497,317	$485,075
Change in Net Assets	47,840	(33,200)	14,640	79,207
Net Assets (Deficit)				
Net Assets, Beginning of Year	47,614	50,000	97,614	18,407
Net Assets, End of Year	$ 95,454	$ 16,800	$112,254	$ 97,614

- On the other hand, FCO's contributed and event income are practically unchanged from the prior year, while grants are slightly down. Since ticket sales are also down, a reader might want to look at several more years and see if this is a trend and if FCO is working hard enough to build its funding base. This might be an organization that is coasting, which could make it hard for them to attract significant new grants.

- On the expense side, we'd need to know more about FCO to tell how much of salaries and benefits are administrative vs. program, and if all musicians are listed under contract services. As an arts organization, FCO is not required to provide a Statement of Functional Expenses, which would have separated these categories.

Statement of Financial Position

FCO's Statement of Financial Position is shown in Figure 2-9.

This Statement of Financial Position is a little more complex than that of Billy's Mother, separating Net Assets into Unrestricted, Temporarily Restricted, and Permanently Restricted. Since SFAS 117, grants are not listed as deferred revenue, but instead as temporarily restricted net assets. Since SFAS 116, the total amounts of multiyear grants must be shown as assets, which can skew the net assets and make it seem like the organization has more cash on hand that it actually does. (See Appendix C for a complete list of these changes.)

FCO's Balance Sheet tells us the following:

- FCO is relatively secure for a mid-sized arts organization, with no debt and cash in the bank.

- FCO has enough cash to meet their current liabilities easily. If we know that their performing season is Fall/Winter and that many season subscription revenues don't come in until September, this seems a safe proportion of their annual budget.

- FCO has a policy of immediately selling any stock donations and converting them to cash, a common practice for nonprofits to deal with marketable securities.

- On the other hand, FCO has some long-term investments resulting from a bequest that set up an endowment with assets that can't be sold. These are reflected under Net Assets as Permanently Restricted.

Figure 2-9. FCO—Statement of Financial Position

Florentine Chamber Orchestra
Statement of Financial Position
As of June 30, 2005

ASSETS	2005	2004
Cash and Cash Equivalents	$102,655	$ 93,802
Marketable Securities	—	2,517
Pledges Receivable.	19,603	18,937
Grants Receivable	6,000	25,000
CD Inventory	1,299	1,587
Prepaid Expenses	12,603	14,687
Property and Equipment, Net.	30,971	16,990
Long-Term Investments	77,643	72,940
TOTAL ASSETS	$250,774	$246,460
LIABILITIES AND NET ASSETS		
Liabilities		
Accounts Payable.	28,111	3,298
Accrued Payroll Taxes	9,645	7,633
Deferred Revenue	100,764	105,722
Note Payable	—	32,193
Total Liabilities	$138,520	$148,846
Net Assets		
Unrestricted	17,629	(326)
Temporarily Restricted	16,982	25,000
Permanently Restricted.	77,643	72,940
Total Net Assets	112,254	97,614
Total Liabilities and Net Assets	$250,774	$246,460

- Under Liabilities, FCO's large Deferred Revenue line reflects ticket sales for future concerts. Since these don't affect cash, FCO's actual available cash is much larger than the Unrestricted Net Assets might make it seem.

Jefferson County Community Action

Our third and largest organization, Jefferson County Community Action (JCCA), has the most complicated financial statements. A large, multiservice agency, JCCA began in 1966 as part of the War on Poverty. JCCA has an annual operating budget of $13.5 million, owns its own headquarters building, and rents other space for programs around Jefferson County. Most of its funding (82 percent) is from local, state, and federal grants and contracts.

In the mid-1990s, JCCA found itself in the situation of many social service providers. It was almost completely dependent on government contracts, which were getting more stringent in their requirements. Local governments were reimbursing for services slowly, often months late, but JCCA had to pay its staff and vendors in a timely manner. Despite its long history, JCCA had trouble getting short-term bank loans to meet its obligations because it had no assets with which to secure them. Further, despite its long history, good reputation, and high visibility, most Jefferson County residents didn't know what it did and vaguely thought it was a government agency. Finally, JCCA was paying thousands of dollars annually for rent. The JCCA management and Board realized that they were functioning almost as a wholly owned subsidiary of government agencies, with little control over their finances or even their destiny.

JCCA responded by launching a capital campaign to build a new building for its administration, child care programs, and most other services. This allowed it to reintroduce itself to the community and tell its story, create a highly visible headquarters, launch a private fundraising program, and dramatically reduce its rent expenses. But the biggest change was in JCCA's financial status. The largest item on their balance sheet was no longer accounts receivable, but their building. They used the equity in this building to secure a low-interest line of credit, so that meeting payroll when the County was slow to pay was no longer a crisis. With a capacity building grant from a foundation, JCCA built on the success of its capital campaign to create a strong development program, which increased contributed income and helped strengthen its community image.

All of these factors put JCCA in a stronger negotiating position with local governments when contracts came due. While government grants and contracts remain by far the organization's largest source of income, JCCA now has more stability and freedom of action.

Statement of Activities

JCCA's Statement of Activities and Changes in Net Assets (see Figure 2-10) follows the same format as FCO's, but the differences in funding are significant. Here is what the statement shows us:

- Government grants and contracts are 87 percent of total income and have increased since the prior year. This is typical of social service agencies. Since this total is so large, JCCA needs to track the diversification of its government funding is among local, state, and federal grants, as well as among program areas such as child care, antipoverty, and other programs.

Figure 2-10. JCCA—Statement of Activities

Jefferson County Community Action
Statement of Activities and Changes in Net Assets
For the Fiscal Year Ended June 30, 2005
with Comparative Totals for 2004

	Unrestricted	Temporarily Restricted	2005 Total	2004 Total
SUPPORT AND REVENUE				
Government Grants and Contracts	$12,589,075		$12,589,075	$11,879,204
United Way	269,938		269,938	293,005
Contributions	95,385	$ 34,872	130,257	177,625
Foundation Grants.	10,000	340,973	350,973	150,000
Corporate Grants and Contributions.	54,697		54,697	56,132
In-Kind Revenue.	857,955		857,955	748,732
Fees.	125,479		125,479	116,859
Reimbursements	118,462		118,462	34,685
Net Assets Released from Restrictions:				
Satisfaction of Time Restrictions	91,455	(91,455)	—	
Satisfaction of Program Restrictions.	334,987	(334,987)	—	
Total Support and Revenue	14,547,433	(50,597)	14,496,836	13,456,242
EXPENSES				
Program Services	12,556,074		12,556,074	12,067,672
Administration	1,643,255		1,643,255	1,206,843
Resource Development.	365,670		365,670	287,281
Total Expenses	14,564,999	—	14,564,999	13,561,796
Change in Net Assets	(17,566)	(50,597)	(68,163)	(105,554)
Net Assets, Beginning of Year	2,529,552	1,088,796	3,618,348	3,723,902
Net Assets, End of Year	$ 2,511,986	$1,038,199	$ 3,550,185	$ 3,618,348

- All contributed income, including in-kind, is 11 percent of total revenues. At over $1.6 million dollars, this allows JCCA to start new programs and provide services outside the limitations of its government contracts. The $340,973 in restricted foundation grants are probably for such innovation or program expansions. A challenge for JCCA is to keep these private funds from being captured by government matching funds requirements.

- On the expense side, Program Services are 86 percent of the total, a good ratio.

- Administration is 11 percent of total expenses, and Resource Development is 3 percent, for a total of 14 percent. This is a low percentage for a direct service agency and a sign of good management.

- Resource Development (fundraising) at $365,670 brought in $1,663,820 in cash and in-kind support, more than 4.5 times its cost. Given that this department also handles public relations and marketing, as well as contributing to writing some government grant applications, the development department is earning its keep.

- JCCA has lost money the last two years, reducing net assets. Although the amounts are relatively small, this trend should be watched over time.

Statement of Financial Position

Here are the main lessons from JCAA's Statement of Financial Position (here called the Statement of Assets, Liabilities, and Net Assets), shown in Figure 2-11:

- JCCA's balance sheet is relatively strong. Its cash, including restricted cash for programs, is more than enough to pay the cash portion of its current liabilities.

- JCCA's main building and equipment are owned free of any mortgage. A small mortgage is for a second program office in another part of the county.

Statement of Functional Expenses

Under SFAS 117, JCCA, a health and welfare organization, is required to provide a Statement of Functional Revenues, Expenses, and Changes in Net Assets. This document takes the Statement of Activities and breaks each "natural" line item into functional areas. The required functions are Administration, Resource Development, and Program Services. As a multi-service agency, JCCA further divides Program Services to show its major program areas.

Figure 2-12 shows the resulting Statement of Functional Revenues, Expenses, and Changes in Net Assets.

This presentation of income and expense by function gives a much clearer idea of how funding and expenses are broken down among programs. It also shows the allocation of income from Resource Development to support programs and the allocation of administrative costs to programs,

Figure 2-11. JCCA—Statement of Financial Position

Jefferson County Community Action
Statement of Assets, Liabilities, and Net Assets
As of 6/30/2005
with Comparative Totals for 2004

ASSETS	2005	2004
Current Assets		
Cash and Cash Equivalents	$ 584,294	$ 318,729
Restricted Cash.	349,021	381,022
Accounts Receivable	562,777	738,273
Pledges Receivable.	56,425	71,926
Prepaid Expenses	3,000	3,000
Total Current Assets	$1,555,517	$1,512,950
Property and Equipment		
Property and Equipment, Net.	3,485,829	3,527,863
Other Assets		
Long Term Pledges Receivable	85,201	104,972
Total Assets	$5,126,547	$5,145,785
LIABILITIES AND NET ASSETS		
Current Liabilities		
Accounts Payable.	603,978	678,539
Accrued Vacation Payable	139,822	132,845
Payroll Tax Payable	58,553	53,907
Deferred Revenue	216,883	42,977
Current Portion of Long-Term Debt.	12,044	10,978
	1,031,280	919,246
Long-Term Liabilities		
Notes and Mortgages Payable, Net.	545,082	608,191
Total Liabilities	$1,576,362	$1,527,437
Net Assets		
Unrestricted Net Assets.	2,511,986	2,529,552
Temporarily Restricted Net Assets	1,038,199	1,088,796
Total Net Assets	3,550,185	3,618,348
Total Liabilities and Net Assets	$5,126,547	$5,145,785

Figure 2-12. JCCA—Statement of Functional Expenses

Jefferson County Community Action
Statement of Functional Revenues, Expenses, and Changes in Net Assets
For the Fiscal Year Ended June 30, 2004, with Comparative Totals for 2003

	Early Childhood Development	Family & Community Resources	Community Partners
SUPPORT AND REVENUE			
Government Grants & Contracts	$6,498,316	$5,608,913	$ —
Private Revenue			
United Way			
Contributions			
Foundation Grants.			
Corporate Grants & Contributions			
Total Private Revenue.			
Income			
Fees.	85,492	39,987	
Reimbursements		54,399	
Total Income	85,492	94,386	—
In-Kind Revenue.	435,669	54,227	302,497
Transfers Between Funds	37,564	384,661	
Total Support and Revenue	$7,057,041	$6,142,187	$302,497
EXPENSES			
Employee Costs	4,756,984	1,709,466	144
Professional Costs	20,188	11,247	487
Travel	61,377	32,648	
Occupancy	269,641	101,699	7,249
Other Rent.	154,266	42,647	
Depreciation			
Supplies	58,436	34,617	33
Communications	112,784	87,498	819
Marketing	7,954	5,314	
Insurance.	31,298	5,017	300
Repairs & Maintenance	28,346	642	
Miscellaneous.	65,779	43,187	
Client Expenses	648,555	3,424,052	
Bad Debt Expense			
Capital Outlay.	41,007		
In-Kind Expenses	435,669	54,227	302,497
Total Expenses	$6,692,284	$5,552,261	$311,529
Other Transactions			
Transfers from CSBG	(66,547)	(80,314)	
Administrative Allocation	614,234	516,433	
Other Fund Sources & Transfers.	10,007	(7,219)	(9,293)
Total Other Transactions	557,694	428,900	(9,293)
Change in Net Assets	(192,937)	161,026	261
Net Assets, Beginning of Year	84,651	687,431	(44)
Net Assets, End of Year	$ (108,286)	$ 848,457	$ 217

Total Program Services	Administration	Resource Development	2005 Total	2004 Total
$12,107,229	$ 481,846	$ —	$12,589,075	$11,879,204
		269,938	269,938	293,005
		130,257	130,257	177,625
		350,973	350,973	150,000
		54,697	54,697	56,132
		805,865	805,865	676,762
125,479			125,479	116,859
54,399	64,063		118,462	34,685
179,878	64,063	—	243,941	151,544
792,393	45,317	20,245	857,955	748,732
422,225		(422,225)	—	
$13,501,725	$ 591,226	$ 403,885	$14,496,836	$13,456,242
6,466,594	774,578	204,977	7,446,149	7,021,945
31,922	194,397	15,642	241,961	174,216
94,025	18,446	5,913	118,384	121,448
378,589	72,647	7,864	459,100	377,964
196,913	99,211		296,124	229,461
—	77,350		77,350	75,483
93,086	51,712	15,233	160,031	331,024
201,101	41,448	30,578	273,127	232,479
13,268	421	15,079	28,768	19,487
36,615	51,267		87,882	46,413
28,988	1,837	525	31,350	54,971
108,966	34,781	5,247	148,994	149,478
4,072,607	3,781	4,610	4,080,998	3,855,009
—		20,000	20,000	11,200
41,007	176,062	19,757	236,826	112,486
792,393	45,317	20,245	857,955	748,732
$12,556,074	$ 1,643,255	$ 365,670	$14,564,999	$13,561,796
(146,861)	308,451	(161,590)		
1,130,667	(1,241,679)	111,012		
(6,505)	241	6,264		
977,301	(932,987)	(44,314)		
(31,650)	(119,042)	82,529	(68,163)	(105,554)
772,038	2,530,683	315,627	3,618,348	3,723,902
$ 740,388	$ 2,411,641	$ 398,156	$ 3,550,185	$ 3,618,348

so that these costs can be included in government contracts. The grantwriter's interest in this statement is to see which programs have deficits that could be filled with additional government or foundation and corporate grants.

Statement of Cash Flows

If we had looked at these preceding statements closely, we might have noticed that, although the Statement of Activities showed a decrease in net assets of $63,163 from the prior year, the Statement of Assets, Liabilities, and Net Assets showed that JCCA ended the year with $233,546 more cash in the bank. The Statement of Cash Flows reconciles these differences by removing noncash transactions such as depreciation, translating accrual items such as accounts receivable into cash transactions, and recognizing nonoperating activities such as financing.

Figure 2-13 shows the JCAA Statement of Cash Flows.

Figure 2-13. JCCA—Statement of Cash Flows

Jefferson County Community Action **Statement of Cash Flows** **For the Year Ended 6/30/2005**		
	2005	**2004**
CASH FLOWS FROM OPERATING ACTIVITIES		
Change in Net Assets	$ (63,163)	$(105,554)
Adjustments to Reconcile Changes in Net Assets to Net Cash Provided by Operating Activities:		
Depreciation	77,350	75,483
(Increase) Decrease in Accounts Receivable	175,460	34,597
(Increase) Decrease in Pledges Receivable	175,496	5,429
Increase (Decrease) in Accounts Payable	(74,561)	152,477
Increase (Decrease) in Accrued Vacation Payable	6,977	24,971
Increase (Decrease) in Payroll Liabilities	4,646	(4,257)
Increase (Decrease) in Deferred Revenue	173,906	(97,231)
Total Adjustments	539,274	191,469
Net Cash Provided by Operating Activities	476,111	85,915
CASH FLOWS FROM INVESTING ACTIVITIES	—	—
CASH FLOWS FROM FINANCING ACTIVITIES		
Payments on Long-Term Debt	(11,823)	(9,937)
Payments on Line of Credit	(230,724)	(33,304)
Net Cash Used by Financing Activities	(242,547)	(43,241)
Net Increase in Cash and Cash Equivalents	233,564	42,674
Cash and Cash Equivalents, Beginning of Year	699,751	657,077
Cash and Cash Equivalents, End of Year	$ 933,315	$ 699,751

What the JCCA Statement of Cash Flows shows is that the organization has been successful in collecting on government contracts (Accounts Receivable) and outstanding pledges from the prior year, while becoming more current on its own accounts payable.

There was also an increase in deferred revenue, reflecting grants income for which program services have not yet been performed.

Using Financial Statements to Determine an Organization's Financial Health

In-Depth Analysis

In each of the examples, we found some information that gave us some idea of how the organization was doing financially, but we can do a more in-depth analysis. There are several generally accepted methods of assessing a nonprofit's financial condition. If you have access to the organization's financial statements, these are all fairly easy to check on and calculate. Since almost all nonprofits' 990 forms (discussed in detail later in this chapter) are now posted online by GuideStar, many of these can be reviewed without formal access to the organization's books.

Four Key Indicators of Financial Health

Kay Sohl, an accountant and consultant who is considered Oregon's nonprofit guru, says she looks for four things in determining an organization's financial health.

- **Are they achieving their mission?** Isn't that interesting, an accountant saying that the mission is the most important thing? Kay's reasoning is that if they aren't carrying out their mission, either they aren't able to raise enough money or they aren't using what they have effectively—or both.

- **What is their cash position?** Do they have enough money to pay their current bills? If not, the organization is likely to run in a state of constant crisis that distracts from their mission work.

- **What are their net assets?** Do they have a nest egg to fall back on if a major funding source fell through? Or on the other hand, do they have the resources to take advantage of a sudden opportunity?

- **Are they in compliance with their contracts and restrictions (if any)?** Many nonprofits, especially social service agencies, operate under several government contracts and grants that have multiple conditions and restrictions. In addition, there are foundation program grants and restricted individual donations, among other things. Keeping track of them can be complex, but an organization that is seriously out of compliance is in danger of losing major grants or contracts or even being required to pay back funds that were spent on unallowable expenses.

Basic Questions about a Nonprofit's Financial Statements

Are their financial statements audited? If so, do they have a clean audit (i.e., no adverse management letter)? Have they had several years of clean audits?

Being audited isn't proof of being financially solvent or profitable, but it does tell you that they pay attention to their finances and that the numbers you get are reliable. Look at the auditor's opinion letter at the beginning; it will say if there are any exceptions. Also look at the notes in the back, which will give details about any major loans, long-term lease obligations, or other factors that could affect their financial condition.

Do their financial statements show comparative data? Do they show both the latest year and the prior year?

Audited financial statements always include two years of comparative information. With comparative statements, you can see if their income from important sources is up or down, if their assets are growing or declining, and so forth.

Here are some things to check in comparative statements:

- Do the amounts or percentages of major categories differ significantly from one year to the next?

- Does this year include line items that didn't exist last year, or vice versa?

- If investments show major changes, does the Statement of Cash Flows show significant sales or purchases?

- Were there significant purchases of property or equipment during the year?

- Has long- and/or short-term debt increased or decreased?

- Have contributions and earned income changed significantly (either up or down) from last year?

- Have program, administrative, or fundraising expenses changed significantly from last year?

- Did revenues exceed expenses, and is this a change from last year?

- Did net assets increase or decrease, and is this a change from last year?

- Did unrestricted net assets increase or decrease, and is this a change from last year?

Any of these cases could have a good explanation with no cause for concern. But making these comparisons tells you what questions to ask if you want to know more.

Key Financial Ratios

Key financial ratios are a quick indicator of the financial condition of a nonprofit, which you can figure out with a little work. They are useful for assessing how the organization manages its funds and its fiscal stability. Considered over a longer term, they are useful in understanding a nonprofit's financial progress from year to year. Of course, financial ratios are affected by the unique circumstances of each organization—its size, age, market, programs, and so forth. Their usefulness is also affected by the accounting practices of the nonprofit.

Key financial ratios are used in business by both outsiders and internal management for making decisions on investing, lending, expansion, changing operations, and many other areas. They are an excellent means for comparing two companies in the same business or comparing a company to industry averages.

For this exercise we'll look at Jefferson County Community Action, the largest of our three organizations. The underlined text tells how to figure the ratios. Text in (parentheses) tells where to find the numbers to use.

Program Ratio: Program Expense ÷ Total Expense (Statement of Activities). The Program Ratio measures the relationship between direct service and total expenses, including administration, fundraising, and other areas. In general, a nonprofit should try to achieve high program ratios, devoting as much of its efforts to program as possible. Over 0.8 is considered very good in most nonprofits.

JCCA's Program Ratio: $12,724,454 ÷ $14,564,999 = 0.87

For a large social service agency running several programs and working with multiple government funders and regulators, this is quite good.

Contributions & Grants Ratio: Contributions and Grants ÷ Total Income (Statement of Activities). The Contributions & Grants Ratio tells us the percentage of total revenue that comes from private sources. This can vary widely depending on the type of organization. After considering its circumstances, a nonprofit should set targets for its Contributions & Grants Ratio.

JCCA's Contributions & Grants Ratio: $805,865 ÷ $14,496,836 = 0.06

This seems very low, but in fact almost any major social service organization will get the vast majority of its funding from government sources.

This ratio varies widely among types of nonprofits. For example, let's look at our other two groups:

FCO's Contributions & Grants Ratio: $280,993 ÷ $511,957 = 0.55

A performing arts organization, FCO has a strong earned income component in ticket sales. However, this pays less than half of their expenses, leaving the rest to be raised privately. Arts organizations typically receive very little government funding.

Billy's Mother's Contributions & Grants Ratio: $85,440 ÷ $85,440 = 1.0

Billy's Mother receives 100 percent of its funding privately. Because it has a small budget and strong support from the church, it doesn't really need to expand its funding sources. This gives the organization great freedom in how it chooses to operate and handle its finances.

Debt Ratio: Total Liabilities ÷ Total Assets (Statement of Financial Position). The Debt Ratio is an indication of an organization's solvency. In general, a nonprofit should try to have low debt ratios. However, such things as mortgages to acquire property and lines of credit to manage cash flow can be solid management practices. (Since nonprofits don't pay income taxes, their interest expenses aren't tax deductible, making borrowing slightly different than with for-profit businesses.)

JCCA's Debt Ratio: $1,576,362 ÷ $5,126,547 = 0.31

JCCA's total debt is almost one-third of its assets, but when we look at the balance sheet, we see that $545,000 is long-term debt, $216,833 is deferred revenues, and $139,822 is employees' accrued vacation.

Quick Ratio: Quick Assets ÷ Total Current Liabilities (Statement of Financial Position). The Quick Ratio or acid test compares an organization's most liquid assets (ordinarily cash, any marketable securities, and receivables) to its current debt. It is called the quick ratio because only cash and assets that can be quickly convertible to cash are included. The general rule of thumb is that the quick ratio should be 1:1 or higher. (A related ratio is the Current Ratio, <u>Current Assets ÷ Current Liabilities</u>. In JCCA's case, they're virtually the same.)

JCCA's Quick Ratio: $1,555,517 ÷ $1,031,280 = 1.51

JCCA has more than adequate cash and liquid assets to pay its bills.

Reserve Ratio or Liquid Funds Indicator: <u>Unrestricted Net Assets (not including buildings and equipment) ÷ One Month's Expenses</u> (Statements of Financial Position and Activities). The Reserve Ratio gives an idea (in months) of the nonprofit's operating liquidity. This shows how long the organization could operate if no new income came in, before it had to consider selling assets.

JCCA's Reserve Ratio: $1,555,517 ÷ $1,213,750 = 1.28

JCCA could operate as usual for 1.28 months, or five to six weeks, on its current cash. Given that it depends largely on government grants, which can sometimes be slow to pay, this could be a cause for concern. Having a large line of credit secured by their building is JCCA's insurance against slow payment. But as we'll see next, they also do a good job of collecting, based on the solid relationships built with funders and a strong billing department.

Accounts Receivable Turnover: <u>Total Amounts Billed ÷ Average Accounts Receivable</u> (Statement of Financial Position). The Accounts Receivable Turnover is relevant for organizations that are reimbursed for services provided. Turnover is a key concept from retailing: to make a profit, a store must sell all of its inventory (turn it over) several times a year. For a nonprofit, this ratio tells how many times per year the organization is paid for its services.

JCCA's Accounts Receivable Turnover: $12,589,075 ÷ $650,525 = 19.35

JCCA turns over its accounts receivable more than 19 times annually. We used their Government Grants and Revenues as Total Amounts Billed and figured average accounts receivable by adding the numbers for 2004 and 2005, then dividing by 2. This gives us the number we can use for the next ratio.

Average Collection Period of Receivables: <u>365 ÷ Accounts Receivable Turnover</u> (Accounts Receivable Turnover ratio). The Average Collection Period of Receivables tells how long it takes for the organization to get reimbursed for services, which can be a key component in cash flow management.

JCCA's Average Collection Period of Receivables: 365 ÷ 19.35 = 18.86

This means JCCA gets paid on the average about 19 days after submitting an invoice. This is an excellent record. Many social service providers will wait two months or longer to be paid. If JCCA is billing in a timely manner, they don't have to worry too much about their cash flow.

Accounts Payable Aging Indicator: [Accounts Payable Balance ÷ Total Expense] × 12 (Statements of Financial Position and Activities). The Accounts Payable Aging Indicator gives an idea (in months) of how fast the nonprofit pays its bills. This may give an indicator of the organization's credit-worthiness. The lower the indicator (fewer months of average payment) the faster the nonprofit pays its bills.

JCCA's Accounts Payable Aging Indicator: [603,978 ÷ 14,564,999] × 12 = 0.48

All of the other ratios and indicators focused on how finances affected JCCA. This looks at how good a customer JCCA is for its vendors. JCCA pays its bills within an average of half a month, or two to three weeks, which makes it a good credit risk. JCCA may have a policy of paying within 10 days for vendors that give discounts for prompt payment (usually listed on an invoice as something like "3% net 10").

Trend Analysis

If comparing two years can tell you a lot, what about looking at five years? What about 10? What are their long-term trends in income and expense? To do trend analysis, you'll need to get five years' worth of financial statements. Then pick out specific items and make multiyear charts showing them.

Figure 2-14 shows JCCA's Average Collection Period of Receivables. You can see, over a five-year period, the average number of days it took JCCA to be paid for their contracted services. They have reduced the days it takes them to get paid from over 44 to less than 19, a 50 percent reduction. This is a real achievement for their billing department and means they will have far fewer cash flow problems.

About Audits

"We're being audited!" These words can strike terror into a manager's heart. While most nonprofits don't have to worry about the truly terrifying kind, IRS audits, even a routine audit requested by the organization itself can be time consuming and expensive. So what is an audit anyway, and how do we know if we should get one, or worry about it if we do? Here are five basic questions to ask about nonprofit financial examinations:

Figure 2-14. JCCA—Receivables Collections in Days, 2001–2005

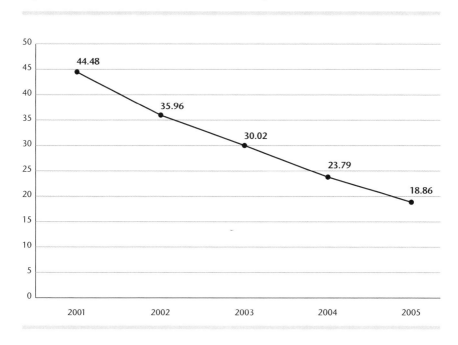

Five Basic Questions about Audits

1. What is an audit?

An audit is a very organized process in which an independent[7] CPA (Certified Public Accountant) looks at your finances and tests selected transactions and internal controls to form an opinion on the accuracy and fairness of the organization's financial statements. Then the auditor expresses this opinion in a letter that becomes part of the financial document.

Steps in the audit include:

- **Testing.** The auditor will check the paper trail on randomly selected or significant transactions. For example, say you bought a computer. The auditor would select that transaction out of your bookkeeping journals, then would want to see the purchase order, the invoice, the check that paid for the invoice, the bank statement showing that the check had cleared, and finally, the computer itself.

---

[7] The auditor cannot work for the organization he or she is auditing, nor be significantly involved in preparing their financial statements.

- **Confirmations.** A confirmation is an independent statement that supports the financial information in your records. Auditors will send confirmation letters on your letterhead to your bank(s), funders, attorney, and the people and organizations to whom you owe money and who owe you money to confirm the amounts reflected in your books. Confirmations are mailed by and returned directly to your auditor to ensure their credibility.

- **Evidence of internal controls.** The auditor will either meet with staff members or request that they complete a questionnaire documenting the procedures related to spending and receiving money and other resources; complying with laws, donor restrictions, and regulations; maintaining property and equipment; and recording financial information in the books.

- **Documentation.** The auditor will request a number of documents related to the following:

  - *Assets:* Accounts receivable, property, and equipment (fixed assets).

  - *Liabilities:* Accounts payable, deferred revenue.

  - *Revenue:* Grants and contributions details; donated services and materials; special events and benefits, showing income and expenses and documentation for the value of goods or services that donors received (and, therefore, are not included in the tax-deductible portion of their payment); documentation of fees from memberships, tuition, performances, and other services; inventory records.

  - *Expenses:* Payroll records, including federal and state tax returns related to payroll; vacation records.

- **Miscellaneous.** The auditor may also review the following items:

  - Board minutes

  - Leases and other contracts

  - Bank statements, bank reconciliations, checkbooks, and canceled checks

  - Financial files for paid bills and deposits

  - Components of your accounting system—chart of accounts, journals and ledgers, printouts if the system is computerized, trial balances, and so forth

  - Budget for the fiscal year being examined.

2. What are the different levels of financial examination?

There are three basic levels of examination a CPA can do for an organization: audits, reviews, and compilations. As listed here, they are progressively less thorough and therefore less reliable, but they are also progressively less expensive. Small- or medium-sized nonprofits with simple finances may choose to have a review rather than an audit, or to have annual reviews and an audit maybe every three or five years.

An audit involves careful analysis and testing of transactions according to strict guidelines. A review involves no testing; it simply compares the internal bookkeeping documents of the organization and performs some quick analysis to see if they have internal consistency. A compilation is little more than collecting and reformatting raw financial records into financial statements; it involves no testing.

3. Does my nonprofit need audited financial statements?

Many foundation guidelines ask for copies of audited financial statements. For smaller nonprofits, however, most funders will accept internally produced, unaudited financial statements. Because audits are expensive (a simple audit may cost $3,000 to $5,000 or more), they are a lot to ask of small organizations applying for smaller grants. I know of one large foundation that added $5,000 to the grants of worthy but unsophisticated grantees and made an audit a condition of their grant. Having audited financial statements gives credibility and a sense of responsibility and maturity to an organization that can be helpful in fundraising and marketing.

Generally speaking, an organization should have its financial statements audited if:

- **It is required to do so.** Many government agencies require audits of their grantees. The federal government requires an A-133 audit (explained later in more detail) of any organization that receives over $500,000 annually in federal money. Because this total can include federal funds passed through state and local government grants, this requirement affects many nonprofits with little or no direct federal funding. Some states are beginning to pass legislation requiring nonprofits with budgets over a certain size, often $500,000, to have independent audits.

- **It is large and complex.** Generally speaking, a nonprofit with a budget of over $1 million annually or one more than five years old with multiple programs should be audited to verify its financial position and practices. Medium-sized organizations without a controller are especially likely to have accounting problems that an audit would uncover.

- **It is considering a major fundraising push.** If you are considering a capital or endowment campaign, or even just a big major donor push, you should be planning an audit as part of the preparation.

4. What should I look for in an audited financial statement?

It surprises many people that an audit doesn't guarantee anything—neither the accuracy of the statements nor the financial health of the organization. Rather, in precise language, the auditor's letter will say, "In our opinion, the financial statements present fairly the financial position of the organization."

This letter will also say, "These financial statements are the responsibility of the organization's management." The auditor doesn't prepare the financial statements; he or she simply examines them. This is what makes the audit independent. Until recent years, many nonprofit accountants were willing to interpret "independent" liberally and help organizations format and draft their statements for auditing. However, with the tightening of accounting regulations after the Enron debacle and other scandals, most CPAs are backing away from this practice. This means that a nonprofit must pay one accountant to prepare their books and another to audit them, greatly increasing their audit-related expenses.

The most significant part of the letter is toward the end. It should say, "In our opinion, these statement present fairly. . . ." If there are no exceptions, the audit is unqualified or "clean." If the word "except" appears anywhere, or if the auditor declines to express an opinion, you have cause for concern.[8] A *qualified audit* will raise red flags with funders. If your organization has a qualified audit, find out why and what can be done to improve your practices.

Figure 2-15 shows a typical auditor's letter.

After the audit letter will come the financial statements. They are the same as those in Chapter 2 and are read and interpreted in exactly the same way. The only difference is that these have been through the audit process.

Notes in the Audited Statement. The last several pages of audited financial statements are the Notes. They give important details to the reader, so you should check these details, even if you don't examine the entire statement closely. Be assured that staff at larger foundations will be looking for these things, and you may have to answer questions about them. Among these details are:

---

[8] A *qualified* opinion is when the auditor takes exception to some aspect of the financial statements, or where records are incomplete or missing. An *adverse* opinion is when the auditor says that the financial statements *do not* present fairly the organization's financial position. A *disclaimer* is included when the auditor is unable to form an opinion.

Figure 2-15. JCCA—Sample Auditor's Letter

INDEPENDENT AUDITORS' REPORT

Board of Directors
Jefferson County Community Action
1234 South Main Street
Anytown, California

We have audited the accompanying statement of financial position of Jefferson County Community Action as of June 30, 2004 and 2005, and the related statements of activities, functional expenses, and cash flows for the years then ended. These financial statements are the responsibility of JCCA's management. Our responsibility is to express an opinion on these financial statements based on our audit.

We have conducted our audit in accordance with generally accepted auditing standards and the standards applicable to financial audits contained in *Government Auditing Standards*, issued by the Comptroller General of the United States, and OMB Circular A-133, *Audits of States, Local Governments and Non-Profit Organizations*. These standards and OMB Circular A-133 require that we plan and perform the audit to obtain reasonable assurance about whether the financial statements are free of material misstatement. An audit involves examining, on a test basis, evidence supporting the amounts and disclosures on the financial statements. An audit also includes assessing the accounting principles used and significant estimates made by management, as well as evaluating the overall financial statement presentation. We believe our audit provides a reasonable basis for our opinion.

In our opinion, the financial statements referred to above present fairly, in all material respects, the financial position of Jefferson County Community Action as of June 30, 2004 and 2005, and its revenues, expenses, and cash flows for the fiscal years then ended in accordance with generally accepted accounting principles.

In accordance with *Government Auditing Standards*, we have also issued our report dated November 15, 2005, on our consideration of Jefferson County Community Action's internal control over financial reporting and our tests of its compliance with certain provisions of laws, regulations, contracts, and grants.

Our audit was performed for the purpose of forming an opinion on the basic financial statements of Jefferson County Community Action taken as a whole. The accompanying schedule of expenditures of federal awards is presented for purposes of additional analysis as required by U.S. Office of Management and Budget Circular A-133, *Audits of States, Local Governments and Non-Profit Organizations*, and is not a required part of the basic financial statements. Such information has been subjected to the auditing procedures applied in the audit of the basic financial statements and, in our opinion, is fairly stated, in all material respects, in relation to the basic financial statements taken as a whole.

Dumbledore and Gandalf, P.C.
Anytown, California

- Was the accrual basis of accounting used? If an organization is big enough to have an audit, it's big enough to need to use accrual accounting.

- Are any related-party transactions indicated? One example is borrowing money from or lending money to a board member. This type of transaction may be perfectly innocent, but check it out.

- Are the organization's borrowing practices detailed? Do they maintain lines of credit? Long-term borrowing should have a purpose, such as purchasing a building, rather than supplementing cash flow. Future indebtedness should decline as this debt is paid off; otherwise there may be a large balloon payment somewhere in the future.

- Is the organization a party to any lawsuits that could seriously affect its finances?

- Does future funding seem uncertain? If the auditors feel that the organization's funding is somewhat shaky, but not enough to warrant mention in the body of the opinion, they may slip in a phrase here about unreliable future funding, especially if it comes from government. This could be a sign of overdependence on one or two sources of funding.

5. What is an A-133 audit?

In 1984, in response to criticism toward the OMB, Congress passed the Single Audit Act, which required audits of state and local governments. The Act required a single audit of each grantee that would be accepted by all federal agencies, rather than the multiple audits by multiple agencies that had been common. OMB promised Congress that it would apply the Act to other contractors and issued OMB Circular A-133, which among other things extended the audit requirements to nonprofits that receive more than $500,000 annually in federal grants.

The A-133 audit is often added to an organization's regular financial audit. It includes a schedule of federal grant awards and covers specific areas that may include compliance with grant conditions, eligibility of service recipients (such as Medicaid or Food Stamps), following Circular A-110 for allowable costs, providing required grant matching funds, uses of program income, and what happened to equipment purchased with federal funds.

Understanding Form 990

Baring Your Finances to the World

Although 501(c)(3) organizations don't have to pay taxes, they do have to file annual returns with the IRS.[9] That return is Form 990, Return of Organization Exempt from Income Tax. This document (commonly called the 990) gives significant information about the organization's finances and operations. Nonprofits have long been required to show their 990s to the public, but until recently this form was obscure and such requests were rare. However, in 1999 the web-based organization called GuideStar (www. guidestar.org) began getting 990s from the IRS and posting them on its website for free downloading as PDF files.

When GuideStar began posting, many nonprofit executives were outraged at having their finances bared to the world. However, as more and more donors and funders began looking at the 990s, it became apparent that if the information was favorable, the posting could be advantageous to the organization. Nonprofits started asking GuideStar, "Why is it taking so long for my 990s to get posted?" Now any 501(c)(3) organization can provide its own PDF file of its 990s to GuideStar, as well as its 501(c)(3) letter, financial audit, annual reports, and other documents.

Importance of Form 990

So what is Form 990 and why should you care? Form 990 is how the IRS tracks a nonprofit's activities to see that they are meeting all of the requirements for their 501(c)(3) and 509(a) "not a private foundation" status. The 990 includes information on sources of income (to meet public support requirements), the amount spent on accomplishments related to the organization's tax-exempt purpose, lobbying activities, and any financial transactions with insiders such as board members.

Form 990 is important to the grant professional for several reasons, so the ability to read this form is invaluable. Many foundations are starting to request copies along with, or instead of, organizational budgets or financial statements (especially for organizations that don't have audits). Of course, funders can also just look at them online at the GuideStar website. A grant-writer can check out a potential consulting client, and an employer can check out similar or competing organizations. Because 990s include information not found in regular financial statements, they are a source of behind-the-scenes information.

---

[9] There are exceptions. Organizations whose gross receipts are "normally not more than $25,000" are not required to file (although they may still have to file with some states). Churches are also not required to file, although some do so.

Much information can be gained from reading one Form 990, but you can get an even better picture of the organization's finances by comparing three or more consecutive years, as shown in the earlier section on organizational financial health.

In addition to the following section, How to Read Form 990, there are two related sections in this book. Appendix B, An Insider's Look at Form 990, is an annotated blank Form 990 produced by Jason Orme, a Portland nonprofit accountant, which gives details on how Form 990 should be filled out. Chapter 6 also includes information on how to read Form 990-PF, the form that private foundations are required to file with the IRS, which is much more detailed than the regular Form 990.

How to Read Form 990

Main Form 990, Return of Organization Exempt from Income Tax

Part I—Revenue, Expenses, and Changes in Net Assets or Fund Balances. This part is basically the same information as the Statement of Activities, in slightly less detail. It gives an idea of the size of the organization and its sources of income. By looking at three years' 990s, you can predict the organization's future income-generating potential. If the income numbers are stable or increasing, it seems likely that the organization will continue to receive financial support in the future and thus remain financially strong. If the numbers are declining, the opposite could be true.

Part II—Statement of Functional Expenses. This part tells how much of its total expenses the organization spends on program services vs. management and fundraising. The program services aren't broken down by program, so it provides less detail than the typical Statement of Functional Expenses.

Part III—Statement of Program Service Accomplishments. This part requires the organization to show how its spending supports its *primary exempt* purpose. It may show a breakdown of program expenses, but is likely to be pretty general.

Part IV—Balance Sheets. These cover the last two years. With three year's 990s, you can look at four years of information and get an idea of trends in net assets, debt, and so forth.

Part IV-A and IV-B—Reconciliation of Revenue & Reconciliation of Expenses per Audited Financial Statements. . . . These parts are only required of organizations that have audited financial statements and are used to reconcile the audited statements with the 990.

Part V—List of Officers, Directors, Trustees, and Key Employees. This part also shows compensation for any of these people. In most nonprofits, the directors will be paid nothing. Key employees are typically the executive director and chief financial officer. (Note: They may be shown at the organization's address to keep their home addresses private.)

If you're really interested in salaries, Question 75 on Part V of the 990 tells if any key employee is partly paid by another related organization (for example, if there is a sister 501(c)(4) for lobbying). Line 89b in Section VI of the 990 asks if the organization paid any excess benefits or unreasonably high compensation, which could be taxable.

You can also get a rough idea of the average salaries in the whole organization by going to Part II of the 990 and adding Lines 25, 26, 27, and 28 in column A (which will give you total compensation), then dividing by line 90b in Part VI (number of employees).

Part VI—Other Information. This is a series of questions about the organization's business activities. In-kind services or donated goods are listed in Line 82. Several questions for other types of 501(c) organizations are included.

Part VII—Analysis of Income-Producing Activities, and Part VIII— Relationship of Activities to the Accomplishment of Exempt Purposes. These parts look at earned income activities such as rents, copays or client fees, Medicare/Medicaid, membership dues, and so forth.

Parts IX and X. These are questions relevant to *self-dealing*, such as the scandal in 1992 where United Way of America set up spin-off operations in which United Way officers had interests and which loaned them money. Most nonprofits will answer NA (not applicable) or No to these parts.

Schedule A, Organization Exempt under Section 501(c)(3)

Part I—Compensation of the Five Highest Paid Employees. . . . These are employees not listed in Part V of the 990 who are paid more than $50,000 annually. Since you get information about key employees in Part V of the 990, you can get an idea of salaries of at least six top staff at the organization.

Part II—Compensation of the Five Highest Paid Independent Contractors for Professional Services. This means an amount over $50,000. Since nonprofits are increasingly using consultants, this could be included in looking at salary information.

Part III—Statements About Activities. This part asks about lobbying and business activities. This includes *self-dealing* such as if a board member or other influential person sold goods or services to the organization. (This isn't necessarily bad; a board member could be selling services or equipment to the organization at a discount.) If any key employee (or director, trustee, or officer) is paid over $1,000, box 2d will be checked.

Part IV—Reason for Non-Private Foundation Status. This part helps the IRS look at the income information in the next section. This should be listed on the organization's 501(c)(3) letter.

Part IV-A—Support Schedule. This part asks questions about sources of income to support the non-private foundation status in Part IV. For this part you must use a cash method of accounting, whereas the rest of the form can use the accrual method.

Part V—Private School Questionnaire. This is only for private schools; it arose in response to the "segregation academies" in the 1960s in the South.

Part VI-A—Lobbying Expenditures by Electing Public Charities, and Part VI-B—Lobbying Activity by Nonelecting Public Charities. These parts ask about lobbying expenses. Lobbying is defined as supporting or opposing legislation. Most nonprofits will mark this NA. Those that do lobby can make a 501(h) election to have the question of whether their lobbying is appropriate determined by how much they spend on lobbying, and fill out VI-A. All other organizations explain their lobbying and fill out VI-B.

Part VII—Information Regarding . . . Noncharitable Exempt Organizations. This part asks about relations with and transfers of assets to other 501(c) organizations that are not charitable. For example, some organizations will establish 501(c)(3) status to carry on exempt activities and receive grants and tax-deductible contributions, and 501(c)(4) status to lobby or 501(c)(6) status to support member activities.

Schedule B, Schedule of Contributors

Schedule B is a listing of individual contributors who gave over $5,000. Organizations meeting the one-third support test as Publicly Supported Organizations or Fee/Activity Supported Organizations that did not receive any contributions over $5,000 are not required to fill out Schedule B. Instead, they check box H on the first page of Form 990 (for details, see Chapter 5).

If you've been using this section to walk through the 990 of an organization you're familiar with, I suggest you look at Appendix B, An Insider's Look at Form 990, for a more detailed view of how the various elements should fit together.

Figure 2-16 is a completed Form 990 for Jefferson County Community Action. I've only provided the first three pages so that you can compare it with their financial statements. For a fuller picture, I suggest that you go to GuideStar and download your organization's most recent 990, or that of another organization that interests you, and use this chapter to walk through its pages. If you do that, I suggest you also use Appendix B, An Insider's Look at Form 990, for a more detailed view of how the various elements should fit together.

Figure 2-16. JCCA—Completed Form 990

Form **990**	**Return of Organization Exempt From Income Tax**	OMB No. 1545-0047
	Under section 501(c), 527, or 4947(a)(1) of the Internal Revenue Code (except black lung benefit trust or private foundation)	20**04**
Department of the Treasury Internal Revenue Service	► The organization may have to use a copy of this return to satisfy state reporting requirements.	Open to Public Inspection

A For the 2004 calendar year, or tax year beginning **June 30.** , 2004, and ending **July 1** , 20 05

B Check if applicable:	Please use IRS label or print or type. See Specific Instruc-tions.	C Name of organization	D Employer identification number
☐ Address change		**Jefferson County Community Action**	95 : 1234567
☐ Name change		Number and street (or P.O. box if mail is not delivered to street address) Room/suite	E Telephone number
☐ Initial return		**1234 South Main Street**	(**222**) **222-2222**
☐ Final return		City or town, state or country, and ZIP + 4	F Accounting method: ☐ Cash ☑ Accrual
☐ Amended return		**Anytown, CA 87654**	☐ Other (specify) ►
☐ Application pending			

• Section 501(c)(3) organizations and 4947(a)(1) nonexempt charitable trusts must attach a completed Schedule A (Form 990 or 990-EZ).

H and **I** are not applicable to section 527 organizations.
H(a) Is this a group return for affiliates? ☐ Yes ☑ No

G Website: ► **www.jeffcca.org**

H(b) If "Yes," enter number of affiliates ► ....
H(c) Are all affiliates included? ☐ Yes ☐ No (If "No," attach a list. See instructions.)

J Organization type (check only one) ► ☑ 501(c) (**3**) ◄ (insert no.) ☐ 4947(a)(1) or ☐ 527

H(d) Is this a separate return filed by an organization covered by a group ruling? ☐ Yes ☑ No

K Check here ► ☐ if the organization's gross receipts are normally not more than $25,000. The organization need not file a return with the IRS; but if the organization received a Form 990 Package in the mail, it should file a return without financial data. **Some states require a complete return.**

I Group Exemption Number ►
M Check ► ☑ if the organization is **not** required to attach Sch. B (Form 990, 990-EZ, or 990-PF).

L Gross receipts: Add lines 6b, 8b, 9b, and 10b to line 12 ► **13,638,881**

Part I	**Revenue, Expenses, and Changes in Net Assets or Fund Balances** (See page 18 of the instructions.)		
1	Contributions, gifts, grants, and similar amounts received:		
a	Direct public support	**1a** 535,927	
b	Indirect public support	**1b** 269,938	
c	Government contributions (grants)	**1c** 12,589,075	
d	**Total** (add lines 1a through 1c) (cash $ **13,394.940** noncash $)	**1d**	13,394,940
2	Program service revenue including government fees and contracts (from Part VII, line 93)	**2**	125,479
3	Membership dues and assessments	**3**	
4	Interest on savings and temporary cash investments	**4**	
5	Dividends and interest from securities	**5**	
6a	Gross rents	**6a**	
b	Less: rental expenses	**6b**	
c	Net rental income or (loss) (subtract line 6b from line 6a)	**6c**	
7	Other investment income (describe ►)	**7**	
8a	Gross amount from sales of assets other than inventory	(A) Securities	(B) Other
		8a	
b	Less: cost or other basis and sales expenses	**8b**	
c	Gain or (loss) (attach schedule)	**8c**	
d	Net gain or (loss) (combine line 8c, columns (A) and (B))	**8d**	
9	Special events and activities (attach schedule). If any amount is from **gaming,** check here ► ☐		
a	Gross revenue (not including $ of contributions reported on line 1a)	**9a**	
b	Less: direct expenses other than fundraising expenses	**9b**	
c	Net income or (loss) from special events (subtract line 9b from line 9a)	**9c**	
10a	Gross sales of inventory, less returns and allowances	**10a**	
b	Less: cost of goods sold	**10b**	
c	Gross profit or (loss) from sales of inventory (attach schedule) (subtract line 10b from line 10a).	**10c**	
11	Other revenue (from Part VII, line 103)	**11**	118,462
12	**Total revenue** (add lines 1d, 2, 3, 4, 5, 6c, 7, 8d, 9c, 10c, and 11)	**12**	13,638,881
13	Program services (from line 44, column (B))	**13**	12,556,074
14	Management and general (from line 44, column (C))	**14**	1,643,255
15	Fundraising (from line 44, column (D))	**15**	365,670
16	Payments to affiliates (attach schedule)	**16**	
17	**Total expenses** (add lines 16 and 44, column (A))	**17**	14,564,999
18	Excess or (deficit) for the year (subtract line 17 from line 12)	**18**	(68,163)
19	Net assets or fund balances at beginning of year (from line 73, column (A))	**19**	3,618,348
20	Other changes in net assets or fund balances (attach explanation)	**20**	
21	Net assets or fund balances at end of year (combine lines 18, 19, and 20)	**21**	3,550,185

For Privacy Act and Paperwork Reduction Act Notice, see the separate instructions.   Cat. No. 11282Y   Form **990** (2004)

Figure 2-16. *Continued*

Form 990 (2004)   Page **2**

Part II **Statement of Functional Expenses** — All organizations must complete column (A). Columns (B), (C), and (D) are required for section 501(c)(3) and (4) organizations and section 4947(a)(1) nonexempt charitable trusts but optional for others. (See page 22 of the instructions.)

	Do not include amounts reported on line 6b, 8b, 9b, 10b, or 16 of Part I.		**(A)** Total	**(B)** Program services	**(C)** Management and general	**(D)** Fundraising
22	Grants and allocations (attach schedule) . . (cash $ _____ noncash $ _____)	22				
23	Specific assistance to individuals (attach schedule)	23				
24	Benefits paid to or for members (attach schedule)	24				
25	Compensation of officers, directors, etc. . .	25	103,546	0	103,546	0
26	Other salaries and wages	26	5,643,262	4,949,140	541,753	146,725
27	Pension plan contributions	27	59,169	50,945	6,686	1,538
28	Other employee benefits	28	991,084	853,323	111,992	25,768
29	Payroll taxes	29	599,088	518,211	64,102	16,774
30	Professional fundraising fees	30				
31	Accounting fees	31				
32	Legal fees	32				
33	Supplies	33	160,031	93,086	51,712	15,233
34	Telephone	34	263,127	201,101	31,448	30,578
35	Postage and shipping	35				
36	Occupancy	36	459,100	378,589	72,647	7,864
37	Equipment rental and maintenance	37	246,124	196,913	49,211	0
38	Printing and publications	38				
39	Travel	39	118,384	94,025	18,446	5,913
40	Conferences, conventions, and meetings .	40				
41	Interest	41				
42	Depreciation, depletion, etc. (attach schedule)	42	77,350		77,350	
43	Other expenses not covered above (itemize): **a**	43a				
b	....	43b				
c	....	43c				
d	....	43d				
e	**See Statement 1.**	43e	6,090,858	5,412,010	536,572	115,276
44	Total functional expenses (add lines 22 through 43). *Organizations completing columns (B)-(D), carry these totals to lines 13—15* .	44	14,564,999	12,556,074	1,643,255	365,670

Joint Costs. Check ▶ ☐ if you are following SOP 98-2.
Are any joint costs from a combined educational campaign and fundraising solicitation reported in **(B)** Program services? . ▶ ☐ Yes ☑ No
If "Yes," enter **(i)** the aggregate amount of these joint costs $_____; **(ii)** the amount allocated to Program services $_____;
(iii) the amount allocated to Management and general $_____ ; and **(iv)** the amount allocated to Fundraising $_____

Part III **Statement of Program Service Accomplishments** (See page 25 of the instructions.)

What is the organization's primary exempt purpose? ▶ **See Statement 2** ....

All organizations must describe their exempt purpose achievements in a clear and concise manner. State the number of clients served, publications issued, etc. Discuss achievements that are not measurable. (Section 501(c)(3) and (4) organizations and 4947(a)(1) nonexempt charitable trusts must also enter the amount of grants and allocations to others.)

Program Service Expenses (Required for 501(c)(3) and (4) orgs., and 4947(a)(1) trusts; but optional for others.)

		Program Service Expenses
a	During the 2004 school year, JCCA's Head Start program brought 925 children to a level of health, social & educational readiness to assure their success in school	
	(Grants and allocations $)	6,692,284
b	See Statement 3 for a list of Family and Community Services to low income families and children.	
	(Grants and allocations $)	5,720,641
c	Partnered with numerous other organizations such as local governments, non-profits and businesses to deliver services to achieve JCCA's mission.	
	(Grants and allocations $)	143,149
d		
	(Grants and allocations $)	
e	Other program services (attach schedule) (Grants and allocations $)	
f	**Total of Program Service Expenses** (should equal line 44, column (B), Program services). . . . . ▶	12,566,074

Form **990** (2004)

Figure 2-16. *Continued*

Part IV   Balance Sheets (See page 25 of the instructions.)

			(A) Beginning of year		(B) End of year
Note:	*Where required, attached schedules and amounts within the description column should be for end-of-year amounts only.*				
	45 Cash—non-interest-bearing		699,751	45	933,315
	46 Savings and temporary cash investments			46	
	47a Accounts receivable	**47a** 562,777			
	b Less: allowance for doubtful accounts .	**47b**	738,273	47c	562,777
	48a Pledges receivable	**48a** 141,626			
	b Less: allowance for doubtful accounts .	**48b**	176,898	48c	141,626
	49 Grants receivable			49	
	50 Receivables from officers, directors, trustees, and key employees (attach schedule)			50	
Assets	51a Other notes and loans receivable (attach schedule)	**51a**			
	b Less: allowance for doubtful accounts .	**51b**		51c	
	52 Inventories for sale or use			52	
	53 Prepaid expenses and deferred charges		3,000	53	3,000
	54 Investments—securities (attach schedule) . . ▶ ☐ Cost ☐ FMV			54	
	55a Investments—land, buildings, and equipment: basis	**55a**			
	b Less: accumulated depreciation (attach schedule)	**55b**		55c	
	56 Investments—other (attach schedule)			56	
	57a Land, buildings, and equipment: basis .	**57a** 4,461,262			
	b Less: accumulated depreciation (attach schedule)	**57b** 975.433	3,527,863	57c	3,485,829
	58 Other assets (describe ▶ _____)			58	
	59 **Total assets** (add lines 45 through 58) (must equal line 74) . . .		5,145,785	59	5,126,547
	60 Accounts payable and accrued expenses		865,291	60	802,353
	61 Grants payable			61	
	62 Deferred revenue		42,977	62	216,883
Liabilities	63 Loans from officers, directors, trustees, and key employees (attach schedule)			63	
	64a Tax-exempt bond liabilities (attach schedule) . . .			64a	
	b Mortgages and other notes payable (attach schedule)		576,602	64b	577,126
	65 Other liabilities (describe ▶ _____)			65	
	66 **Total liabilities** (add lines 60 through 65)		1,484,870	66	1,576,362
	Organizations that follow SFAS 117, check here ▶ ☑ **and complete lines 67 through 69 and lines 73 and 74.**				
	67 Unrestricted		2,529,552	67	2,511,986
	68 Temporarily restricted		1,088,796	68	1,038,199
Net Assets or Fund Balances	69 Permanently restricted			69	
	Organizations that do not follow SFAS 117, check here ▶ ☐ **and complete lines 70 through 74.**				
	70 Capital stock, trust principal, or current funds			70	
	71 Paid-in or capital surplus, or land, building, and equipment fund .			71	
	72 Retained earnings, endowment, accumulated income, or other funds			72	
	73 **Total net assets or fund balances** (add lines 67 through 69 **or** lines 70 through 72; column (A) **must** equal line 19; column (B) **must** equal line 21) . .		3,660,915	73	3,550,185
	74 **Total liabilities and net assets / fund balances** (add lines 66 and 73)		5,145,785	74	5,126,547

Form 990 is available for public inspection and, for some people, serves as the primary or sole source of information about a particular organization. How the public perceives an organization in such cases may be determined by the information presented on its return. Therefore, please make sure the return is complete and accurate and fully describes, in Part III, the organization's programs and accomplishments.

Special Cases

Some types of nonprofit organizations have specific accounting practices that meet the particularities of their fields and apply only to them. The three main types are museums, colleges and universities, and health care organizations. Their accounting practices are described below.

Museums

Collections of art and historical treasures are not required to be capitalized (i.e., listed as capital assets on the balance sheet), although both governments and nonprofits are encouraged to do so. This can be a major issue for museums because of the subjective nature and practical difficulty in valuing art and other collection items. To be considered exempt, the collection must be:

- held for public exhibition, education, or research in furtherance of public service, rather than for financial gain.

- protected, kept unencumbered, cared for, and preserved.

- subject to an organizational policy that requires proceeds from the sale of collection items be used to acquire other items for collection.

When a collection is not capitalized, the organization is required to disclose in its financial statements a description of the collection and the reasons it is not capitalized. If a donation to the collection is not capitalized, it is treated as an in-kind contribution, with equal and offsetting revenue and expense entries.

Colleges and Universities

Colleges and universities fall into three categories: private, public, and public with taxing authority (mostly community colleges). Private universities follow the same accounting rules as other nonprofits. Public universities follow the same rules as other governments (most will report as governmental units engaged in "business activities only" and use accrual accounting). Community colleges may report as "engaged in both government and business-type activities" if they are significantly supported by property taxes. If the college or university has a foundation that receives contributions for the benefit of the school, those contributions must be shown on the school's financial statements.

Student financial aid in the form of scholarship allowances consists of the difference between the official tuition and fees and the amount actually billed to the student. How these allowances are treated in the financial statements depends on whether the student has to perform a service to receive the discount.

- If the tuition or fee reduction is an employee discount, as with work-study students or graduate assistantships, it is treated as a personnel expense.

- If the tuition or fee reduction doesn't require work, as with academic or athletic scholarships, it is treated as a revenue reduction.

Health Care Organizations

Health care organizations such as hospitals can be for-profit, nonprofit, or governmental. Because the lines between nonprofit and for-profit operations can be blurry, large amounts of money are involved, and the operations are complex and unique to the health care field, nonprofit and governmental health care organizations must show some specific information on their financial statements.

A performance indicator such as Excess of Revenues over Expenses must be provided, as well as other changes in net assets. They must show the following nonoperating items below the performance indicator: equity transfers (if the organization is a subsidiary or owner of another organization), receipt of restricted contributions, contributions of long-lived assets, unrealized gains and losses on investments, investment returns restricted by donors or law, and any extraordinary items.

Patient service revenues, minus discounts given to HMOs, must be reported in the statement of activities. Significant revenue under capitation agreements (such as when HMOs pay for the number of individuals or employees served, instead of the services performed) must be reported separately. The methods of revenue recognition and types and amounts of contractual adjustments must be disclosed in the notes.

Patient service revenue does not include charity care. Management's policy for providing charity care and the level of charity care must be disclosed in the notes.

Operating revenues are often classified as net patient service revenue, premium revenue (such as from HMOs under capitation agreements), and nonmedical revenue (gift shop, cafeteria, tuition, and such). If significant, tuition should be reported separately. Unrestricted gifts may be reported as either operating or nonoperating revenue, depending on the organization's policy.

Budget Considerations | 3

Thinking About Budgets

In this section we will talk about two kinds of budgets, the organizational budget for your whole agency and the grant project budget for your proposed project. As a grantwriter you need to be able to read and understand the first, and read and prepare the second. As we will see, there is a fundamental difference between these two, although they both follow many of the same principles.

The *organizational budget* is a prediction of income and expense for a fiscal year, based on past experience, best guesses, and plans for the future. It is usually prepared by top management and financial staff, hopefully with input from program staff. It may or may not include restricted funds. This prediction or plan is presented to an organization's Board of Directors, hopefully before the beginning of the fiscal year. Adoption of the budget is a formal authorization by the board to spend the amounts in the budget. The organizational budget then becomes a monitoring tool for tracking income and expense and for keeping the organization solvent. If circumstances change dramatically during the year, the budget may be amended to reflect new conditions, especially if revenues don't keep up with predictions.

A *grant project budget*, on the other hand, is a request for support of a particular project and a promise to the funder to spend their grant funds according to that budget. It may be prepared by the grantwriter, the financial staff, a program manager, or others. In most cases if a grant proposal is funded, the funds become temporarily restricted. If there are matching requirements, those may have financial consequences for the organization, which will have to raise the additional funds.

The role of the grantwriter in preparing these budgets varies considerably. An outside grantwriter (such as a consultant) needs to understand the organization's budget and its relationship to a major grant proposal, but wouldn't be involved in the budget's preparation and generally might not be too concerned with it. An inside grantwriter employed by an organization would be very concerned with the income side of the budget, particularly that management or board doesn't set unachievable goals for grant income.

On the other hand, every grantwriter needs to be intimately involved in preparing a major grant budget. Even if the budget numbers are being prepared by someone else, the grantwriter needs to match the program narrative and goals to the budget categories. As shown below in the sections on grant project budgets, the budget format can help support the case for foundation funding. (Government agencies generally prescribe budget formats, so you don't have much leeway.)

Organizational Budgets

The annual budget is the most basic tool of organizational planning. Ideally budgeting happens within the context of a multiyear strategic plan, which, as the name implies, includes more than one year's financial projections. But even nonprofit organizations that don't have strategic plans or program goals will generally develop a basic one-year budget. Bylaws will often require the board, treasurer, or finance committee to adopt a budget. How the budgeting process is managed, who's involved, and how the budget is used tells an enormous amount about an organization.[10]

The development of the annual budget is where the staff and board work together to plan the organization's work for the year. It is generally where salaries are set, resources are allocated to particular programs or functions, and goals are established for income from different sources including foundation, corporate, and government grants. The budget document provides a specific written plan for where money will come from and how it will be spent.

The budget is not only a plan, it is an authorization document. When the board of directors or other governing body adopts an annual budget, they are authorizing the management to spend funds on particular things—staff, rent, supplies, and so forth. A more detailed budget may specify which programs and staff positions are to be supported.

An organizational budget is often presented as a simple one-page document showing income and expenses. Larger, more complex or sophisticated organizations may develop several other budgets for management purposes.

---

[10] Years ago when I was a journalist starting to cover local government, I asked the mayor's chief of staff for advice. He said, "Cover the budget hearings; they show the real intentions of the City Council. Commissioners may make pronouncements and speeches about many issues, but where they commit money is where they are actually going to do things. Everything else can be just for show.   ]" I've found this to be true of practically all organizations.

Multiservice agencies may develop a budget at each individual program level. Financial staff may create cash flow budgets to manage cash and ensure that the organization can pay its bills throughout the year. In addition, there are different budgeting processes: zero-based budgeting assumes no funds for any purpose and requires each program to justify its total funding; incremental budgeting assumes spending at current levels and adjusts for inflation. Finally, different organizations organize their budget processes differently and involve different people in the process.

This chapter isn't concerned with how to create an organizational budget, just how to read one. We'll look at a simple budget for a single-purpose organization and a functional budget that allocates costs among programs in a multiservice agency. But first let's consider a few budgeting basics that are of concern to grantwriters:

- The budget should be for the organization's fiscal year, as established with the IRS.

- The budget covers only funds to be spent during the fiscal year. If you have multiyear grants, only the portion to be spent during this year is included in the budget.

- The general annual budget will be for operations only. Things like major building or equipment purchases should be in a separate capital budget.

- If grants already funded require particular staffing and program expenses, these must be included in the budget.

- If you include in-kind income, it must always be matched with an equal expense.

- A grant project budget will generally be designed to break even, but it is desirable for an organization to budget for a surplus to increase its net worth.

- In budgeting for general grant income, include 100 percent of the grants already committed or funded. However, estimate income from grant applications as a percentage based on past experience.

- If you are planning to apply for specific major grants that will be a significant portion of the overall budget (say, 20 percent or more), don't include them in your basic budget. Foundations don't want to be depended on to balance your operating budget. Instead, if you want to show them, create an alternative budget column for each such grant with additions to both revenues and expense.

- Is the organization using its budget to monitor its income and expenses on a monthly basis and making adjustments accordingly? If not, the organization is likely to be financially unstable and prone to looking for emergency grants to cover shortfalls that could (should) have been foreseen and prevented.

Florentine Chamber Orchestra Annual Budget

Figure 3-1 shows the annual budget of the Florentine Chamber Orchestra (FCO) in a common format used for presentation to their board. For publication in their annual report, the same format would be used, but the non-musician salaries could be combined under personnel to preserve confidentiality. The budget identifies major expenses, but combines many small ones into "other costs." Although it groups expenses by category, it doesn't break them out by function nor allocate administrative costs. It doesn't identify restricted grant funds, because most grants are for season support or specific projects included under production or marketing.

FCO presents its budget with the previous year's actual figures for comparison. This allows readers to see whether any major changes are proposed and to judge for themselves if they seem realistic. For the coming year, FCO is proposing a rather status quo budget. There are no major increases in either income or expense. Last year there was a slight deficit of less than 3 percent of expenses, and this year proposes a slight surplus of a little more than 4 percent.

What can a grantwriter tell from looking at this budget?

- Grants (foundation, corporate, and government) comprise about one-third of total contributed support, which is probably a healthy amount for ongoing grant support for an arts organization. On the other hand, the budget reflects no plans for major grant-funded initiatives. Since last year didn't show any major grants either, FCO may be too conservative in its planning.

- FCO enjoys strong community support. Contributed support is 59 percent of total income—a little high but within industry standards. Individual contributions are a healthy 48 percent of total support and 28 percent of total income.

- Aside from the development director (who is probably writing the grants), no funds are identified for fundraising or grantwriting, unless they are hidden in administrative costs or mailings. Again, FCO may be too conservative in its fundraising planning.

Figure 3-1. FCO—Annual Budget

Florentine Chamber Orchestra
Budget 2005–2006

	Last year actual	Budget year
SUPPORT AND REVENUE		
Support		
Contributions	$159,080	$175,000
Foundation Grants.	52,000	75,000
Corporate Sponsorships.	31,000	30,000
Government Grants	20,000	15,000
Fundraising Events, Net of Costs	56,271	70,000
Total Support	318,351	365,000
Earned Revenue		
Ticket Sales		
Subscriptions	124,660	130,000
Single Ticket Sales	39,300	45,000
Special Concert Tickets.	52,400	55,000
Contract Concerts	10,000	10,000
Program Advertising	3,200	5,000
Product Sales	3,718	5,000
Total Earned Revenue.	233,278	250,000
Total Support and Revenue	$551,629	$615,000
EXPENSES		
Personnel		
Executive Director	55,000	60,000
Office Manager	30,000	30,000
Development Director	40,000	45,000
Orchestra Musicians	117,642	120,000
Payroll taxes and benefits at 15%	36,396	38,250
Production		
Guest Conductor Fees	18,900	20,000
Chorus Fees.	7,500	7,500
Soloists Fees	32,050	30,000
Artist Travel	24,399	27,000
Hall Rentals	19,500	18,000
Programs Printing and Design	13,772	15,000
Other Concert Costs	86,500	90,000
Management		
Professional Services, Administation	14,000	15,000
Office Rent	10,000	10,000
Telephone	4,237	5,000
Other Administrative Costs	11,197	12,000
Marketing		
Professional Services, Marketing.	3,500	3,500
Season Brochure	14,922	15,000
Advertising	12,672	16,000
Mailings.	14,022	12,000
Total Expense	$566,209	$589,250
Income – Expense	$ (14,580)	$ 25,750

A new grantwriter or grants consultant talking to FCO would want to explore opportunities for new grant initiatives. It would be helpful to be able to look at five years of past financial statements for trends or significant problems, as well as the balance sheet to see how healthy the bottom line is and if FCO carries significant debt. The grantwriter should ask for a list of regular grant funders going back at least five years and, if one doesn't exist, suggest that it be created. Then perhaps the grantwriter should meet with the executive director, artistic director, and board president to discuss potential artistic or marketing initiatives that could be grant-funded and look at potential funders.

Florentine Chamber Orchestra Cash Flow Budget

The Florentine Chamber Orchestra also creates a cash flow budget for its internal management purposes (Figure 3-2). Because their income and expenses have significant fluctuations driven by ticket sales and contributions on the income side and by concert production costs on the expense side, an annual budget that shows only yearly totals won't give information about when they might need to borrow to meet payroll. A grantwriter might want to understand FCO's cash flow projections to try to bring in grant income for times when cash is needed or to avoid undertaking new initiatives requiring additional expenses when the orchestra is tight on cash.

Jefferson County Community Action Annual Budget

Jefferson County Community Action (JCCA) is a large, multiservice agency serving thousands of clients annually. In contrast to FCO, JCCA is heavily dependent on government contracts, which means that it must track and account for many funds separately and deal with the restrictions of multiple funders.

JCCA uses *functional budgeting*, which means that it distinguishes between the costs projected for different service areas and costs for administration and fundraising. Functional budgeting has several advantages for a large agency. It closely follows the required financial statement format for GAAP, so budget-to-actual statements are readily produced. It shows the allocation to programs of both administrative expenses and fundraising revenues, letting the reader see the true costs of running each program.

Figure 3-3 shows the annual budget for this organization.

This one-page format gives an overview by department (such as Early Childhood Development and Family and Community Resources). A separate page could present budget details for personnel, shown by program area, to be used for board adoption. The single sheet could be used for publication in the annual report and for including in grant applications to potential

Figure 3-2. FCO—Cash Flow Budget

Florentine Chamber Orchestra
Cash Flow Budget, 2005

	July	August	September	October	November	December
Beginning Cash	$ 6,000	$ 2,562	$ (8,376)	$ 89,796	$103,358	$ 97,530
Support						
Contributions	3,000	3,000	10,000	15,000	25,000	60,000
Foundations			15,000			15,000
Corporations.................			5,000	5,000	5,000	5,000
Government	10,000					
Fundraising events............			10,000			50,000
Total Support	13,000	3,000	40,000	20,000	30,000	130,000
Earned Revenue						
Ticket Sales						
Subscriptions		30,000	90,000	10,000		
Single ticket sales...........		9,000		9,000		
Messiah tickets.............			15,000		10,000	30,000
Contract concerts					10,000	
Sales			2,000	1,000	1,000	4,000
Total Revenue	—	30,000	116,000	11,000	20,000	44,000
Total Support and Revenue ..	13,000	33,000	156,000	31,000	50,000	174,000
Expenses						
Personnel....................	12,938	12,938	12,938	12,938	12,938	12,938
Production...................		36,390			36,390	135,560
Management	3,500	3,500	3,500	3,500	3,500	3,500
Marketing		27,500	5,000	1,000	3,000	4,000
Total Expense	16,438	43,938	57,828	17,438	55,828	155,998
Income – Expense	(3,438)	(10,938)	98,172	13,562	(5,828)	18,002
Ending Cash.................	$ 2,562	$ (8,376)	$ 89,796	$103,358	$ 97,530	$115,532

funders. For internal management accounting purposes, JCCA's executive director and fiscal and program managers would have detailed breakouts for each program (such as information and referral services, child care, energy assistance, housing stabilization, its homeless family shelter, and prenatal outreach programs.) These would be used to determine the cost of each unit of service (such as one day of preschool, one month of case management, and one "ready to rent" class.)

What can a grantwriter tell from looking at this budget?

- Both major program areas lost money. This is common with government-funded programs, which frequently require matching funds or reimburse the organization at below actual costs.

Figure 3-3. JCCA—Annual Budget

Jefferson County Community Action
Proposed Budget, Fiscal Year 2006

EXPENSES	Early Childhood Development	Family & Community Resources	Administration	Fundraising	Total
Personnel					
Salaries.........................	$3,553,000	$1,393,000	$ 552,000	$ 157,000	$ 5,655,000
Payroll taxes (13%)..............	461,890	181,090	71,760	20,410	735,150
Benefits (15%)	532,950	208,950	82,800	23,550	848,250
Subtotal Personnel	4,547,840	1,783,040	706,560	200,960	7,238,400
Professional Services	22,000	11,000	180,000	12,000	225,000
Occupancy	285,000	104,500	27,000	58,500	475,000
Travel	60,000	35,000	20,000	5,000	120,000
Communications	100,000	70,000	35,000	30,000	235,000
Supplies.......................	60,000	35,000	40,000	15,000	150,000
Marketing	8,500	5,000	500	15,000	29,000
Insurance......................	30,000	5,000	40,000	—	75,000
Client Expenses	650,000	3,700,000	3,000	4,500	4,357,500
In-kind Expenses	425,000	50,000	45,000	15,000	535,000
Total Expenses	6,188,340	5,798,540	1,097,060	355,960	13,439,900
Administration Allocation.........	658,236	329,118	(1,097,060)	109,706	—
Total Expenses with Allocation ..	6,846,576	6,127,658	—	465,666	13,439,900
SUPPORT AND REVENUE					
Federal Grants, Contracts.........	4,300,000	2,800,000			7,100,000
State and Local Grants, Contracts..	1,500,000	2,500,000			4,000,000
United Way				200,000	200,000
Individual Contributions..........				700,000	700,000
Events.........................				200,000	200,000
Foundation Grants...............				500,000	500,000
Corporate Grants................				50,000	50,000
In-Kind Revenues................	425,000	50,000	45,000	15,000	535,000
Total Support and Revenue	6,225,000	5,350,000	45,000	1,665,000	13,285,000
INCOME					
Fees...........................	85,000	45,000			130,000
Reimbursements		55,000	65,000		120,000
Investment Income				5,000	5,000
Total Income	85,000	100,000	65,000	5,000	255,000
Total Revenue and Income	6,310,000	5,450,000	110,000	1,670,000	13,540,000
Revenue – Expenses	(536,576)	(677,658)	110,000	1,204,334	100,100
Transfers Between Funds	536,576	677,658	(110,000)	(1,104,234)	—
Net Income	$ —	$ —	$ —	$ 100,100	$ 100,100

- The program losses are paid for by fundraising and allocation of administrative surplus (see the next-to-bottom line, Transfers Between Funds).

- Administrative costs are allocated to each program, showing its true cost. If we didn't include this allocation, it would look like the Early Childhood Development program actually made money, and the Family & Community Resources program shortfall would be about half of what's shown.

- The $500,000 of foundation grants are shown under fundraising. In fact, they were probably restricted for different program services, and they could have been presented that way in the budget. Putting them in the budget under fundraising gives the development department credit for grantwriting and sets targets for grant income.

- The income from federal grants isn't included in fundraising. Separating government grants from foundation and corporate grants is a common practice. In many organizations the development department isn't involved in government funding. Government grants are often written by program managers, a government contracts department, or outside contractors. However, a grantwriter would want to be clear about this responsibility.

- A grantwriter would want to know more detail about which specific programs were losing money to target private grants to areas of need.

- Finally, JCCA shows a small surplus for this year, but the amount is insignificant compared to their total budget. The important thing is that they're not predicting a deficit.

Developing Your Grant Project Budget

Some grantwriters treat the grant project's budget as cut and dried. It tells how much money you need to carry out the project described in your narrative. It's often left for the fiscal or program folks to develop. This hands-off approach misses the opportunity to use the budget to support your narrative and strengthen your proposal. It also misses the chance to involve program people in the process. After you've established the basic categories and developed a draft budget, take it to the program manager who will implement it and see if the program staff can identify any possible additions or deletions. Then use the budget categories to judge your narrative. If not everything in the budget is included, revise the narrative to make the two consistent. Of course, make sure everything in the budget is accounted for, even if it's to be paid for from other sources.

Budgeting is another way of telling your story through the process of translating your project into fiscal terms. It's important that it describe the same project as the grant narrative, and the reader should be able to guess what the project is just from reading the budget. This works in three ways:

- A single theme should run through your whole proposal. The written narrative, goals and objectives, timeline, evaluation, and budget should describe the same project and include the same items.

- Your budget categories need to tie to the narrative. Make sure every budgeted item is described in the narrative and, conversely, every activity or piece of equipment in the narrative is included in the budget. Use the same names for categories and job titles as are used by your fiscal department. This will make grants management much easier.

- Since in many grants, personnel can be 80 percent of your costs, "personnel" shouldn't be just one budget line. Each position should be a line item of its own. Be sure that you use the same job titles in the narrative and the budget—don't call a position "counselor" in the narrative, "case manager" in the evaluation, and "MSW" in the budget. If you attach job descriptions, they need to use the same job titles, too. Give each funded position's job title and tell what percentage of the person's time will be spent on the project. If it's not clear what they will do, spell it out in the budget narrative. List the employee fringe benefits and payroll taxes separately from the staff costs.

Other common budget categories are contracted services, travel, rent or occupancy, utilities, telephone, and office supplies. Nonoffice supplies for the project should be listed separately. If you will need equipment (office furniture, computers, copiers, vans, for example), decide whether you will purchase or lease them. If you need to remodel or build for the project, be clear what the funder will pay for—many funders don't want to do major remodeling or construction on rented space where the residual value would go to the landlord. Chapter 4, Federal Grants, includes a more detailed section on budget categories.

Many private funders won't pay for administrative, overhead, or indirect costs. If you've been used to government funding, this can be a shock. However you can often list many of these items (such as a portion of the executive director's time and a portion of the rent and utilities) as line items in the budget. If the funder sees the detail and how it directly relates to your project, in many cases it will be funded.

Your approach to creating the budget will depend partly on the funding source. If you are approaching a major foundation, you will probably design your project, develop goals and objectives, decide how many staff you will need, then do the budget last. If, on the other hand, you are responding to a government RFP that specifies how much money they will award each grantee, you may do a rough projection of staffing and other major items to develop a preliminary budget to match the available funding, use this to define the scope of your project, then complete the final budget.

Rules for Grant Budgeting

Budget conservatively. When figuring a grant budget, estimate your income low and your expenses high. If you're very familiar with the type of project and its costs, you can budget closer to the edge. The more uncertainly there is, the more conservative you should be in your budgeting.

Size of the grant request. The most common question grantwriters are asked is, How much can we ask for? This simple question has several aspects, and you need to consider them all, but it's not a difficult process. Here are a few major ones:

- **How much do you need to do the job right?** The first step is to look at the project you want to undertake and figure out all of its costs: personnel, supplies, rent, for example. You never want to undertake a major project without having a plan of how to pay for it. Resist any temptation to under-budget in order in an attempt to appear worthy or not seem greedy.

  On the other hand, don't be tempted to pad the budget. Don't assume that you'll be granted less than you request. Reviewers will have a good sense of what's reasonable and will assume you don't have a realistic understanding of your project or may be turned off if it seems you're only after money rather than committed to the project.

- **How does this amount relate to your organization's annual budget?** Foundations will seldom make grants of more than 30 percent of an organization's annual budget. They know from experience that most organizations aren't prepared to take on that kind of sudden growth, and that their grant could cause an agency to increase its staff and operations to a level that wouldn't be supportable after the grant period. You should also be concerned about whether your agency can take on a project that would increase its size by more than a third. (Also check out the section on Tipping in Chapter 5.)

- **What is the funder's capacity?** If a foundation has assets of $2 million and an average grant of $5,000, don't ask it for $50,000. That shows ignorance of the grant process and is disrespectful— they'll assume you didn't bother to find out enough about them to know their capacity. If you need $50,000, either find a larger funder or bundle together several $5,000 and $10,000 requests to smaller foundations.

- **Are there limits to the amount for this project?** Most government grants have a set amount they will grant to one agency's project. This amount will be stated in the agency's RFP.

In-Kind Contributions. Many nonprofits use large amounts of volunteer time. I've personally worked for two organizations where almost all of the agency's real work was done by volunteers, and the paid staff were mainly in supporting roles. Other organizations receive significant amounts of donated goods or services. You want to include these noncash contributions for two reasons: They give a truer picture of your actual operations, and they demonstrate community support. In-kind contributions are also useful as matching funds, especially when a match is required by government funders. Be sure the funder will accept a noncash match before submitting your proposal.

There are two rules to budgeting in-kind contributions, similar to valuing them on financial statements.

- Clearly identify them as in-kind, either in the budget notes or by including them in a separate column.

- Show in-kind contributions under both income and expenses as balancing entries. If you don't, you'll distort your cash needs and income.

As we'll see later, there are strict rules about what in-kind services can be listed on formal financial statements, but for budgeting purposes, you can do whatever makes the most sense.

Equipment. As a rule, funders don't want you to use their grant funds for equipment without knowing that you shopped for the best deal. If you can avoid it, don't propose to use grant money to pay full retail price for big-ticket items (say, over $2,000) such as a van or computers. If you can't get them donated outright, ask the vendor for the wholesale price or a nonprofit discount. Then get a letter you can include with the grant proposal showing the funder how careful you'll be with their money.

Allocating Costs. If you're including agency costs in your grant budget as line items, how should you figure them? There are many different approaches; here are three pretty common ones:

- **Staff time.** If your executive director will spend 10 percent of her time on the project, include 10 percent of her salary and fringe in your personnel costs.

- **Rent and utilities.** These are often allocated by percentage of floor space. If you have a 3,000-square-foot building and the project office will occupy 600 square feet, include 20 percent of rent and utilities.

- **Other expenses.** Some examples are telephone, office supplies, and copying. If you can't easily figure their actual cost, allocate them by percent of personnel. Let's say you have six staff costing $300,000; two of these are for your project, and their salary and fringe benefits are $50,000. You could use either 33 percent (two of six staff) or 16.7 percent ($50,000 or $300,000 or one-sixth of salary and fringe benefits), depending on what seems more accurate.

Cash Flow. Cash flow and how to project it was explained previously in the section on organizational budgets. In some cases you will want to do a cash flow projection before submitting a grant proposal.

For most foundation grants where checks are issued upfront, cash flow isn't a problem. Just don't spend the grant funds faster than needed for the project. For government "grants," which are actually contracts for services, you need to be concerned about planning for cash flow before you apply if the grant will be a significant part of your organizational budget. Many government agencies, at any level from federal to local, pay by reimbursement. This process frequently takes one to several months after you've spent your money. Do a cash flow analysis and see if you can afford to support the program from agency funds. If this looks like a potential problem, you can ask for an advance or some other arrangement to cover your expenses. If the funder won't do this, don't apply for the grant (or, in extreme circumstances, don't accept it).

Budget Notes and Records. When you're developing the budget, especially for a complex project, keep your notes and calculations that show how you arrived at each line item. If you used a spreadsheet program such as Excel, save it and print a copy for your notes. This is important not only for negotiating with funders, but also for explaining to the program people operating the funded program, or to the financial staff tracking it, what your sources and assumptions were for the budget.

Matching Funds. Both government and foundation funders often require matching funds, but they have different motivations. Governments want you to share the cost of the program, and they generally don't care where the money comes from. You can already have the money in the bank, get private funding, or use state or local government funds. (An exception is that most federal agencies won't allow other federal agencies' funds to be used as match.)

Foundations, on the other hand, can have two motivations. One is to know that you're asking other funders to participate, and often which sources you're approaching—this is often called "cost sharing." The other is to use their grant to build your fundraising capacity by specifying a challenge grant and requiring you to raise new dollars before they will release their funds.

I urge organizations to be careful in requesting a challenge grant. Do so only if you have a plan for where the matching funds will come from and think it will help your fundraising efforts (which in many cases it will). The pitfall is to ask for a challenge grant because you think it will make your grant more fundable, then find yourself struggling to raise additional funds outside your budget just to fulfill the grant conditions.

Capacity to Match Government Grant Funds. Just as with cash flow from reimbursement, agencies can get in trouble by applying for grants that require matching. Program RFPs will specify match requirements (e.g., 1 to 1 or 2 to 1). If an organization can't raise the match, they can be out of compliance with their grant and not get reimbursed or even lose the grant. Since many RFPs fund up to a certain amount, you can adjust your budget request to an amount you're comfortable matching. In some cases smaller grant amounts may only recommend a match, but over a certain dollar amount, a match will be required. Check if the funder requires the funds to be committed. If they don't, are you comfortable applying for funds when you don't know how you will match them?

Future Funding or Sustainability. If you're developing a new program or expanding an existing one, you need to be thinking about continuation funding after the grant runs out. Many funders will ask for sources of future funding, but even when they don't, it's important to address the issue and let them know you're planning ahead. As one program officer said to me, "It's OK not to know. It's not OK to not think about it."

A vague statement that future funds will come from "a variety of sources such as individuals and corporations" isn't adequate. Be as specific as you can about strategies such as fee for service, targeted direct mail, major donor programs, corporate sponsor tie-ins, potential government support, and so forth.

Capital campaign grants must often specify both funds to maintain the building and funds to operate programs in the building. A major capital campaign should have developed an operating *pro forma*,[11] which you could include or summarize.

Formatting the Grant Budget to Tell Your Story

Part of your grant strategy is deciding how to use your budget to support your program narrative. Here are some of the characteristics of this project's finances that will be important for the reader to understand: Do you have other sources of funding? Are you putting your own resources into the project? Do you have a plan, a pro forma, for operating the project after grant funding runs out? How will this grant-funded project fit into your agency's overall operations?

There is no right answer for any of these questions, nor are these all of the important questions that could arise. Here are a few examples of ways to format your grant budget to improve your proposal.

Formatting to Show Project Income

Decide whether you're going to show only project expenses or both income and expenses. If you're asking a funder to support the entire project, you can just show the expenses. But if you're going to approach multiple foundations or expect the project to generate revenues, you want to include them. This shows the funder that you have a fundraising plan in place, that you're not entirely dependent on their continued funding, and that other funders have interest in your project.

In the next two examples, the Florentine Chamber Orchestra is applying for a foundation grant to fund marketing and audience development, including direct mail, advertising, and building marketing capacity. The budget categories make it obvious that this is a marketing and advertising grant, and you can get an idea of their project strategy without even looking at the narrative. If you knew this was a performing arts organization, you could guess it was for audience development. Note that they have included some administrative expenses as individual line items, such as the executive director's time spent on the project and rent. FCO anticipates paying for about 40 percent of the project from other sources and wants to demonstrate this commitment.

---

[11] A formal operating plan is called a *pro forma*, which projects income and expenses for several years into the future.

Figures 3-4A and B show two different budget presentations, each of which shows other sources of funding. Figure 3-4A shows both total income and its sources, separated from the expenses; this format is commonly used to demonstrate support from other funders.

Figure 3-4A. FCO—Marketing Grant Budget, Version 1

Florentine Chamber Orchestra
Marketing and Audience Development

	Year 1	Year 2	Year 3
INCOME			
This Grant	$22,973	$32,696	$ 32,696
Other Foundations	10,000	15,000	15,000
Earned Income	6,846	9,362	9,362
Total Income	$39,819	$57,058	$ 57,058
EXPENSES			
Direct Mailings	9,500	16,000	16,000
Print Ads	5,000	5,000	5,000
Bus Ads	1,760	2,000	2,000
PR Materials	1,500	1,000	1,000
Programs	2,700	3,000	3,000
Marketing Plan	1,000	—	—
Graphic Design	1,000	1,000	1,000
Development	4,000	6,000	6,000
Executive Director	9,999	19,998	19,998
Rent	1,200	1,200	1,200
Telephone	1,200	1,200	1,200
Postage	240	240	240
Supplies	600	300	300
Copying	120	120	120
Total Expenses	$39,819	$57,058	$ 57,058

Three-Year Total	$153,935
Three-Year Other Funding	$ 65,570
Three-Year This Grant	$ 88,365

An alternate approach is to show the division of spending for each line item. FCO was already spending 10 percent of its total annual budget on marketing, so the "other funds" didn't require any extra expense. Figure 3-4B shows that the foundation was being asked to support only 60 percent of the project. This approach allowed FCO to take credit for spending its own money and demonstrated the project's importance to the orchestra.

Demonstrating Project Sustainability

Increasingly, funders are asking about project sustainability. They want to know how your project will continue to be funded after their grant period,

Figure 3-4B. FCO—Marketing Grant Budget, Version 2

Florentine Chamber Orchestra
Marketing and Audience Development

	Year 1 Other Funding	Year 1 Grant Funds	Year 2 Other Funding	Year 2 Grant Funds	Year 3 Other Funding	Year 3 Grant Funds
Mailings	$ 6,500	$ 3,000	$ 6,500	$ 9,500	$ 6,500	$ 9,500
Print Ads	—	5,000	—	5,000	—	5,000
Bus Ads	—	1,760	—	2,000	—	2,000
PR Materials	—	1,500	—	1,000	—	1,000
Programs	—	2,700	—	3,000	—	3,000
Marketing Plan	—	1,000	—	—	—	—
Graphic Design	—	1,000	—	1,000	—	1,000
Development	2,000	2,000	3,000	3,000	3,000	3,000
Executive Director	6,666	3,333	13,332	6,666	13,332	6,666
Rent	600	600	600	600	600	600
Telephone	600	600	600	600	600	600
Postage	120	120	120	120	120	120
Supplies	300	300	150	150	150	150
Copying	60	60	60	60	60	60
Total Expenses	$16,846	$22,973	$24,362	$32,696	$24,362	$ 32,696

Three-Year Total	$153,935
Three-Year Other Funding	$ 65,570
Three-Year This Grant	$ 88,365

and how the grant project will help strengthen your organization. Since this is often a question in the funder's guidelines, it's generally addressed in the narrative (perhaps with some hemming and hawing). If you know how you're planning to continue funding, you can strengthen your case by showing future funding in the budget.

For example, Jefferson County Community Action was seeking funding to build a development program. In a common scenario in recent decades, as their government funding was cut, they were looking to preserve programs by aggressively seeking private funds. The proposal was for a three-year grant to develop fundraising capacity, that is, to strengthen their development program and increase their private funding across the board. JCCA wanted to show how the development program would not only pay for itself, but also strengthen the agency's social service programs during and after the grant period.

As Figure 3-5 shows, the budget layout for this three-year grant covers seven years: the two years before the grant; the grant period, including two years of declining grant funding; and two years afterward.

Aside from a big jump in corporate giving (on which they had already been working hard), there isn't a huge income increase in the first grant year (2000). But by the end of the grant period, every category has been incrementally strengthened, building a diversified funding base that continues to support the agency's services. This format is especially suited to capacity-building grants, since the ability to raise increased funds will be demonstrated by meeting the budget.

Figure 3-5. JCCA—Development Grant Showing Future Funding

JCCA Development Department
Funding Diversification Project

Income from Fundraising	1998 Actual	1999 Actual	Period of Grant			2003	2004
			2000	2001	2002		
Direct Mail.........	$ 35,444	$ 39,696	$ 50,000	$ 70,000	$ 100,000	$ 110,000	$ 120,000
Events.............	57,414	43,211	50,000	57,000	75,000	100,000	110,000
Major Donors......	26,600	20,000	40,000	77,000	120,000	170,000	175,000
United Way........	70,000	232,938	182,000	182,000	182,000	190,000	200,000
Corporations.......	11,500	95,751	145,000	185,000	195,000	200,000	210,000
This Grant			120,000	80,000	50,000		
Other Foundations .	18,428	25,760	20,000	90,000	140,000	160,000	170,000
Community........	33,036	51,031	60,000	92,000	138,000	120,000	125,000
Total Income	252,422	508,387	667,000	833,000	1,000,000	1,050,000	1,110,000
Development Expense	$170,000	$170,000	$310,000	$320,000	$ 330,000	$ 340,000	$ 350,000
Funds Contributed to Agency Programs...	$ 82,422	$338,387	$357,000	$513,000	$ 670,000	$ 710,000	$ 760,000

Integrating Your Grant Project into the Organization's Budget

Foundation program officers will often want to see the relationship of their grant to your organizational budget. They want to look at its size relative to your overall budget and at the project's impact on your agency's programs. On the other hand, they don't just want to see their grant assumed in your organization's budget; they want to know how you would operate without it. They especially don't want to see your organization dependent on their grant to maintain your operations.

Figure 3-6 presents one way of showing a grant-funded project within the context of an organizational budget. It inserts a new marketing grant into the Florentine Chamber Orchestra's operating budget, showing one year without the grant, total project funds (including money from other funders), and the combined numbers. This format can be adapted for different funders by simply changing the support lines.

Figure 3-6. FCO—Budget Integrating a Grant Project

	Florentine Chamber Orchestra Budget Integrating Grant Project		
SUPPORT	Budget without This Grant	This Grant	Budget with This Grant
Contributions from Individuals......................	$ 159,080		$ 159,080
Foundation Grants................................	52,000		52,000
This Grant	—	$30,000	30,000
Other Grants for this Project........................	—	25,875	25,875
Corporate Sponsorships...........................	31,000		31,000
Government Grants................................	20,000		20,000
Fundraising Events, Net of Costs	56,271		56,271
Total Support	318,351	55,875	374,226
EARNED REVENUE			
Ticket Sales			
Subscriptions	124,660		124,660
Single Ticket Sales	39,300		39,300
Special Concert Tickets...........................	52,400		52,400
Contract Concerts	10,000		10,000
Program Advertising	3,200		3,200
Product Sales	3,718		3,718
Total Earned Revenue...........................	233,278	—	233,278
Total Support and Revenue	$ 551,629	$55,875	$ 607,504
EXPENSES			
Personnel			
Executive Director*	55,000	5,500	55,000
Office Manager*.................................	30,000	3,000	30,000
Development Director*	40,000	4,000	40,000
Orchestra Musicians	117,642		117,642
Payroll Taxes and Benefits at 15%	36,396	1,875	38,271
Production			
Guest Conductor Fees	18,900		18,900
Chorus Fees.....................................	7,500		7,500
Soloists Fees	32,050		32,050
Artist Travel.....................................	24,399		24,399
Hall Rentals	19,500		19,500
Programs Printing and Design	13,772		13,772
Other Concert Costs..............................	86,500		86,500
Management			
Professional Services, Administration...............	14,000		14,000
Office Rent	10,000	2,000	12,000
Telephone	4,237	500	4,737
Other Administrative Costs	11,197		11,197
Marketing			
Professional Services, Marketing...................	3,500	4,000	7,500
Season Brochure	14,922	5,000	19,922
Advertising	12,672	10,000	22,672
Mailings..	14,022	20,000	34,022
Total Expenses	$ 566,209	$55,875	$ 609,584
INCOME – EXPENSES	$ (14,580)	$ —	$ (2,080)

* Personnel costs are allocations of staff time to this project and do not increase totals.

Federal Grants | 4

Budgeting for Federal Grants

Private funders can allow, or even invite, creative grant budget formats, but the feds—and most state and local governments—are absolutely rigid. Federal RFPs prescribe exactly what, where, and how to put everything. As with everything about government grants, it's important to follow the directions to the letter.

Examples of federal budget forms 424 and 424A, which are standard for virtually all federal grant applications, and instructions on filling them out are included later in this chapter. The federal categories for budgeting are detailed in the section on filing out the form 424A. Also included are definitions of "allowable costs" in publications of the OMB. In most cases they're common sense, but it's a good idea to download the applicable circular(s) to have for reference (see the section entitled "OMB Circulars").

Documentation is key to federal grant budgeting. Keep careful track of the assumptions and calculations you use in preparing the budget and *save them*. It's a good idea to do all of your calculations using spreadsheet (one popular product is Excel), and include the assumptions you made in doing them. If you'll be hiring a consultant, get a letter from her or him detailing their work on the project and their hourly rates. If you'll be buying equipment, get bids or do some comparison shopping and save and include copies of these pages with your proposal (pages printed off company websites will do). Keep copies of everything you use in preparing the proposal.

Many federal grants will have a required match listed in the RFP, which specifies that you'll have to put up your own resources according to some formula (such as 1 to 1 or 2 to 1). See if you can use in-kind goods and services for this match. If the RFP doesn't say, call the program officer listed in the RFP. You can use your administrative costs (e.g., your executive director's time) or forgo your indirect costs to provide a match. In some cases, you'll have to tell how you plan to come up with the matching funds.

OMB Circulars

Grants awarded by federal agencies have numerous policy and performance requirements, including allowable costs, which are the kinds of things that can be charged to a grant. Although these are intended for grant management, a grant-writer needs to be aware of them when assembling a budget so that he or she does not include cost items that would be disallowed during grant negotiations—or worse, when seeking reimbursement.

These requirements are included in a series of OMB circulars. Because these circulars are periodically revised, it's a good idea to download the current ones for use in preparing budgets and managing grants. Six of these circulars are relevant; any given organization is covered by only three of them, depending on its type, as explained by the OMB website:

Nonprofit organizations:

* A-122 for cost principles
* A-110 for administrative requirements
* A-133 for audit requirements.

States, local governments, and Indian tribes:

* A-87 for cost principles
* A-102 for administrative requirements
* A-133 for audit requirements.

Educational institutions (even if part of a state or local government):

* A-21 for cost principles
* A-110 for administrative requirements
* A-133 for audit requirements.

Copies of these and other OMB circulars can be found and downloaded from http://www.whitehouse.gov/omb/circulars/.

The Common Rule

In 1987, all federal grant-making agencies issued a grants management "common rule" to adopt government-wide terms and conditions for grants to states and local governments, so that they would not have to negotiate different rules for each agency. Ironically, there are still slight differences in application among different agencies. OMB maintains a chart that includes the locations of federal agency codifications of the grants management common rule. This chart can be found at http://www.whitehouse.gov/omb/grants/chart.html.

You can't use federal dollars from one grant as match for another federal grant.[12] However, different federal agencies treat federal funds passed through states in different ways. Be sure to check if you're planning to use state grant funds or programs such as Medicaid as match.

You can't use federal grant dollars to replace or supplant other funds, especially other government funds. This means you can't use federal grant funds to pay for something you're already doing, then use the replaced funds for other purposes. Using sentences like "This grant will free up agency funds to [do something else]" is death to your proposals. The exception is in administration, where you can allocate a percentage of your executive director's time or your office rent to the project. Obviously, these are expenses you'd be paying anyway, but strictly speaking, you're not replacing them. And of course, you can use indirect funds for anything, since they're intended to pay for your organization's operating expenses.

Indirect Costs in Federal Grants

Unlike many private foundations, the federal government acknowledges that it costs money to run your agency, above and beyond the costs of providing direct services. These administrative overhead, or indirect, costs are the things that keep your organization operating smoothly and efficiently, but are not tied to any one project or program area. They can include such things as:

- Administrative staff: the executive director, finance director, human resources staff, the receptionist, and clerical staff not dedicated to specific programs

- Office space used by those staff, including costs of rent and utilities

- Equipment and services used by everyone: copiers, phone systems, janitorial service, IT support, and so on

- Board of directors expenses

- Fundraising and marketing expenses

- Grants management, the audit, liability insurance, staff training, and so on.

The federal government has a standardized, and fairly complex, method of determining your indirect costs, which results in a negotiated Indirect

---

[12] There are rare exceptions, and they require the permission of both federal agencies' legal and finance departments.

Cost Rate. As a grantwriter, you don't have to know how to negotiate Indirect Cost Rates, but you certainly need to understand how they work.

Once a federal Indirect Cost Rate is negotiated with one government agency, that rate is honored in any grant from any federal agency. This may be the agency that is awarding your first federal grant, or if you have multiple grants, the agency that awards the greatest share of your federal funding, which is called your *cognizant audit agency*.[13]

If you're working on a federal grant proposal, ask the organization's financial manager if the agency already has an approved federal Indirect Cost Rate. If so, in most cases you can just plug that percentage into your budget on the Indirect Costs line. If not, talk to the finance director and executive director about whether to apply for one. If you and they decide the organization needs an approved rate, work with the controller or accountant to pursue an application.

An agency can apply for several types of indirect cost rates: provisional, final, predetermined, fixed with carry-forward, or multiple indirect. The provisional and final rates are preferable for most nonprofits because they are easier to budget and account for actual costs. You can choose between two calculation methods—Direct Salaries & Wages and Total Modified Direct Costs—depending on your organization's finances. This will be a decision for your controller or chief financial officer.

To obtain a negotiated indirect cost rate, an organization's program and financial staff work together to develop a pool of costs by department,[14] then allocate them according to a reasonable formula. Then they figure an indirect cost rate by one of the two calculation methods and propose it to the appropriate federal agency. After negotiations, an official of the federal agency approves the rate, and the organization receives an indirect cost agreement.[15] The approval will be formalized by a rate agreement that is signed by an agency official and an authorized representative of your organization. Each agreement will include:

---

[13] The *cognizant audit agency* is the federal agency that deals with your organization for audit purposes, representing all federal agencies under the Single Audit Act. For auditees with more than $50 million in federal awards, this agency is assigned by the OMB.

[14] Refer to the appropriate OMB circular (indicated in the section on OMB circulars) to make sure you include only allowable costs.

[15] This description, of course, does not constitute complete instructions for developing your indirect cost rate, which will vary from agency to agency. If you are involved in developing an indirect cost rate, contact the agency you're working with and ask for guidance. A good overview and instructions from the U.S. Department of Labor are downloadable from: http://www.dol.gov/oasam/programs/boc/costdeterminationguide/main.htm.

- The approved rate(s) and information directly related to the use of the rates (e.g., type of rate, effective period, and distribution base)

- The treatment of fringe benefits as direct and/or indirect costs, or an approved fringe benefit rate

- General terms and conditions

- Special remarks (e.g., composition of the indirect cost pool).

Figure 4-1 is a sample indirect cost rate agreement from one of our model organizations, Jefferson County Community Action.

Special Considerations

Of course, it's not always this straightforward. After all, we're talking about the federal government. Here are a few exceptions or special cases:

- If you don't have a negotiated indirect cost rate, some federal agencies will let you use a temporary administrative fee, often 15 percent of the project budget's direct costs. In some cases, if you don't expect to apply for many federal grants, you can simply use this rate and not apply for a negotiated rate. If you're doing this, be sure to exclude all indirect cost items from the budget.

- Some federal agencies will cap the indirect costs they will pay, often at 20 percent of the project budget's direct costs. A few agencies or specific RFPs may not pay any indirect costs at all. If a funder refuses to acknowledge eligible indirect costs when negotiating a grant award, you have to be prepared to bargain—or even to walk away if absorbing the administrative costs is too much of a burden for your agency.

Using Line Items Instead of Indirect Costs

Some organizations assume that because they don't have an indirect cost rate agreement or a particular RFP doesn't allow indirect costs, they can't recover any administrative costs. In fact, many of these expenses can be included as line items under direct costs. For example, figure out how much of the executive director's or accountant's time will be spent administering the grant and include the value of those hours under personnel expenses. If, for example, the grant will force you to pay for an A-133 audit, that's a cost of the grant. Calculate a reasonable percentage of your telephone, copying, insurance, janitorial, and other operating expenses and include them as direct cost line items. Make sure these are all legitimate costs and reasonable allocations of operating the grant project. In some cases you'll recover most or all of what you would have received under a percentage using an indirect cost rate.

Figure 4-1. JCCA—Indirect Cost Rate Agreement

INDIRECT COST RATE AGREEMENT
NONPROFIT ORGANIZATION

ORGANIZATION: Jefferson County Community Action 1234 South Main Street Anytown, CA 87654	DATE: August 23, 2004 FILE REF: This replaces the agreement dated April 15, 2003

The rates approved in this Agreement are for use on grants, contracts, and other agreements with the Federal Government to which OMB Circular No. A-122 applies, subject to the conditions in Section II, A below. The rates were negotiated by Jefferson County Community Action and the U.S. Department of Health and Human Services in accordance with the authority contained in Attachment A, Section E.2 (a), of the Circular.

SECTION I: INDIRECT COST RATES

TYPE	EFFECTIVE PERIOD FROM	TO	RATE (%)	LOCATION	APPLICABLE TO
Final	7/1/00	6/30/01	36.5%	All	All Programs
Final	7/1/01	6/30/02	36.5%	All	All Programs
Provisional	7/1/02	6/30/03	36.5%	All	All Programs
Provisional	7/1/03	6/30/05	36.5%	All	All Programs

(SEE SPECIAL REMARKS)

* BASE:
Total direct costs excluding capital expenditures (buildings, individual items of equipment; alterations and renovations), and that portion of each sub-award in excess of $25,000.

SECTION II: SPECIAL REMARKS

TREATMENT OF FRINGE BENEFITS:
Fringe benefits applicable to direct salaries and wages are treated as direct costs.

TREATMENT OF PAID ABSENCES:
Sick leave, holiday, and other paid absences are included in salaries and wages and are claimed on grants, contracts, and other agreements as part of the normal cost for salaries and wages. Separate claims for these absences are not made. Vacation pay is accrued and charged the same as other fringe benefits.

SECTION III: GENERAL

A. LIMITATIONS:
Use of the rate(s) contained in the Agreement is subject to all statutory or administrative limitations and is applicable to a given grant or contract only to the extent that funds are available. Acceptance of the rate(s) agreed to herein is predicated upon the following conditions:

(1) that no costs other than those incurred by the grantee/contractor or allocated to the grantee/contractor via an approved central service cost allocation plan were included in its indirect cost pool as finally accepted and that such incurred costs are legal obligations of the grantee/contractor and allowable under the governing cost principles,
(2) that the same costs that have been treated as indirect costs have not been claimed as direct costs,
(3) that similar types of costs have been accorded consistent treatment, and
(4) that the information provided by the grantee/contractor, which was used as a basis for acceptance of the rate(s) agreed to herein, is not subsequently found to be materially inaccurate.

The elements of indirect cost and the type of distribution base(s) used in computing provisional rates are subject to revision when final rates are negotiated.
The rates cited in this Agreement are subject to audit.

B. CHANGES: The grantee/contractor is required to provide written notification to the indirect cost negotiator prior to implementing any changes that could affect the applicability of the approved rates. Changes in the indirect cost recovery plan, which may result from changes such as the method of accounting or organizational structure, require the prior written approval of the Division of Cost Determination (DCD). Failure to obtain such prior written approval may result in cost disallowance.

Figure 4-1. *Continued*

C. NOTIFICATION TO FEDERAL AGENCIES: A copy of this document is to be provided by this organization to other Federal funding sources as a means of notifying them of the Agreement contained herein.

D. PROVISIONAL-FINAL RATES: The grantee/contractor must submit a proposal to establish a final rate within six months after their fiscal year end. Billings and charges to federal awards must be adjusted if the final rate varies from the provisional rate. If the final rate is greater than the provisional rate and there are no funds available to cover the additional indirect costs, the organization may not cover all indirect costs. Conversely, if the final rate is less than the provisional rate, the organization will be required to pay back the difference to the funding agency.

Indirect costs allocable to a particular award or other cost objective may not be shifted to other Federal awards to overcome funding deficiencies, or to avoid restrictions imposed by law or by the terms of the award.

E. SPECIAL REMARKS:
1. Indirect costs charged to Federal grants/contracts by means other than the rate(s) cited in this Agreement should be adjusted to the applicable rate(s) cited herein and be applied to the appropriate base to identify the proper amount of indirect costs allocable to the program.

2. Contracts/grants providing for ceilings as to the indirect cost rate(s) or amount(s), which are indicated in Section I above, will be subject to the ceilings stipulated in the contract or grant agreements. The ceiling rate or the rate(s) cited in this Agreement, whichever is lower, will be used to determine the maximum allowable indirect cost on the contract or grant agreement.

3. The indirect cost pool consists of its allocable share of the following administrative expenses (all costs identifiable to a specific contract or grant are charged directly):
1) Salaries;
   a. 100% indirect—President, Executive Director, Administrative Assistant, Personnel Staff, Office Services, Accounting, Network Support, Receptionist.
   b. The remaining salaries are charged either to direct or indirect costs by individual time sheets.
2) Employee fringe benefits for indirect employees—FICA, Unemployment Insurance, Workers Compensation, health insurance, pension, long term disability, and life insurance. Vacation pay is accrued and charged like other fringe benefits.
3) Professional fees and contract services
4) Supplies and materials
5) Telephone
6) Postage and shipping
7) Occupancy
8) Rental and maintenance of equipment
9) Printing and publication, visual aids
10) Travel
11) Training and educational assistance costs
12) Depreciation and amortization costs

ACCEPTANCE:

BY THE ORGANIZATION

Jefferson County Community Action
(Grantee/Contractor)

_____
(Signature)

Janet Smith
(Name)

Executive Director
(Title)

August 23, 2004
(Date)

BY THE COGNIZANT AGENCY
ON BEHALF OF THE FEDERAL GOVERNMENT:
Department of Health and Human Services
(Government Agency)

_____
(Signature)

David. S. Low
(Name)

Director, Division of Cost Allocation
(Title)

July 30, 2004
(Date)

Negotiated By: John Jones
Telephone No.: 202-555-5555

Standard Forms 424 and 424A

The Standard Form 424 (SF 424) and its companion budget sheet, SF 424A, are required on virtually all federal grant applications.

Filling Out Standard Form 424

SF 424 (see Figure 4-2) is used as the cover page on most applications. You can download a PDF version that can be completed from www.whitehouse.gov/omb/grants/sf424.pdf.

Although most of the form is self-explanatory, here are some pointers for filling it out.

Block 1. Type of Submission. Most grants to nonprofits are Non-Construction. Most Non-Construction grants don't require a pre-application unless the application specifies otherwise.

Block 2. Date Submitted / Applicant Identifier. Date Submitted is the date you mail it—pretty obvious. Applicant Identifier is for large agencies whose grants management offices use internal numbering systems. If your agency doesn't, leave this blank.

Blocks 3 and 4. Dates Received by State, and by Federal Agency / Applicant Identifiers. These are for state and federal internal use, so leave them blank.

Block 5. Applicant Information.

- Legal Name: For nonprofits, use the one from your 501(c)(3) letter.

- Organizational DUNS: In 2003, the federal government started requiring all applicants to have a Dun and Bradstreet Number as part of a move to automate the federal payment process. You can apply for one free at https://eupdate.dnb.com/requestoptions/government/ccrreg/ or by calling 1-866-705-5711. If you're in a hurry, telephoning gets a faster response. Since this number is required, if you anticipate applying for federal grants in the future, you might as well get it now.

- Address: Use the organization's main office, where the grant would be managed.

- Organizational Unit: Department and Division are for large organizations. If your agency isn't this big, leave these boxes blank.

- Name and telephone number of person to be contacted . . . : This will probably be either your agency's chief executive, department manager, or the person who will be managing the grant. This person should be familiar with the proposal and have the authority to answer questions and make decisions.

Figure 4-2. Standard Form 424 for Federal Grants

APPLICATION FOR FEDERAL ASSISTANCE			Version 7/03

APPLICATION FOR FEDERAL ASSISTANCE	2. DATE SUBMITTED	Applicant Identifier
1. TYPE OF SUBMISSION: Application / Pre-application ☐ **Construction** ☐ **Construction** ☐ **Non-Construction** ☐ **Non-Construction**	3. DATE RECEIVED BY STATE	State Application Identifier
	4. DATE RECEIVED BY FEDERAL AGENCY	Federal Identifier

5. APPLICANT INFORMATION

Legal Name:	**Organizational Unit:** Department:
Organizational DUNS:	Division:
Address: Street:	**Name and telephone number of person to be contacted on matters involving this application (give area code)**
	Prefix: / First Name:
City:	Middle Name
County:	Last Name
State: / Zip Code	Suffix:
Country:	Email:

6. EMPLOYER IDENTIFICATION NUMBER *(EIN)*: ☐☐–☐☐☐☐☐☐☐	Phone Number (give area code) / Fax Number (give area code)
8. TYPE OF APPLICATION: ☐ **New** ☐ **Continuation** ☐ **Revision** If Revision, enter appropriate letter(s) in box(es) (See back of form for description of letters.) ☐ ☐ Other (specify)	**7. TYPE OF APPLICANT:** (See back of form for Application Types) Other (specify)
	9. NAME OF FEDERAL AGENCY:
10. CATALOG OF FEDERAL DOMESTIC ASSISTANCE NUMBER: ☐☐–☐☐☐ TITLE (Name of Program):	**11. DESCRIPTIVE TITLE OF APPLICANT'S PROJECT:**
12. AREAS AFFECTED BY PROJECT *(Cities, Counties, States, etc.):*	

13. PROPOSED PROJECT		**14. CONGRESSIONAL DISTRICTS OF:**	
Start Date:	Ending Date:	a. Applicant	b. Project

15. ESTIMATED FUNDING:		**16. IS APPLICATION SUBJECT TO REVIEW BY STATE EXECUTIVE ORDER 12372 PROCESS?**	
a. Federal	$ .00	a. Yes. ☐ THIS PREAPPLICATION/APPLICATION WAS MADE AVAILABLE TO THE STATE EXECUTIVE ORDER 12372 PROCESS FOR REVIEW ON	
b. Applicant	$ .00	DATE:	
c. State	$ .00		
d. Local	$ .00	b. No. ☐ PROGRAM IS NOT COVERED BY E. O. 12372	
e. Other	$ .00	☐ OR PROGRAM HAS NOT BEEN SELECTED BY STATE FOR REVIEW	
f. Program Income	$ .00	**17. IS THE APPLICANT DELINQUENT ON ANY FEDERAL DEBT?**	
g. TOTAL	$ .00	☐ Yes If "Yes" attach an explanation. ☐ No	

18. TO THE BEST OF MY KNOWLEDGE AND BELIEF, ALL DATA IN THIS APPLICATION/PREAPPLICATION ARE TRUE AND CORRECT. THE DOCUMENT HAS BEEN DULY AUTHORIZED BY THE GOVERNING BODY OF THE APPLICANT AND THE APPLICANT WILL COMPLY WITH THE ATTACHED ASSURANCES IF THE ASSISTANCE IS AWARDED.

a. Authorized Representative			
Prefix	First Name	Middle Name	
Last Name		Suffix	
b. Title		c. Telephone Number (give area code)	
d. Signature of Authorized Representative		e. Date Signed	

Previous Edition Usable
Authorized for Local Reproduction

Standard Form 424 (Rev.9-2003)
Prescribed by OMB Circular A-102

Block 6. Employer Identification Number (EIN). For nonprofits, this number will be in the upper right hand corner of your 501(c)(3) letter (see examples in Chapter 5).

Block 7. Type of Applicant. Choose from the list provided on the second page of the form.

Block 8. Type of Application. Choose from the options provided.

Block 9. Name of Federal Agency. If it's a main agency, give the full name (e.g., Department of Education). If it's a subagency, abbreviate the main agency and spell out the subagency (e.g., HHS [for Health and Human Services], Bureau of Primary Health Care).

Block 10. Catalog of Federal Domestic Assistance Number. Often called the CFDA Number, this should appear on the RFP, along with the title of the program.

Block 11. Descriptive Title of Applicant's Project. This mini-abstract will end up being what's listed in the agency computer, and the name used when your project is discussed. Make it truly descriptive of what you're doing, but limit yourself to six to ten words.

Block 12. Areas Affected by Project. This information should be as specific and meaningful as possible, covering the whole geographic range of your project activities or impact. If your project is national, say so.

Block 13. Proposed Project Start and Ending Date. The start date is sometimes given in the RFP. If it isn't, list the month starting about 90 days from your submission. Be sure your ending date matches the right time period. A three-year project might go from October 1, 2005, to September 30, 2008 (note the month/day/year format). Since application decisions are often delayed, then grants negotiated, the actual dates are often different and usually later that these proposed dates.

Block 14. Congressional Districts of Applicant and Project. This information is important because the agency will notify your congressional representative, who may want to make a courtesy call on you, or even a formal announcement. It can't hurt to list more than one district (if that is the case) to get more congressional offices familiar with you. (You should also contact your congressional offices, both House and Senate, to let them know that you're submitting the grant. Offer to provide some information about it, and ask them for a letter of support.)

Block 15. Estimated Funding. This is your budget for the first year of the project. It only includes the funding for this project, not any other federal or other type of funding you may have. Make sure that these numbers match those on your SF 424A and your budget narrative.

Block 16. Review by State Executive Order 12372 Process. Also called the State Clearinghouse Review or Single Point of Contact (SPOC), this process varies from state to state. Half of the states (actually 25) don't have an SPOC. Many RFPs list the state SPOCs, or you can find them at http://www.whitehouse.gov/omb/grants/spoc.html.

You have three options here:

- Among SPOC states, the review process varies. Before checking the "Yes" box and entering the date, contact the listed SPOC and ask how they want to be notified and if they have any written procedures.

- The RFP should say whether the program requires SPOC notification. If it is exempt, just check the box: Program is not covered by E.O. 12372.

- If your state doesn't have an SPOC, check the box: Program has not been selected for review.

Block 17. Delinquent on Any Federal Debt. Hopefully the answer is no. If you have to answer yes, you must attach an explanation. Call the listed program officer and see if the agency will still do business with you—some will, some won't.

Block 18: Signature Block. A person authorized to commit the organization must sign here. For nonprofits, this is usually the executive director or board president; for local governments, it's the mayor or city manager. If you have a board resolution authorizing this application or a general resolution authorizing application for grants, you can include it (unless it puts you over your page limit). You can also refer to the resolution in your cover letter, which doesn't affect your page count.

Filling Out Standard Form 424A

If you write federal grant proposals, you will inevitably come across Standard Form (SF) 424A, the companion to SF 424. This two-page basic federal budget form (shown in Figure 4-3) has been part of the common grant application package since 1988. In the bad old days, you had to fill out all those little boxes with a typewriter, fitting everything into the spaces provided. Today you can download from various government websites PDF or MS Word forms that you can fill out directly on your computer. Some versions will even do the math for you. A central source is www.whitehouse.gov/omb/grants/sf424a.pdf.

Figure 4-3. Standard Form 424A for Federal Grants

BUDGET INFORMATION - Non-Construction Programs						OMB Approval No. 0348-0044

SECTION A - BUDGET SUMMARY

Grant Program Function or Activity (a)	Catalog of Federal Domestic Assistance Number (b)	Estimated Unobligated Funds		New or Revised Budget		
		Federal (c)	Non-Federal (d)	Federal (e)	Non-Federal (f)	Total (g)
1.		$	$	$	$	$
2.						
3.						
4.						
5. Totals		$	$	$	$	$

SECTION B - BUDGET CATEGORIES

6. Object Class Categories	GRANT PROGRAM, FUNCTION OR ACTIVITY				Total
	(1)	(2)	(3)	(4)	(5)
a. Personnel	$	$	$	$	$
b. Fringe Benefits					
c. Travel					
d. Equipment					
e. Supplies					
f. Contractual					
g. Construction					
h. Other					
i. Total Direct Charges (sum of 6a-6h)					
j. Indirect Charges					
k. TOTALS (sum of 6i and 6j)	$	$	$	$	$
7. Program Income	$	$	$	$	$

Authorized for Local Reproduction

Standard Form 424A (Rev. 7-97)

Previous Edition Usable

Prescribed by OMB Circular A-102

SECTION C - NON-FEDERAL RESOURCES

(a) Grant Program	(b) Applicant	(c) State	(d) Other Sources	(e) TOTALS
8.	$	$	$	$
9.				
10.				
11.				
12. TOTAL (sum of lines 8-11)	$	$	$	$

SECTION D - FORECASTED CASH NEEDS

	Total for 1st Year	1st Quarter	2nd Quarter	3rd Quarter	4th Quarter
13. Federal	$	$	$	$	$
14. Non-Federal					
15. TOTAL (sum of lines 13 and 14)	$	$	$	$	$

SECTION E - BUDGET ESTIMATES OF FEDERAL FUNDS NEEDED FOR BALANCE OF THE PROJECT

(a) Grant Program	FUTURE FUNDING PERIODS (Years)			
	(b) First	(c) Second	(d) Third	(e) Fourth
16.	$	$	$	$
17.				
18.				
19.				
20. TOTAL (sum of lines 16-19)	$	$	$	$

SECTION F - OTHER BUDGET INFORMATION

21. Direct Charges:	22. Indirect Charges:
23. Remarks:	

Authorized for Local Reproduction

Standard Form 424A (Rev. 7-97) Page 2

Here are some pointers for filling out SF 424A.

Section A—Budget Summary. This section asks for the grant program name (program function or activity) and Catalog of Federal Domestic Assistance (CFDA) Number. These should be on the program RFP. For a typical application of a new proposal, use line 1. If you're working with multiple activities or programs, use one line for each—and call the agency program officer to see how they want this handled.

Estimated Unobligated Funds is for carry-over funds of existing multiyear grants. If you're doing a new proposal, leave these spaces blank. New or Revised Budget is the total funds for the first year of a new grant or the next year of a continuing grant.

Section B—Budget Categories. Item 6 in this section asks for a detailed outline of your project budget, broken down by the categories listed: Personnel, Fringe Benefits, Travel, Equipment, Supplies, Contractual, Construction, Other, and Indirect Charges. Detailed information on what belongs in each of these categories is included in the following section on the budget narrative. The feds force all of your direct project costs into the same eight categories, regardless of what your project is actually doing. As a result, you may end up with a substantial number of items thrown into Other.

Item 7, Program Income, should list any anticipated income related to the project, such as client fees.

Section C—Non-Federal Resources. This section tells the funding agency the source(s) of your matching funds. Be as specific as possible in each category. Applicant and State are self-explanatory. Other Sources could be local governments or private foundation grants for the project, for example. You may need to document these with letters of commitment from those funders.

Section D—Forecasted Cash Needs. This section guides your payment schedule for the first grant year, which can be vital to your organization's cash flow (see the discussion of cash flow budgets on page 74). The easiest approach is to divide the total by four and put the same amount in each box. However, if you anticipate heavy startup costs (remodeling, equipment purchases, and such), the first quarter amounts could be larger. Conversely, if the first quarter involves mostly planning and recruiting, and program staff will be hired later, the first quarter amounts could be smaller.

Section E—Budget Estimates of Federal Funds Needed for Balance of the Project. For a one-year project, this section should be marked NA. For a multiyear project, it should show your estimates of funding needs for up to a total of five years. Note that in the Future Funding Periods, (b) First means the second grant year, and so forth.

Section F—Other Budget Information. These tiny spaces are for you to explain anything unusual about your project budget. If you have longer remarks to make, you should refer to a section in your budget narrative where you have more room for explanations.

Budget Narrative and Justifications for Completing SF 424A

Federal grants ask for expansion on the numbers in SF 424A, using some variation of language like "Detail budget by line item along with detailed narrative explaining why each line item is necessary/relevant to the proposed project." This expansion can be in a format of your choosing, as long as it includes information about the same nine Object Class Categories: Personnel, Fringe Benefits, Travel, Equipment, Supplies, Contractors, Construction (if applicable), Other, and Indirect Costs.

Figure 4-4 is a template, with minor variations, that is provided by several federal agencies.

Notes for the SF 424A Budget Narrative

These notes for the budget narrative relate to the categories in the SF 424A. The initial, quoted paragraphs are from sample worksheets provided by various federal agencies. The regular text that follows is mine. The text in italics is from OMB Circulars.

A. Personnel. "This budget category refers to the applicant's employees only. List each position by title and name of employee, if available. Show the annual salary and the percentage of time to be devoted to the project. Compensation paid for employees engaged in grant activities must be consistent with that paid for similar work within the applicant organization."

This category includes only organization staff directly working on the project. Outside consultants of any type are included in the contractual category (f). Don't forget to include management and administrative staff costs, such as a percentage of your executive director's or finance officer's time. Because managing federal grants requires significant amounts of time in negotiating and reporting, your agency can get burned if you don't cover these.

B. Fringe Benefits. "Fringe benefits should be based on actual known costs or an established formula. Fringe benefits apply only to employees listed in the personnel category (a) and only for the percentage of time devoted to the project. Fringe benefit costs for overtime hours are limited to FICA, Worker's Compensation, and Unemployment Insurance."

This category includes required costs such as Social Security and Medicare (FICA), Unemployment Insurance (FUTA), Worker's Compensation and any state and local payroll taxes. It also includes any benefits your agency provides such as health insurance, retirement, and child care. On the SF 424A,

Figure 4-4. Budget Narrative and Justification Charts for SF 424A

A. Personnel: List employees of the applying agency whose work is tied to the application.

Position	Name	Annual Salary/ Rate	Level of Effort	Cost	Justification*

* Describe the role and responsibilities of each position.

TOTAL _____

B. Fringe Benefits: List all components of fringe benefits rate.

Component	Rate	Wage	Cost	Justification*

* Fringe reflects current rate for agency.

TOTAL _____

C. Travel: Explain need for all travel other than that required by this application. Local travel policies prevail.

Purpose of Travel	Location	Item	Rate	Cost	Justification*

* Describe the purpose of travel and how costs were determined.

TOTAL _____

D. Equipment: List each piece of equipment and the means of computation.

Item(s)	Computation	Cost	Justification*

* Explain the need for each piece of equipment and how it relates to the overall project. (Federal definition: an article of tangible, nonexpendable, personal property having a useful life of more than one year and an acquisition cost of $5,000 or more per unit). Explain how you arrived at the price and if applicable, the procurement process to be used

TOTAL _____

E. Supplies: List all materials costing less that $5,000 per unit and often having one-time use.

Item(s)	Rate	Cost	Justification*

* Describe need and how costs were estimated.

TOTAL _____

F. Contractual: List all non-employees and amount paid for services or products. A consultant is a non-employee who provides advice and expertise in a specific program area.

Name	Service	Rate	Other	Cost	Justification*

* Explain the need for each agreement and how it relates to the overall project.

TOTAL _____

G. Construction: Not allowed for non-construction projects.

H. Other: Expenses not covered in any of the previous budget categories

Item	Rate	Cost	Justification*

* Break down costs into cost/unit (e.g., cost per square foot). Explain the use of each item requested.

TOTAL _____

Figure 4-4. *Continued*

I. Total Direct Charges: This is simply the total of lines A through H.

TOTAL _____

J. Indirect Charges: If your organization has an indirect cost rate, use it to figure the indirect costs and include a copy of the fully executed, negotiated, indirect cost agreement. If your organization has no indirect cost rate, indicate if you intend to waive the indirect costs or negotiate and establish an indirect cost rate with the funding agency within 90 days of award issuance, if the grant is awarded.

Description	Computation	Cost

TOTAL _____

BUDGET SUMMARY
When you have completed the budget worksheet, transfer the numbers here for calculating totals. This information goes in Section B of Form 424A.

Category	Amount
Direct Costs	
Personnel	
Fringe Benefits	
Travel	
Equipment	
Supplies	
Contractors	
Other	
Total Direct Costs	
Indirect Costs	
TOTAL PROJECT COST*	

* Total Direct Costs + Indirect Costs = Total Project Cost

CALCULATION OF FUTURE BUDGET PERIODS

Category	Project Yr. 2	Project Yr. 3	Project Yr. 4	Project Yr. 5
Direct Costs				
Personnel				
Fringe Benefits				
Travel				
Equipment				
Supplies				
Contract				
Other				
Total Direct Costs				
Total Indirect Costs				
TOTAL PROJECT COST				

most agencies figure these benefits as a single percentage of salary, for example, 25 percent of the personnel line. In the budget narrative, give a detailed breakdown.

C. Travel. "Itemize travel expenses of project personnel by purpose (e.g., travel for staff training, field interviews, advisory group meetings, etc.). Show the basis of your computation (e.g., six people to a 3-day training at $X airfare, $X lodging, $X subsistence allowance). In training projects, travel and meals for trainees should be listed separately. Show the number of trainees and the unit costs involved. Identify the location of travel, if known."

This category includes travel and lodging costs associated with the project. Some federal grants require that project staff attend meetings of federal program officers and grantees (the RFP will say if this is so), and you have to include these costs in your budget. Travel can be both local and national. Local travel is often figured as mileage, using the current federal rate[16] for a privately owned vehicle (POV). National travel often includes airfare and ground transportation (taxi, shuttles, rental cars), which are figured at cost. National and out-of-town travel can also include living expenses such as food and lodging. These costs are often figured at either your agency's rate or the federal per diem rate for the continental United States (CONUS).[17] Both the CONUS and POV are administered by the Government Services Administration (GSA).

D. Equipment. "List non-expendable equipment that needs to be purchased. Non-expendable equipment is tangible property having a useful life of more than 1 year and an acquisition cost of $5,000 or more per unit. However, lower limits may be established if they are consistent with the applicant organization's policy. Expendable items should be included in the Supplies or Other categories. Applicants should analyze the cost benefits of purchasing vs. leasing equipment, especially high cost items and those subject to rapid technical advances. Rented or leased equipment costs should be listed in the "Contractual" category. Explain how the equipment is necessary for the success of the project. Attach a narrative describing the procurement method to be used."

Equipment includes capital items of significant value (often over $500 for smaller organizations) that will have a residual value after the project is finished, such as computers and furniture.

---

[16] The current federal POV mileage rate can be found at http://www.gsa.gov/Portal/gsa/ep/contentView.do?contentId=9646&contentType=GSA_BASIC, or by doing a Google search for "GSA Privately Owned Vehicle mileage reimbursement rate."

[17] The current federal per diem rates for CONUS (the continental United States) can be found at http://policyworks.gov/org/main/mt/homepage/mtt/perdiem/perd05d.html, or by doing a Google search for "Domestic per diem rates."

NOTE: The applicant should establish property management standards (capitalization policy) that establishes the criteria for inventoried items (equipment), procurement procedures, and equipment depreciation. Title to equipment acquired by the applicant with federal funds shall vest with the recipient, however the federal agency retains its share of interest. Equipment may be used on other programs or projects if such other use will not interfere with the work of the program, which originally acquired the equipment. (OMB Circular A-110, Property Standards)

E. Supplies. "List items by type (office supplies, postage, training materials, copying paper, and expendable equipment items costing less than $5,000 such as books and hand-held tape recorders) and show the basis for computation. (Note: Applicant's own capitalization policy may be used for items costing less than $5,000.) Generally, supplies include any materials that are expendable or consumed during the course of the project."

Supplies are items that you will use up during the project, such as office supplies (stationary, pens, printer toner, stamps). This can also include nonoffice supplies for the project such as medicine for a clinic, toys for a children's program, and art supplies. As a general rule, if something costs under $500, it's a supply, even if it will last beyond the project (e.g., staplers and tape dispensers).

NOTE: Title to supplies and other expendable property shall vest in the recipient upon acquisition. If there is a residual inventory of unused supplies exceeding $5000 in total aggregate value upon termination or completion of the project or program and the supplies are not needed for any other federally-sponsored project or program, the recipient shall retain the supplies for use on non-Federal sponsored activities or sell them, but shall, in either case, compensate the Federal Government for its share. (OMB Circular A-110, Property Standards)

F. Contractual. "Indicate whether the applicant's formal, written procurement policy or the Federal Acquisition Regulations are followed."

This category includes anyone you will pay who is not an employee. (If you pay them for work or services, and you don't pay payroll taxes on them, they're contractual.) Consultants, independent contractors, and computer experts are obvious. Less obvious might be maintenance contracts on your copier, janitorial services, or the accountant you hire to audit the grant.[18] Contractual also includes leased equipment or vehicles. If you lease your big photocopier, you can allocate a portion of that cost to the grant. Explain how you made the decision to lease rather than buy.

---

[18] If your agency receives more than $500,000 of federal funds annually, you will be required to have an A-133 audit.

G. Construction. "As a rule, construction costs are not allowable on non-construction grant projects. In some cases, minor repairs or renovations may be allowable. Check with the program officer before budgeting funds in this category."

Most nonprofit program grants are for non-construction projects. Some programs allow project-related new construction or remodeling, some only minor repairs, and some prohibit any construction spending. If you're in doubt, call the program officer.

H. Other. "List items by major type (e.g., rent; document reproduction, telephone, janitorial, or security services; and investigative or confidential funds). Explain the basis of the computation. For example, provide the square footage and the cost per square foot for rent or provide a monthly rental cost and how many months of occupancy."

This catch-all category includes any costs not found in the first seven categories, except those found in Indirect Charges below.

I. Total Direct Charges. This is simply the sum of lines A through H.

J. Indirect Charges. "Indirect costs are allowed only if the applicant has a federally approved indirect cost rate. A copy of the rate approval, (a fully executed, negotiated agreement) must be attached to the budget. If the applicant does not have an approved rate and receives an award, the applicant can request one by contacting the cognizant federal agency, which will review all documentation and approve a rate for the recipient organization, or if the recipient's accounting system permits, costs may be allocated in the direct costs categories."

NOTE: Indirect costs are those costs that have been incurred for common or joint objectives and cannot be readily identified with a particular final cost objective. Because of the diverse characteristics and accounting practices of non-profit organizations, it is not possible to specify the types of cost which may be classified as indirect cost in all situations. However, typical examples of indirect cost for many non-profit organizations may include depreciation or use allowances on buildings and equipment, the costs of operating and maintaining facilities, and general administration and general expenses, such as the salaries and expenses of executive officers, personnel administration, and accounting. In general, small non-profit organizations will not qualify for an indirect rate because they can easily identify administrative costs as direct costs. (OMB Circular A-122, Attachment A, Section C, Indirect Costs)

Demonstrating Fiscal Capability

Funders, both government and private, will often ask something about your ability to manage their grant's finances. You need to assure them that you have the equipment, staff, and know-how to manage their money wisely and well. For the federal government, you want to be sure to start with an affirmative declaration like "JCCA has the fiscal capability to administer this grant." Look at the RFP language and echo it back to them. For example, if they ask you to "affirm," say, "JCCA *affirms* it has the capacity to administer this grant."

Below are three examples for Jefferson County Community Action, with increasing levels of detail.

Jefferson County Community Action

Example 1. Jefferson County Community Action (JCCA) has the fiscal capacity to administer this grant project to a successful conclusion. JCCA manages an operating budget of approximately $14.5 million, encompassing 21 different grants and contracts that range in size from $15,000 to $3 million, with multiple and diverse funding sources that require different reporting systems. JCCA uses a computerized, automated, accrual-based fund accounting system and has received unqualified annual financial audits with no adverse opinions for 10 consecutive years.

Example 2. JCCA offers extraordinary fiscal capacity to administer this grant. JCCA currently has an annual operating budget of over $14.5 million and employs 130 individuals. Approximately 85 percent of JCCA's revenues come from contracts with federal, state, county, and city agencies; third-party billing and private fundraising make up the rest. The agency meets all of the numerous fiscal and reporting requirements from over 21 different funding sources that require different reporting and invoicing systems. JCCA operates according to GAAP using a computerized, automated, accrual-based fund accounting system. The 2003/2004 audit had no findings, nor were there any findings in the past nine audits, including the A-133 audit that meets all federal requirements.

Example 3. JCCA affirms that it is fully capable of managing this grant's finances. JCCA has a sophisticated computerized accounting system capable of managing an array of programs. Contracts with the City of Jefferson, Jefferson County, and the State of California, as well as private foundations, have required structures and systems in fund accounting and reporting that have consistently passed the audits and reviews of independent auditors and the funding agencies.

The accounting system has the capacity to budget and track funding sources, programs, restrictions, funds (fund accounting), and several levels of allocations, as well as natural accounts through Micro Information Products' NPS Pro accounting software, with the support of Excel spreadsheets customized to meet the needs of the organization. All systems are in compliance with generally accepted accounting principles. The Board of Directors, Fiscal Committee, directors, and managers receive monthly financial statements with detailed program analysis. Sufficient capacity exists to maintain current receivables, payables, and inventories and to report on all aspects of the financial position and activities of the organization in a timely manner.

JCCA ensures that all grant funds will be utilized to meet the needs of eligible individuals as defined in the statute and Program Expectations and will not be directed to other activities of the organization. The accounting system has the capacity to ensure compliance with this and other fiscal requirements of Health and Human Services and the privacy requirements of HIPPA.

The fiscal policies and procedures are reviewed annually by the Fiscal Committee. Independent auditors are engaged annually, and the resulting financial statements are disseminated to interested parties. There have been no adverse opinions on the audited statements.

JCCA's Chief Fiscal Officer Bill Buckcounter came to the agency in 1994 with a master's degree in business, four years' experience as a nonprofit accountant, and 16 years' experience in nonprofit management. Mr. Buckcounter is supported by an experienced financial staff, including a supervisor of billing, billing specialists, and Medicaid eligibility screeners at both JCPC clinic sites.

Understanding Tax-Exempt Status

Nonprofit charitable organizations are curious institutions in American law, defined more by what they *aren't* than what they *are*, because of the way the Internal Revenue Code has evolved. If you think about it, a nonprofit institution is: *not* for profit, *exempt* from taxes, and *not* a private foundation. So what does this mean, and how does it work?

Terminology of 501(c)(3) Organizations

Nonprofit (or not-for-profit) doesn't mean that an organization can't take in more money than it spends—what we usually think of as "profit." If that were the requirement, most, if not all, nonprofits would soon fail. What it means is that profit can't be the *reason* for its existence, and any surplus funds have to stay in the organization or be spent for charitable purposes. No owners or shareholders can share in these funds, and if the organization fails or is sold, the remaining assets must go to other similar nonprofit organizations.

Tax-exempt generally means that the organization is exempt from federal income tax under Section 501(c)(3)[19] of the Internal Revenue Code. To be exempt from paying state or local business sales, income, and property taxes, you must receive a separate tax exemption from the government involved. In most cases, receiving federal tax exemption automatically gets you state income tax exemption and makes it much easier to receive sales and property tax exemptions from state and local governments.

Not a private foundation is the least understood part of tax exemption. To be totally tax exempt and to receive grants, among other things, a 501(c)(3) organization cannot be a private foundation. When Congress laid the

---

[19] All nonprofits in Section 501(c) are tax-exempt, but in common usage "tax-exempt" refers to charities.

History of Federal Tax-Exempt Status

1917: When the first permanent federal income tax was enacted in 1913, it affected less than one-half of 1 percent of the population. When Congress expanded the tax code in 1917, it also initiated a deduction for charitable contributions.

1938: The Internal Revenue Code (IRC) of 1938 introduced tax exemption language for nonprofit organizations in Section 101(6).

1954: The tax code was revised, and Section 501(c)(3) was derived from the 101(6) language of the IRC of 1938. This language has continued without substantial change.

1969: The Tax Reform Act of 1969 introduced the classification of "private foundation" in Section 509(a) of the IRC and added a wide array of restrictions, requirements, taxes, and penalties affecting private foundations. It also exempted organizations found to be "not a private foundation."

1984: Congress required nonprofit organizations to deduct and pay FICA (Social Security) taxes.

1996: The Taxpayer Bill of Rights legislation required tax-exempt organizations to make their tax forms (990s) public.

groundwork for modern private foundations in 1969, the IRS developed a better sense of what a private foundation is than a public charitable organization. As a result, public charities came to be described as nonprofit corporations that are *not* private foundations.

Federal 501(c)(3) Requirements

To qualify for 501(c)(3) tax-exempt status, an organization must meet the following requirements set by Congress:

- The organization must be organized and operated exclusively for religious, educational, scientific, or other charitable purposes.

- Net earnings may not inure to the benefit of any private individual or shareholder.

- No substantial part of its activity may be attempting to influence legislation.

- The organization may not intervene in political campaigns.

- The organization's purposes and activities may not be illegal or violate fundamental public policy.

The first step in forming a nonprofit is to incorporate in some state as a "nonprofit corporation" under that state's laws. Once incorporated, the nonprofit applies for tax-exempt status by filing a Form 1023 with the IRS. If approved, the organization receives a letter granting it 501(c)(3)[20] tax exemption as a Public Charity (see Understanding Your 501(c)(3) Letters later in this chapter). The organization must stay within the purposes described in its Form 1023, and the Form 1023 must be available for public inspection. If you are being asked to write grants that seem to be far afield from the organization's mission, check the original Form 1023 to see if the grant project is within the scope of the original application. If it isn't, the organization should not apply for that grant or, with much deliberation and after consulting an attorney, seek to modify its purpose.

Other Tax-Exempt 501(c) Organizations

There are many other types of organizations exempted under section 501(c) of the Internal Revenue Code, for example, civic leagues under 501(c)(4) and credit unions under 501(c)(14). Two important differences distinguish 501(c)(3)s from all the rest: Donations made to 501(c)(3)s may be deductible from the donor's taxable income as charitable contributions, and 501(c)(3)s are eligible to receive foundation grants.

Sometimes an organization will set up parallel nonprofit corporations for related purposes. For example, a 501(c)(3) will be created to do educational and service work and to receive grants and contributions, and a 501(c)(4) will be created to do lobbying and support candidates. If you are working for such an organization, be careful to distinguish its grant-supported activities from its ineligible lobbying work.[21]

"Not a Private Foundation" Status

The IRS assumes that all nonprofits are taxable entities until proven otherwise and that all 501(c)(3) tax-exempt organizations are private foundations until proven otherwise. The differences in proof are significant: Tax-exempt status is based on where your money goes, whereas private foundation status is based on where your money *comes from*.

Public charities are defined in the tax code by the things that distinguish them from private foundations. These can be either or both of the following:

---

[20] Under U.S. Code, Title 26 (Internal Revenue Code), Subtitle A (Income taxes), Chapter 1 (Normal taxes), Subchapter F (Exempt organizations), Part I (General Rule), § 501 (Exemption from taxation), c (list of exempt organizations).

[21] Although there are restricted situations in which 501(c)(3) nonprofits can lobby, most foundations are reluctant to fund these activities.

- **What they are:** The Internal Revenue Code lists churches or associations of churches; schools, colleges, and universities; hospitals or medical research institutions; governmental units; supporting organizations; public safety organizations; development foundations for state or local colleges or universities.

- **Where their funding comes from:** Publicly Supported Organizations (PSOs) and Fee/Activity Supported Organizations (FASOs).

There are complex income tests for PSOs and FASOs, but as a general rule, they must receive a minimum percentage of their total support in contributions from the general public, with limited amount from any one person. If a nonprofit doesn't meet these tests, the IRS can reclassify it as a private foundation (see the section on Tipping).

Nonprofit 501(c)(3) organizations realize significant advantages by not being private foundations:

- They are exempt from paying federal taxes (except for income taxes on any unrelated business).

- They are generally exempt from paying state and local taxes.

- Donations from individuals and corporations are deductible from the donor's federal and state income taxes as charitable contributions, with fewer restrictions than donations to private foundations.

- They are eligible to receive grants from private foundations.

- They are eligible to apply for certain restricted government grants and contracts.

Being classified as a private foundation means loss of most of these advantages. Of particular importance to the grant professional is the loss of eligibility to apply for and receive foundation and government grants.

State Corporate Status

There's another vitally important but often overlooked factor, not directly involving the IRS, that can affect an organization's tax-exempt status. This is whether the organization is keeping its corporate status current with the state in which it is incorporated. *If your corporate status expires, so does your tax exemption!*

Requirements vary from state to state, but most require that you file a form on a regular basis. For example, nonprofit registration is maintained in Oregon with the Department of Justice, and corporate status with the Corporate Division. Failure to stay current can result in the organization's

Tipping

Tipping isn't about whether to leave 15 or 20 percent for your waiter. In nonprofit financial terms, it's the problem of getting too much of your income from one source, which can *tip* you into being considered a private foundation. The U.S. Tax Code requires an organization seeking treatment as a public charity based on the nature of its funding to demonstrate annually that, over the past four years, it has received at least one-third of its total support in contributions from the general public (defined in the code as "qualified people"), with limit of 2 percent of total support from any one person. The proportion of this public support can drop as low as 10 percent of total support (the total of all public support, plus endowment and other income) if the charity meets a facts-and-circumstances test that suggests it is publicly supported.

In this public support test calculation, a private foundation's grant is capped like an individual's gift—any part of the grant that is more than 2 percent of the organization's total support will not count as public support. Since all of a foundation's grant will count toward total support, a big grant can decrease the percentage of funds considered public support and potentially *tip* a charity into private foundation status. One of the 13 factors the IRS reviews in granting non-private foundation status is the amount of public support it plans to attract compared with contributions from substantial donors and other "disqualified" people.[22] For this instance, foundations can be considered disqualified people because they are "substantial contributors." There are exceptions for unusual grants such as startup, nonrecurring, capital campaigns and major bequests, but it's still good to be careful. If you have any questions about tipping, talk to a knowledgeable nonprofit attorney or accountant.

corporate status being revoked. For example, the State of Michigan Corporation Division website says they dissolved 2,638 nonprofit corporations in 2000 for failure to file their annual reports within a two-year grace period.

State corporate status is becoming an increasingly important factor, as states are posting their databases of corporate status on their websites. An auditor from the Oregon Department of Justice told me that the IRS is starting to inspect these public databases, looking for expired corporations. A nonprofit

---

[22] People who are "in a position to exercise substantial influence over the affairs of" a 501(c)(3) or 501(c)(4) nonprofit organization are considered "disqualified persons." They include, but are not limited to: the board president, treasurer, chief executive officer, chief operating officer, and chief financial officer; voting members of the nonprofit's governing body; people with more than 35 percent of a nonprofit organization's combined voting power, profits, or beneficial interests; substantial contributors; and a disqualified person's spouse and family members.

attorney told me the story of a fairly large nonprofit that had operated for 13 years, unaware that its corporate status had expired, filing 990s and using its 501(c)(3) letter. When this was discovered, the organization was faced with the prospect of telling all its donors that their gifts were not deductible and renegotiating or returning foundation and government grants. Although it was able to reach an accommodation with the state and the IRS to restore retroactively its corporate status, legally it ran a huge risk.

Understanding Your 501(c)(3) Letters

Every grantwriter is familiar with the IRS 501(c)(3) determination letter. Foundations and corporations always ask for a copy with grant proposals, as do some government grant programs. But before you mail it off with your application, look it over and make sure it's current and has no unpleasant surprises.

When an organization first applies for tax-exempt status by filing Form 1023, the IRS may either directly grant tax-exempt and "not a private foundation" status, or they may issue an advance ruling stating that you will be treated as exempt until the end of the advance ruling period (about five years), at which time you'll have to file additional information (Form 8734). One of the major reasons to examine your letter is to make sure your advance ruling period hasn't expired.

This section will look at a few examples and point out things to look for, but first here are a few hints and observations.

- One of the first and easiest things a grantwriter or development director can, and should, do is protect the organization's 501(c)(3) letter. Make 25 copies of the original letter. Give one to your lawyer, give one to your accountant, put the original (or a clean copy) in a safety deposit box, and take one home with you. Then place a sticky note saying, "Master—Use Only for Making Copies" on a clean copy and put it at the back of a file folder with the remaining the copies. When you get down to a few copies, make 25 more.

  It is unfortunately very common for an organization to lose its 501(c)(3) letter. A common scenario is that someone takes the original and makes ten copies, then puts them all in a file folder. People use them all for grants, and when the eleventh one is mailed out, the letter is lost. (Not the end of the world, but embarrassing— we'll address this later).

- Make sure you have all the pages of the letter. Many are one page, but they often go on for two or three (sometimes unnumbered) pages.

- Occasionally, a funder will ask for your 501(c)(3) tax exempt ruling and your 509(a) non-private foundation ruling separately. Don't look for two documents because these are almost always included in the same letter. Long ago, some IRS offices issued separate letters, but they are very rare.

- The sample letters in this chapter are representative, but your letter may look quite different, especially if your organization has been around for a long time. I have a folder of 501(c)(3) letters from many organizations, and virtually every one is different. As long as it says your organization is tax exempt under 501(c)(3) and not a private foundation under 509(a), the format doesn't matter.

- Some old letters may say your organization is exempt from paying Social Security taxes for its employees. This stopped being true in 1984, when the nonprofit organization law changed.

Figures 5-1 through 5-4 on the following pages are examples of what different determination letters can look like. They are copied from actual letters. In cases where a letter was more than one page, just the first page is shown, since that contains all of the information you need to check.

Sample A—Advance Ruling Letter

1. **Name and Address.** Make sure this is the organization's current legal name and address. If it isn't, contact the IRS with changes.
2. **Employer Identification Number (EIN).** This is how the IRS keeps track of your organization for all correspondence, your employees' tax with-holding, and your annual 990s. If someone asks for your tax-exempt number, this is what they mean.
3. **Accounting Period Ending.** This is your fiscal year end. You can't change your fiscal year without IRS permission.
4. **Foundation Status.** More detail is given in the previous section, Understanding Tax-Exempt Status.
5. **Advance Ruling Period Ends.** This is a biggie—you don't want to let it expire without applying for permanent status. If this date is fairly far into the future, make a note of it for future reference. If it is in the near future, say less than six months away, tell your management staff they need to fill out and file Form 8734, Support Schedule for Advance Ruling Period, to make your status permanent. The IRS is supposed to notify you when the expiration date gets close, but if they don't, it's your problem.

Figure 5-1: IRS Determination Letter—Advance Ruling

Internal Revenue Service
District Director

Department of the Treasury

Date: 14 March, 1988

Florentine Chamber Orchestra ❶
654 West Alder Street
Anytown, CA 87653

Employer Identification Number: ❷
95-7654321
Accounting Period Ending: ❸
June 30
Foundation Status Classification: ❹
509(a)(2)
Advance Ruling Period Ends ❺
June 30, 1993
Person to Contact: ❻
Bob Oliver
Contact Telephone Number:
(213) 555-5555
Caveat Applies: ❼
None

Dear Applicant:

Based on information supplied, and assuming your operations will be as stated in your application for recognition of exemption, we have determined that you are exempt from Federal income tax under section 501(c)(3) of the Internal Revenue Code. ❽

Because you are a newly created organization, we are not now making a final determination of your foundation status under section 509(a) of the Code. However, we have determined that you can reasonable be expected to be a publicly supported organization described in section 509(a)(2). ❾

Accordingly, you will be treated as a publicly supported organization, and not as a private foundation, during an advance ruling period. This advance ruing period begins on the date of your inception and ends on the date shown above.

Within 90 days after the end of your advance ruling period, you must submit to us information needed to determine whether you have met the requirements of the applicable support test during the advance ruling period. If you establish that you have been a publicly supported organizations, you will be classified as a section 509(a)(1) or 509(a)(2) organization al long as you continue to meet the requirements of the applicable support test. If you do not meet the public support requirements during the advance ruling period, you will be classified as a private foundation for future periods. Also, if you are classified as a private foundation, you will be treated as a private foundation from the date of your inception for purposes of sections 507(d) and 4940.

Grantors and donors may rely on the determination that you are not a private foundation until 90 days after the end of your advance ruling period. If you submit the required information within the 90 days, grantors and donors may continue to rely on the advance determination until the Service makes a final determination of your foundations status. However, if notice that you will no longer be treated as a section 509(a)(2) organization is published in the Internal Revenue Bulletin grantors and donors may not rely on this determination after the date of such publication. Also, a grantor or donor may not rely on this determination if he or she was in part responsible for, or was aware of, the act or failure to act that resulted in the loss of your 509(a)(2) status, or acquired knowledge that the Internal Revenue Service had given notice that you would be removed from the classification as a section 509(a)(2) organization.

P.O. Box 486, Los Angeles, CA 90053   (over)   Letter 1045 (D) (6-77)

If the advance ruling period date has passed, your "not a private foundation" status has technically run out. Don't panic. First ask around and look in files to see if you are using the most recent IRS determination letter—there may be a permanent letter that for some reason isn't being used. If not, contact a nonprofit attorney or accountant for advice, then call the IRS and file a late Form 8734. In most cases, the IRS will accept it and make the status retroactive. If they impose an excise tax or penalties, appeal it. If you're persistent, they'll usually drop the penalties.

6. **Person to Contact and Telephone Number.** Most often this information will be out of date. The IRS moves its offices and employees so often that it is unlikely the same person will be available. But if you need help, try calling the number anyway; you might get lucky. Then check out the IRS website for contact information or call the IRS Exempt Organization Customer Service at 1-877-829-5500.

7. **Caveat Applies (sometimes called Addendum).** If it says None, great—ignore it. If it says Yes, look on the last page of your letter for any conditions applied to your tax exemption. This designation means that when your organization first applied for tax-exempt status, it mentioned some activity that the IRS questioned. For example, I worked with a national educational organization whose application said its activities would include doing research, publishing books, and producing audio and videotapes, without being sufficiently specific about how these related to its mission. Its letter contained addendums that said its tax-exempt status was predicated on the results of its research being made available to the public, that the content of their publications and tapes had to be educational and "germane to their purpose," and that their distribution had to be "distinguishable from ordinary commercial practices." The organization must comply with any restrictions in the addendum in order for its activities to be tax exempt.

8. You'll usually find the magic phrase "501(c)(3)" in the first paragraph of the letter.

9. The wording on your "not a private foundation" status may vary, but it should be there in the first couple of paragraphs. It may refer to 509(a) or 170(b)(1)(A). If you're in any doubt, ask your accountant.

Sample B—Permanent Letter

1. **Name and Address.** Check the name and address again. This letter was written five years after the organization was formed; have there been changes?

2. **Our Letter Dated.** This refers to the date of your advance ruling letter.

3. Receipt of the permanent letter means that the IRS has received your Form 8734 and has made your "not a private foundation" status permanent. This letter is good forever, as long as the organization keeps to its purpose and operates soundly, and the law doesn't change.

Note: If the upper right part of your tax exemption letter has neither an advance ruling period nor an "Our Letter Dated" reference, it merely means that your group was granted permanent status without an advance ruling period.

Sample C—Group Ruling Letter

Some large national or regional organizations that have chapters or other local units will request a group exemption on behalf of the central organization and its subordinates. Subordinate organizations may be separate corporations, or they may be established in some other framework. Churches and religious organizations are often included in group rulings issued annually to a state, regional, or national body, which must submit a list of exempt subordinates to the IRS annually.

In this example, the United States Catholic Conference publishes a thick book, the *Official Catholic Directory*, which lists all of the thousands of churches, monasteries, convents, schools, hospitals, and so forth that are sponsored by the Roman Catholic Church. Even though some of them may have their own separate incorporation and tax exemption, they're also covered by the *Directory*.

Sample D—Lost Letter

If a tax-exempt organization loses its 501(c)(3) letter, it can request a replacement from the IRS. Although the IRS will not issue a new determination letter or a copy of the one you lost, it will send a letter stating that their records show your tax-exempt status is still in effect. This is very common with organizations more than 20 or 30 years old.

Figure 5-2: IRS Determination Letter—Permanent

**Internal Revenue Service
District Director**

Department of the Treasury
P O Box 486
Los Angeles, CA 900530486

Date: May 17, 1972

Jefferson County Community Action ❶
1234 South Main Street
Anytown, CA 87654

Employer Identification Number:
  95-1234567
Case Number:
  987654321
Contact Person:
  John Jones
Contact Telephone Number:
  (213) 555-5555

Our Letter Dated:
  March 25, 1967 ❷
Caveat Applies:
  None

Dear Applicant:

This modifies our letter of the above date in which we stated that you would be treated as an organization which is not a private foundation until the expiration of your advance ruling period. ❸

Based on the information you have submitted, we have determined that you are not a private foundation within the meaning of section 509(a) of the Internal Revenue Code, Because you are an organization of the type described in 509(a) (2). Your exempt status under section 501(c) (3) of the code is still in effect. ❸

Grantors and contributors may rely on this determination until the Internal Revenue Service publishes notice to the contrary. However, a grantor or contributor may not rely on this determination if he or she was in part responsible for, or was aware of, the act o failure to act that resulted in the loss of your 509(a) (2) status, or acquired knowledge that the Internal Revenue Service had given notice that you would be removed from classification as a section 509 (a) (2) organization.

Because this letter could help resolve any questions about your private foundation status, please keep it in your permanent records.

If the heading of this letter indicates that a caveat applies, the caveat below or in the enclosure is an integral part of this letter.

If you have any questions, please contact the person whose name and telephone number are shown above.

Sincerely yours,

Frederick C. Nelson

Frederick C. Nelson
District Director

Figure 5-3: IRS Determination Letter—Group Ruling

Internal Revenue Service	**Department of the Treasury**
District Director	Baltimore District
	31 Hopkins Plaza
	Baltimore, MD 21201

Ms. Deirdre Halloran
Associate General Counsel
United States Catholic Conference
3211 4th Street, N.E.
Washington, D.C. 20017-1194

Dear Ms. Halloran:

In a ruling dated March 25, 1946, we held that the agencies and instrumentalities and all educational, charitable and religious institutions operated, supervised, or controlled by or in connection with the Roman Catholic Church in the United States, its territories or possessions appearing in the Official Catholic Directory for 1946, are entitled to exemption from federal income tax under provisions of sections 101(6) of the Internal Revenue Code of 1939, which corresponds to section 501(c)(3) of the 1986 Code. This ruling has been updated annually to cover the activities added to or deleted from the Directory.

The Official Catholic Directory for 1994 shows the names and addresses of all agencies and instrumentalities and all educational, charitable and religious institutions operated, supervised, or controlled by or in connection with the Roman Catholic Church in the United States, its territories or possessions in existence at the time the Directory was published. It is understood that each of these is a non-profit organization, that no part of the net earnings thereof inures to the benefit of any individual, that no substantial part of their activities is for the promotion of legislation, and that none are private foundations under section 509(a) of the Code.

Based on all information submitted, we conclude that the agencies and instrumentalities and educational, charitable and religious institutions operated, supervised, or controlled by or in connection with the Roman Catholic Church in the United States, its territories or possessions appearing in the Official catholic Directory for 1994 are exempt from federal income tax under section 501 (c) (3) of the Code.

Donors may deduct contributions to the agencies, instrumentalities and institutions referred to above, as provided by section 170 of the Code. Bequests, legacies, devises, transfers, or gifts to them or for their use are deductible for federal estate and gift tax purposes under sections 2055, 2106 and 2522 of the Code.

Figure 5-4: IRS Determination Letter—Lost Letter

Internal Revenue Service
District Director

Department of the Treasury
P O Box 486
Los Angeles, CA 90053-0486

Forgetful Nonprofit
500 West Alder Street
Anytown, CA 87653

RE: Forgetful Nonprofit

Person to Contact:
  Bob Oliver
Contact Telephone Number:
  (213) 555-5555
Refer Reply to:
  EO000000
Date:
  November 1, 1998
EIN:
  93-0987654

Dear Taxpayer:

This letter is in response to your request for a copy of the determination letter for the above named organization.

Our records indicate that this organization was recognized to be exempt from Federal Income tax in June, 1968 as described in the Internal revenue Code 501 (c)(3). It is further classified as an organization that is not a private foundation as defined in Section 509(a) of the code, because it is an organizations described in Section 170(b) (1) (A) (i).

The exempt status for the determination letter issued in June 1968 continues to be in effect.

If you need further assistance, please contact our office at the above address or telephone number.

Sincerely,

Frederick Fredericson

Frederic Fredericson
Disclosure Assistant

Local Government Accounting

This book is written mostly for the grant professional working with nonprofit organizations. However, many grantwriters work inside local governments (cities, counties, school districts, and so forth), and their government's financial statements look somewhat different than what's been described so far. Also, nonprofits are increasingly contracting or partnering with local governments, so this section can be helpful for understanding them and working with them.

This section is an overview of a complex subject and doesn't include examples because they would be too lengthy. I suggest reading it through, then getting a copy of a recent government financial statement to use in studying the financial statements section. If you want to look at a city's financial statements, many are available as free PDF files through the Governmental Accounting Standards Board website at http://www.gasb.org/repmodel/cities.html. You can find the financial statements of other government entities (such as counties and public universities) at http://www.gasb.org/repmodel/implementers.html.

Tax Exemption for Local Governments

Local governments are exempt from federal taxes under Internal Revenue Code Section 115(1), and contributions or grants to them are tax deductible under Section 170(c)(1). Local governments do not have to apply for tax-exempt status, so they don't routinely receive IRS determination letters. Local governments will usually apply for federal or state grants, which don't require them to give proof of tax exemption, rather than for foundation grants.

If they do apply for foundation grants or receive donations, the funders may ask for a determination letter. The IRS will issue, at no charge, a "government affirmation letter" that describes government entity exemption and deductible contributions.[23] Most funders will accept this general letter as proof of tax exemption. For a government entity to receive an *official* determination of its status as a political subdivision, instrumentality of government, or an entity whose revenue is exempt under Section 115, it must pay a fee to obtain a letter ruling.

Government-Supporting Foundations

Increasingly, local governments or citizen groups are establishing separate foundations to raise funds for their most popular departments, such as libraries, parks, and schools—often because the government itself is strapped for funds and can't raise the necessary taxes. These foundations seek individual contributions and grants to support the work of the named beneficiary, the governmental entity, in the form of grants. They are set up as separate nonprofit corporations with 501(c)(3) tax exemption. In terms of private foundation status, some are 509(a)(1) like most nonprofits, and others are 509(a)(3) "supporting organizations." These foundations are not legally tied to the government itself, so they follow nonprofit accounting rules, have their own separate financial statements, and file Form 990s. Some blur the lines by having government employees as their staff, so they don't show administrative costs on their statements.

Private foundations take a mixed view of these organizations. Most don't like to make grants directly to governments. Some see these supporting foundations as legitimate nonprofits, but others view them as attempts by governments to make an end run around private foundation restrictions. Public colleges and universities have long used such separate foundations for fundraising and related purposes with no resistance, so in time, these others may also come to be accepted.

Accounting Differences

Local government accounting is different from nonprofit accounting in several ways, including:

- Local governments use fund accounting, which most nonprofits stopped using after SFAS 117.

- Local governments use a system of modified accrual accounting for governmental funds in which revenues are recognized only when measurable and available (i.e., when taxes are collected), and expenditures are recognized when they are incurred. For enterprise

---

[23] A local government may request this letter by calling the IRS Office of Federal, State and Local Governments at 1-877-829-5500.

funds, which resemble private businesses in that they are self-supporting from user fees, governments report on a full accrual basis, in which revenues are recognized as earned, and expenses are recognized when the liability is incurred.

- Local governments also use budgetary accounting, in which they need to show compliance with laws and legislatively approved expenditures.

Governmental Accounting Standards Board Statement 34

In 1999, the GASB issued Statement 34, which had as much impact on governments as SFAS 117 did on nonprofits. Its major impacts were these:

- Governments are required to provide consolidated, government-wide financial statements in addition to the fund-based statements they had traditionally issued. Fund-based statements are presented on a modified accrual basis, but government-wide ones are required to be presented on a full accrual basis, which means they have to show general capital assets and long-term debt.

- On the government-wide statements, governments are required to list and value their infrastructure assets (roads, bridges, sewer and water systems, and so forth). Previously, they were not required to report these assets at all in the financial statements.

Types of Funds

Governments operate with a mix of restricted funds, which are accounted for separately. A fund is defined as a fiscal entity that:

- represents a part of the activities of some larger organization.

- is an accounting entity of its own, with a self-balancing set of accounts that reflects the assets, liabilities, net assets, and changes in those balances.

- may be segregated for specific activities in such a way that ensures compliance with appropriate laws, regulations, or restrictions.

Every government is required to have an unrestricted General Fund, which handles most of the ongoing activities of the government. It contains all monies that are not in other funds. In addition, a government may have one or more of the following funds:

- **Special Revenue Fund** is used for legally restricted revenues, such as gas taxes dedicated to road building.

- **Capital Projects Fund** is used for construction or acquisition of buildings, bridges, and so forth.

- **Debt Service Fund** pays for long-term debt, such as bonds.

- **Permanent Fund** operates like an endowment; for example, privately raised or donated money is invested and used to maintain a cemetery or to acquire library books.

- **Fiduciary Fund** is monies the government holds in trust for others, such as employees' retirement funds or joint ventures with other entities.

- **Proprietary Fund** is for business-like activities that are wholly or partially supported by user fees. These are divided into:

  - **Enterprise Fund** for goods and services sold to individuals or others outside the government, such as water and sewer.

  - **Internal Services Fund** for services provided to other departments or agencies within the same organization, such as a motor pool.

Reading Government Financial Statements

The required government-wide financial statements for local governments under GAAP are the Statement of Net Assets and the Statement of Activities. A government-wide Statement of Cash Flows, like that required of nonprofits and businesses, is not required of local governments.

Government financial statements include information that is not required in for-profit or nonprofit statements.

- The introduction will include an organization chart and the names of government officials.

- A statistics section will include any information the government thinks would be of use to readers, even if it is not financial. This might include unemployment rate, levels of education, population trends, miles of paved roads, and numbers of schools or fire stations, for example.

- The audited financial statements will include both government-wide and fund-level statements.

There are advantages to both government-wide and fund-level statements:

- Government-wide statements use full accrual accounting and list long-term assets and liabilities for all fund types. This allows readers to see the long-term effects of the decisions and actions of the government.

- Fund-level statements use modified accrual accounting that shows budget-oriented current spending effects. Under modified accrual:

  - Bond monies received are treated as inflows, and bond repayments are treated as outflows.

  - Purchases of long-term assets are treated as outflows.

  - Long-term debt is not listed on the fund's balance sheet

  - Long-term assets are not listed on the fund's balance sheet.

Government-Wide Statements

Let's consider the government-wide statements first, since they're the most like what we've been looking at in this book. They are configured on a consolidated basis and don't separate out any individual funds. A separate column is provided for governmental activities and business-type activities. As mentioned previously, these statements are prepared using full accrual accounting, so they reflect long-term assets and infrastructure, as well as long-term debt.

The Statement of Net Assets has three categories: Invested in Capital Assets, Restricted, and Unrestricted.

- Capital assets are generally recorded at historical cost and depreciated in a manner similar to nonprofit or business accounting.

- Infrastructure assets such as bridges, tunnels, drainage systems carry a depreciation exception. Under this exception, if the government can document that these assets are adequately maintained, their maintenance costs are expensed, not depreciated.

The Statement of Activities shows the operations of the government as a whole.

- This statement shows the net "cost" of activities after deducting the revenues that can be directly attributed to each function.

- General revenues, such as property taxes, are then added at the bottom to get the Change in Net Assets.

- Adding the change in net assets to beginning assets reconciles the Statement of Activities with the Statement of Net Assets.

Fund-Level Statements

The fund-level statements use a major fund reporting concept: There must be one column for the general fund and a separate column for each other major fund. Major funds are defined as 10 percent of the total assets, liabilities, revenues, or expenditures in the government category and 5 percent of the same in the combined government *and* business-type categories. Funds can also be qualitatively determined as "major" by the government for informational or political purposes. Remaining smaller funds are added together and shown in one column as non-major. Fund balances are shown as reserved or unreserved.

The fund-level statements must also reflect budget vs. actual comparisons in the required supplemental information for the general fund and special revenue funds for which an annual budget is adopted. A reconciliation schedule reconciles the changes in net assets shown on the accrual-based government-wide statement and the modified-accrual-based fund-level statement.

Fiscal Sponsorship

Sometimes a nonprofit will be asked to act as a fiscal sponsor for another group that wants grant funding, or to allow use of its tax-exempt status to facilitate contributions to another group or individual. The fiscal sponsor relationship is often assumed to be simple, but it isn't. So if you're considering entering into this arrangement from any role, read this first.

Although the fiscal sponsor relationship can be beneficial to the sponsor, the funder, and the ultimate recipient, it must be approached carefully to avoid both IRS problems and misunderstandings among the parties involved. In the past this has been called a "fiscal agent" or a "pass-through" relationship, but these are not good terms to use: they raise questions with both the IRS and auditors, and they create misunderstandings among the partners.

If a nonprofit is considering entering a fiscal sponsor relationship, either as the sponsor or as the sponsored group (referred to as the "project"), these two conditions must be met:

- The sponsor must maintain fiscal control and some degree of program control.

- The project must be within the sponsor's mission as set forth in its articles of incorporation, bylaws, and original 501(c)(3) application papers (IRS Form 1023).

Examples of Fiscal Sponsorship

Below are models of five common types of fiscal sponsorship that show the relationships between the sponsor and the project.

1. A small organization asks a larger one to sponsor a project that is too large or complex for the small one.

The amount of money involved may be so large that it could "tip" the small organization into private foundation status (see the discussion of Tipping in Chapter 5). The project may have complex bookkeeping, administrative, or evaluation requirements that the small organization doesn't want to undertake. Or they may hope that funders will be reassured by the larger organization's reputation, size, and management expertise.

Billy's Mother has learned of a large national foundation with an interest in programs for street youth. The staff have been aware of a growing problem in Jefferson County, and the organization has been trying some innovative approaches, but thinks a realistic program would have to span several years, would require several hundred thousand dollars, and would be more fundable if it had a solid program evaluation. Billy's Mother approaches Jefferson County Community Action (JCCA) about acting as fiscal sponsor for the project, to handle the accounting and contract with the state university for an evaluation. Billy's Mother volunteers who are close to the street youth would be hired to operate the program from the church-owned houses, giving the project the "street cred" that Billy's Mother has earned.

2. A donor is interested in giving money to a particular individual, but cannot take a charitable deduction for the gift.

The prosperous Evans family would like to sponsor a talented local oboist as a tax-deductible donation. Such a gift, from one private individual to another, is not tax deductible. The family has established the Evans Family Foundation as its private giving vehicle, but the foundation also cannot give directly to individuals. The Foundation approaches the Florentine Chamber Orchestra (FCO) to accept the gift and pass on the funds to the oboist. Although the FCO cannot accept funds to be given to a specific recipient, it can set up criteria for individuals to apply for funding, and it can pre-qualify the oboist. As long as any other person meeting the criteria could apply for those funds and have the same chance of receiving them, this arrangement is acceptable. The Evans Family Foundation and FCO contact a lawyer to set up the arrangement.

3. An individual or group has an idea for a project, but isn't ready to apply for tax-exempt status.

The person or group approaches a large, established nonprofit organization to take the project under its wing and apply for funding, with the understanding that the organization will either hire or contract with the original individual or group to carry out the project. This type of arrangement is not infrequently made by community foundations, United Ways, and Councils of Churches, and is the way many community social service organizations get started.

Bob Smith and Ron Jones have started an after-school basketball program in their neighborhood as a way of keeping kids off the streets. They call the project TeamBuilders and so far have provided all the funding. After two successful years, they decide to add an academic component, requiring an hour of homework with volunteer tutors before each practice. They also would like to expand the program in the summer. They approach the Jefferson Council of Churches (JCC) to sponsor the project and receive some small grants to fund it.

This relationship could be handled two ways. The simplest way is for TeamBuilders to become a project of the JCC with no separate legal existence, and for Bob and Ron to become employees of the Council. The second way is for the JCC to accept grant funds and re-grant them to TeamBuilders. But JCC cannot just write a check to TeamBuilders (called a "pass-through"). For the process to pass IRS scrutiny, these steps must be followed:

- TeamBuilders must make a formal request to the JCC.

- The JCC board must approve the grant.

- The JCC and TeamBuilders should sign a contract setting grant terms and reporting responsibility.

- The JCC must inform the original foundation funder of its control of the project.

Bob and Ron elect to use the second method.

After 10 years, the project has grown so large that Bob and Ron form their own nonprofit corporation, apply for tax-exempt status, and arrange with the JCC to spin the TeamBuilders program off as an independent organization. Because they foresaw this possibility, they already have a written agreement with the JCC describing the process, including what happens to any property and funds acquired by the project.

4. An individual or group wants to donate and solicit large contributions for a particular project, but doesn't want to create a private foundation.

Three wealthy business people want to preserve the old Davis Estate in East Jefferson County and establish it as a museum and nonprofit conference center. They would like to do this by forming the Friends of the Davis Estate (FDE). However, they and their friends would be contributing so much of the funding that the IRS would qualify the FDE as a private foundation. They approach the Jefferson County Community Foundation (JCCF) and establish within it a "supporting organization" that has independent 501(c)(3) status as a separate 509(a)(3) organization. The FDE has its own office, staff, checkbook, investment manager, and letterhead, but contributions are made to the JCCF, which has control legally, if not in practice. This type of organization-within-an-organization naturally requires legal assistance to establish and to meet strict reporting requirements.

5. A foundation with a particular interest may want to establish and fund a new program, but doesn't want it subject to private foundation restrictions.

The private Murray Foundation has an interest in elderly homeless people and wants to establish a housing and counseling program for this group. To avoid IRS restrictions put on private foundations, they ask Jefferson County Community Action, which operates both homeless and Meals on Wheels programs, to create and operate the program with Murray Foundation support.

Issues of Fiscal Sponsorship

Lost Grant Opportunities. This is a serious issue for many potential sponsors. Many funders have a policy of one grant to an organization at a time. If a sponsor applies for a grant for that project, it may be giving up the opportunity to approach that funder for its own programs for the life of the project. An organization that is considering being a sponsor should ask the staff of any foundation that they plan to approach if that sponsorship would disqualify it from receiving other grants from that foundation.

Conditions of the Original Grant. The funder can make an unrestricted grant to the sponsor, with the informal understanding that it will be used for that particular project. Or the funder can make a restricted grant, specifying that funds must be used for that project. For this to not be an illegal "pass-through" transaction, the sponsor must pre-approve the project before funds are received and must exercise expenditure and oversight responsibility.

Recordkeeping. If the project itself is a 501(c)(3) organization, project funds will not show up on the sponsor's financial statements. If the project is not tax-exempt, both grant revenues and project expenses will be shown in the sponsor's formal financial statements, audit, and Form 990.

Property. At the end of the sponsorship relationship, any property and funds acquired with project grant funds must go to a 501(c)(3) organization. This can be the sponsor, the project organization (if it is tax-exempt), or an agreed upon third party 501(c)(3) organization (for example, if the project moves to a new fiscal sponsor).

Payments to the Sponsor. A sponsor can and should be appropriately paid for its services. If the project is tax exempt and the sponsor is not handling funds, it might take minimal or no fees. If the project isn't tax exempt, or if the sponsor is handling funds or managing the project, there should be a written compensation agreement. Amounts up to 15 percent of the grant funds are common. Project organizations should be careful about working with large sponsors like universities that have high overhead and indirect costs.

Liabilities. The sponsor should get legal advice concerning responsibilities and liabilities and in some cases consider additional insurance.

Public Relations. The project will be associated with the sponsor, so both parties need to consider whether the relationship helps or hurts their reputations. They might set up agreements on press relations and printed materials.

Misuses of Fiscal Sponsorship

Fiscal sponsorship can be knowingly or unknowingly misused, with serious consequences for all concerned. Here are a few common pitfalls:

- Acting as a conduit for gifts or grants to specific individuals.

- Channeling funds to an organization without tax-exempt status in the absence of proper controls.

- Avoidance of the public support test and allowing large donors to contribute more than allowed to the project organization.

The consequences of misuse of fiscal sponsorship include the following:

- The reputations of all concerned could be damaged.

- The foundation could be subject to penalty tax.

- The project organization could be reclassified and lose its not-a-private-foundation status.

- The sponsor could be subject to unrelated business income tax or, in extreme cases, lose its tax-exempt status.

- The IRS could impose excise taxes on the boards of both organizations for misuse of funds.

Private Foundations

Private foundations first came into being in the early 20th century when business tycoons like John D. Rockefeller and Andrew Carnegie formed trusts to support their charitable activities. When Congress revised the tax code in 1939, it created the first definitions of tax-exempt organizations, with few distinctions between grant-making foundations and public-benefit nonprofits, and no reporting requirements. This changed in 1969, when Congressional hearings suggested that a growing number of private foundations had been established by wealthy families for tax avoidance purposes. It was claimed that these "foundations" were not using their funds for public purposes and in some cases were improperly using those funds to benefit their creators.

The Omnibus Tax Reform Act of 1969 created a distinction between private foundations and non-private foundations by adding provisions to the Internal Revenue Code to make it impossible for private foundations (i.e., section 501(c)(3) groups that receive their funds from only a few sources) to hoard funds. This was done by requiring private foundations to distribute a portion of their assets to the public for charitable purposes and by other restrictions that laid the groundwork for private foundations as we know them today. Definitions of private foundations and their differences from other 501(c)(3) organizations are included in the Internal Revenue Code under a section commonly called 509(a)[24] in the nonprofit world.

Requirements for Private Foundations

Private foundations *must*:

- Keep detailed financial records and file detailed annual reports with the IRS (Form 990-PF).

- Divest themselves of all but a small portion of shares in their founding corporation and limit the combined holdings of the foundation and "disqualified persons."

- Make minimum distributions (grants) of at least 5 percent of their noncharitable assets annually.

- Pay an excise tax on their net investment income.

Private foundations *must not*:

- Make risky investments that could jeopardize carrying out their exempt purposes.

---

[24] The entire title is U.S. Code, Title 26 (Internal Revenue Code), Subtitle A (Income taxes), Chapter 1 (Normal taxes), Subchapter F (Exempt organizations), Part II (Private Foundations), § 509 (Private Foundation defined), a (General rule).

- Engage in self-dealing (i.e., making various payments to "disqualified persons").

- Engage in lobbying or election activities.

- Make grants to individuals or to organizations that are not public charities.

- Spend money on noncharitable purposes.

Violating these requirements and prohibitions is punished by taxes and penalties on the offending transaction.

Private Foundations Compared with Charitable Trusts

You may notice that some of the foundations you apply to are called "charitable trusts." The difference between foundations and trusts is in the way they are legally established. A foundation is a corporation based in *civil law*, established like any other nonprofit organization. A trust is established by a private contract based in *common law*. Charitable trusts are often established in wills and estates. The IRS treats grant-making charitable trusts as private foundations under the law. Trusts file the same Form 1023 application for tax exemption as private foundations and nonprofit corporations, and are required to file Form 990-PFs annually. (Note: This is different in Canada; see the following section on Canadian nonprofits.)

Like other 501(c)(3) organizations, private foundations are required to file reports with the IRS. However, their reporting requirements are more stringent and detailed than other nonprofits, because they are generally formed by very wealthy individuals and have a much higher possibility of being used as a tax avoidance tool. As part of Form 990-PF, private foundations are required to list all of their assets and grants paid out. Unlike other 501(c)(3)s, private foundations are subject to some taxes, although at much lower rates than private corporations.

Reading a Private Foundation's Form 990-PF

The 990-PF gives a real insight into a foundation's inner workings, and some grantseekers spend hours pouring over them. If you're not sure it's worth your time and trouble to review the 990-PF, think about this: Representatives of the foundation have spent weeks, or even months, compiling data and filling out the report. In a half hour or less spent reviewing the highlights of this massive document, you can glean information that may be invaluable to your success in seeking grants from this funder. The information in the 990-PF is generally one or two years more current than that in most foundation directories or even databases, and if your state doesn't have such a directory, the 990-PF provides the most current information on staff, trustees, address, and phone numbers. For smaller foundations, which don't produce annual reports, the 990-PFPFs are the primary source of information on their giving history. Some major foundations that produce annual reports will include copies of their annual report grant pages as part of their 990-PF. These attached pages, in Section XV, are probably the most heavily perused portion section of 990-PFs.

By looking at the sizes of grants and the types of organizations funded, grantseekers can get an idea of their organization's likelihood of being funded. For instance, if most of a foundation's grants are under $5,000, a new applicant has very little chance of obtaining a $100,000 grant. If most grants are for the arts, an arts organization might be encouraged, but an environmental group might be better off looking elsewhere. If all of a foundation's grants are in Tennessee, an Idaho organization is probably wasting its time applying. Looking at the actual grants is also a good way of comparing a foundation's stated interests and giving territory to its actual behavior and grants history. It's not uncommon for a foundation to say it gives nationally, but in fact make grants almost exclusively in its local area.

Let's go through the form and pick out some particular details. I haven't provided an example of a 990-PF because they are much too long. Instead, I suggest you go to www.guidestar.org and download the form of a foundation that interests you, such as the largest one in your state. Then use this chapter to walk through it.

Even the first few boxes contain valuable information. The very first line, Fiscal Year, can be useful. If a foundation is near the end of its fiscal year, it may have spent its required 5 percent payout, and you might do better waiting to apply until early the next year. Conversely, it may have underspent and be looking to make some last-minute grants. Of course, you won't know this unless you ask someone from the foundation, but knowing the fiscal year prepares you to know what to ask.

Question I, Fair Market Value of All Assets, gives you an overview of the foundation's capacity. If its total assets are $100 million, then it is likely to make $5 million in annual grants. But if its total assets are only $500,000, it might grant $25,000 a year.

Part I, Analysis of Revenue and Expenses, is a summary of other sections of the report. If Line 1 shows significant contributions during the year, it could mean that a trustee is doing estate planning or has died and left a portion of her estate to the foundation, which in turn could mean larger assets and proportionately greater grants in the future. With a family foundation, it could also mean significant changes in direction or interests, as other family members take control of the grants process. (There may be much more detail of contributions to the foundation in an Attachment B.) The rest of this section gives basic information about income and expenses, including total grants made.

Part II, **Balance Sheets**, give an overview of the foundation's capacity and practices. Lines 10 to 13 show how assets are allocated. Are they heavily invested in stocks for growth at higher risk, or more conservatively in corporate and government bonds for income and security?[25] Any program-related investments will probably be on line 15, "other." Line 18, Grants Payable at the beginning and end of the year, shows if they're over or under the required 5 percent payout (the large majority will be very close). If they're significantly higher, it could be a sign of many committed multiyear grants, which could signal fewer grants in the near future. Less likely, it could mean the foundation is spending down its assets. Either way, the situation merits more research.

Parts III and IV are bookkeeping, probably not of much interest to us.

Part V gives more detail on the foundation's distribution rate. How close was it to the 5 percent payout over the last five years, and is there any pattern? It's also a quick glance at their asset growth (or loss) over that time.

Part VI figures the foundation's excise tax, which is tiny (1 percent of income).

Part VII-A and B are check-off boxes about their activities. This part also gives you the name of the person who keeps their books, if that's of interest.

Part VIII names the board or trustees and discloses their compensation. These people are the decision-makers for grant making, so this part of the form may be one of the most important sources of information for local foundations, where you or your board might actually know someone. By looking at the last names, you may be able to guess who are members of the family that established the foundation.

This part of the form is also the juicy part—the compensation of the five highest paid employees, the five highest paid independent contractors (attorneys, brokers, etc.), and the total number of people paid over $50,000 a year. In strategizing how to approach a trustee, it's useful to understand the nature of that person's relationship to the foundation—who's donating time, who's representing the foundation as a full-time job, and who's billing

---

[25] The list of investments in Part II often will be included as attachments. If you're really curious, you can see where they invest and make inferences about the values of the organization. For instance, a foundation heavily invested in defense contractors might not be a good match for a peace organization; one heavily invested in tobacco and liquor may be more focused on profits than social values. Because of tax laws, foundations are not allowed to keep large portions of stock in their founder's companies, so the investments will generally be made to produce income and may or may not reflect the trustees' values.

$300 per hour. Volunteers or members of the family may be motivated to perform differently than people who work for the foundation as employees. You can also gauge someone's importance by that person's salary and infer how seriously the trustees may take her or his recommendations.

Part IX-A tells if the foundation engages in any direct charitable activities. Most do not, but some have scholarship programs, host conferences, publish research papers, or sponsor institutes in areas of particular interest.

Part IX-B lists program-related investments. If the foundation loans or invests money with the nonprofits whose programs it supports, rather than making grants to them, that will be shown here. This situation is rare, but it is becoming more common among larger foundations. These transactions can be a source of creative financing for a nonprofit with a large or unusual entrepreneurial project.

Parts X, XI, XII, and XIII are all concerned with seeing whether the foundation is making, or has made, the required 5 percent average payout in grants. If it doesn't, part of its income is subject to taxes.

Part XIV applies to Private Operating Foundations, rather than purely grant-making foundations. Most will leave this part blank or mark it "not applicable."

Part XV lists all current and future grant commitments. This part often refers to an attachment, which may be a copy of the foundation's annual report or a computer printout of its grants. For foundations that don't produce an annual report, the 990-PF is the only detailed source of information on their giving history.[26] This information is often one or two years more current than that in most foundation directories or even databases, and if your state doesn't have such a directory, the 990-PF provides the most current information on staff, trustees, address, and phone numbers.

As mentioned at the start of this section, the 990-PF is where you find out whether a foundation regularly funds groups similar to yours, the average size of its grants, and its multiyear commitments (or if it ever makes multi-year grants). It can be extremely useful in your planning or in talking to program officers if you know the foundation's funding limitations in current or subsequent year(s) as a result of multiyear commitments.

Part XVI-A is a summary of the sources of the foundation's income, which will generally be investments.

Part XVI-B asks if and how any of the income-producing activities in Part XVI-A were related to tax-exempt purposes. In most cases this part will be left blank or marked "not applicable."

---

[26] The 990-PFs are the source material for the privately published state and national foundation directories.

Part XVII asks for transfers, transactions, and relationships with non-charitable tax-exempt organizations. Those are organizations in other 501(c) categories such as 501(c)(4)s, which can engage in lobbying.

This 12-page form will be followed by attachments, referring to parts of the form that didn't provide enough space for a full answer. These can run from a couple of dozen pages for smaller foundations into several hundred pages for larger ones. Typically they will include:

- Details from answers in Part I about finances

- A list of investments from Part II, Question 13

- The foundation's application guidelines from Part XV

- A list of grants made during the year from Part XV.

Canadian Nonprofits

Canadian nonprofits operate similarly to those in the United States, but there are some differences in both tax exemption and financial reporting. Canada has a large and active nonprofit sector, accounting for 6.85 percent of gross domestic product and more than 12 percent of employment. Measured by the percentage of the workforce, Canada's nonprofit sector is larger than that in the United States and second only to that in the Netherlands.

Canada is more of a European-style "welfare partnership" state than the United States, with the government assuming responsibility for health care and more of its housing and social services. On the other hand, it is closer to the United States than many European countries in using charities to carry out many social service activities. Government accounts for 51 percent of Canadian nonprofits' income, with fees bringing in 39 percent and philanthropy 9 percent.[27]

Incorporation and Tax Exemption

Canadian tax exemption differs from U.S. tax exemption in several ways, although the systems operate very similarly in practice. In Canada, an organization can incorporate at either the federal or provincial level. Larger national or international nonprofits find it advantageous to incorporate federally, whereas smaller ones usually do so only in their province. Canadian nonprofits can be established as corporations, trusts, or unincorporated groups of individuals. Canadian corporations or societies must have members as well as directors, although they can be the same people. Canadian

---

[27] When the value of volunteer labor is included, philanthropy rises to 20 percent.

nonprofits must have constitutions, which in some provinces are combined with their articles of incorporation. Some provinces require charities to appoint an auditor as part of incorporation.

To qualify as a registered charity, 50 percent of the directors or trustees "must deal with each other at arms length." This is a significant difference from the United States, where nonprofit boards can be all family members or business associates.

Incorporation is also called "registration as a society" in Canada, and application for tax exemption is called "registration as a charity." It is possible to be a charitable organization without being incorporated; however, such an organization isn't eligible for the same tax benefits. To register as a charity, an organization files a Form T2050E, similar to the U.S. Form 1023 for tax-exempt status. Registered charities must file an annual T3010 Report with the federal government, similar to U.S. Form 990.

Nonprofit Operations

Canadian charities have some specific differences from U.S. nonprofits. Registered charities can give receipts for contributions to donors, which the donors must use to get income tax deductions. Without these receipts, donations are not tax deductible.

Charities are required to spend 80 percent of their receipted donations and 80 percent of contributions from other charities on charitable activities (although this is not a severely limiting factor, since the 51 percent of income from government and the 39 percent from fees are not included).

Foundations

Foundations in Canada operate similarly to those in the United States, but again there are some differences. Private foundations must give away 4.5 percent of their assets annually (compared to 5 percent for U.S. foundations), but in addition they must calculate and donate 80 percent of donations received during the year and 100 percent of donations received from other registered charities. These amounts can be cumulative, as long as all of the requirements are met.

Foundations that are organized as trusts are treated somewhat differently than those organized as corporations because of Canadian court decisions. Trusts' giving is limited to registered charities, defined as organizations with one or more of the following goals: the relief of poverty, the advancement of religion, the advancement of education, or other purposes beneficial to the community as a whole (e.g., disaster relief, social welfare, animal welfare, historic preservation).

Foundations that are organized as corporations can make grants not only to registered charities, but also to "qualified donees," which include: Canadian amateur athletic associations; not-for-profit senior housing corporations; Canadian municipalities, provinces, and the federal government; the United Nations and its agencies; certain foreign universities; and certain foreign charitable organizations.

Canadian public foundations are similar to community foundations in the United States. They must meet the same requirement as registered charities that 50 percent of the directors or trustees "must deal with each other at arms length."

Nonprofit Accounting

Financial accounting for nonprofits in Canada is similar to that in the United States, with standards set by the Accounting Standards Board of the Canadian Institute of Chartered Accountants (CICA). Canadian accounting standards setters generally look to the United States and international standards setters when setting Canadian accounting standards for for-profit enterprises. Notwithstanding this, there are significant differences between Canadian and U.S. generally accepted accounting principles. No attempt has been made to match Canadian and U.S. accounting standards for nonprofit organizations.

Canadian nonprofit organizations follow standards in the *Handbook of the Canadian Institute of Chartered Accountants*. In 1996, at about the same time as SFAS 116 and 117 were issued in the United States, CICA published six new sections to the Handbook that affected nonprofit organizations. They didn't parallel the FASB changes, but were similarly significant. The most important ones are explained below.

Section 4400, Presentation of Financial Statements. The required financial statements are the Statement of Financial Position, Statement of Operations, Statement of Changes in Net Assets, and Statement of Cash Flows. There is no requirement for a Statement of Functional Expenses, although for organizations choosing Restricted Fund accounting (see the next section), there is a very similar effect.

Section 4410, Contributions—Revenue Recognition. This section requires nonprofits to follow either the Deferral Method or the Restricted Fund Method of accounting for contributions. Under the deferral method, organizations are required to:

- Recognize externally restricted contributions and externally restricted investment income as revenue in the same period in which the related expenses are incurred;

- Recognize unrestricted contributions and unrestricted investment income as revenue in the current period;

- Recognize endowment contributions as direct increases in net assets.

Under the restricted fund method, organizations are required to:

- Recognize externally restricted contributions and externally restricted investment income for which there is a corresponding restricted fund as revenue of that fund;

- Recognize externally restricted contributions and externally restricted investment income for which there is no corresponding restricted fund in the general fund, in accordance with the deferral method;

- Recognize unrestricted contributions and unrestricted investment income as revenue of the general fund;

- Recognize endowment contributions as revenue of the endowment fund.

All organizations are required to measure contributions at fair value and to disclose:

- The policies followed in accounting for each type of contribution;

- Contributions by major source;

- The nature of changes to any deferred contributions balances;

- Total investment income earned on resources held for endowment and how it was recognized in the financial statements.

Contributed materials and services (in-kind) may be recognized, but only when fair value at the date of contribution can be reasonably estimated, when they are used in normal operations, and when they would otherwise have been purchased. (There is no "professional services" restriction as required by SFAS 116.)

Section 4420, Contributions Receivable. This section requires organizations to recognize contributions receivable when the amount to be received can be "reasonably estimated and collection is reasonably assured." Specific guidance is provided on the recognition of pledges and bequests. Nonprofits are required to disclose the amount of pledges and bequests recognized as assets, and the amount is included in revenue.

Section 4430, Capital Assets Amortization.[28,29] This section requires nonprofits to:

- Record capital assets on the Statement of Financial Position at cost (for a contributed capital asset, cost is considered to be fair value at the date of contribution);

- Amortize capital assets with limited lives;

- Recognize amortization as an expense in the Statement of Operations;

- Write down capital assets that no longer have any long-term service potential;

- Disclose the amount of amortization expense, the amount of any write-downs, and information about major categories of capital assets and contributed capital assets.

Section 4440, Collections. Collections are specifically excluded from the definition of capital assets. This section defines collections, and sets out certain disclosure requirements for collections and the proceeds therefrom. It does not specify how collections should be accounted for.

Other Differences

Several other differences between Canadian financial statements and the U.S. statements described in this book are noteworthy:

- Canadian statements don't require recognizing capital gains (or losses) from investments because there is no requirement to show investments at market value.

- Temporarily and permanently restricted net assets and income are not required to be shown separately. The awkward conversion of temporarily restricted to unrestricted income and assets required by SFAS 117 isn't used in Canada.

- Externally restricted and internally restricted assets are differentiated, with the board allowed to designate funds "not available for general operations." In the United States, internal restrictions are not recognized on financial statements, so the funds must be listed as unrestricted.

---

[28] Under the Exemption Provision, small nonprofits may limit the application of this Section to certain required disclosures about capital assets if the average annual revenues recognized in the Statement of Operations in the current and preceding year of the organization and any entities it controls is less than $500,000.

[29] Amortization is the same as depreciation in this case. U.S. nonprofits were required to depreciate capital assets by SFAS 93 in 1988.

This section is obviously not a comprehensive study of Canadian non-profit financial accounting. I found several books on U.S.-oriented nonprofit accounting, but there seemed to be none for Canada. The best book I found, *Forming and Managing a Non-Profit Organization in Canada*, is out of print. In addition, I live and work in the United States, so I don't have the same first-hand knowledge of Canada. The *Handbook of the Canadian Institute of Chartered Accountants* is a resource for those who want to get deeper into the subject. If you live in Canada, Imagine Canada (formerly the Canadian Centre for Philanthropy), at http://www.imagine.ca, is another great resource.

Canadian Applicants to U.S. Foundations

Canadian nonprofits wishing to apply for grants from U.S. foundations must establish their eligibility as charities or nonprofit organizations. Canadian groups have a relatively easy time with this, compared to those in developing countries, because of the similarity between U.S. and Canadian laws, the shared use of the English language, relatively common cultures, and the fact that both are advanced societies with solid accounting and banking systems.

In fact, all Canadian registered charities are deemed to be the equivalent of tax-exempt organizations under the *United States–Canada Income Tax Treaty*, spelled out under IRS Notice 99-47. Unfortunately, the Notice does not address whether private foundations may rely on this equivalency, so most U.S. grantmakers still undertake equivalency determinations.

The IRS Revenue Procedure 92-94 provides three main ways for foreign nonprofits to establish their tax-deductible status. They are:

1. Apply directly for 501(c)(3) status. This is time consuming and carries the requirement of filing annual Form 990s. Only organizations that expect to seek multiple grants over several years would be likely to find this an attractive approach.

2. File an Affidavit of Equivalency. This signed document states that the organization is the equivalent of a U.S. public charity. If the foreign organization is a church, school, or hospital, this is fairly simple. If the organization needs to qualify based on its sources of income, the form is more complex. Some larger U.S. foundations have their own affidavit forms, or the organization can find samples at the U.S. International Grantmaking Project (USIG), whose website is www.usig.org.[30]

---

[30] The U.S. International Grantmaking Project is a project of the Council on Foundations. The web site has a great deal of information, and any Canadian or other foreign nonprofit interested in seeking grants from U.S. sources should explore it.

3. Enter into an Expenditure Responsibility relationship with the granting foundation, in which the foundation oversees the grant funds. This is very useful for organizations in developing countries, which might have a hard time complying with U.S. laws or documenting their income sources, but most Canadian nonprofits could easily show their equivalency. Details on expenditure responsibility are also found on the USIG website.

Foreign organizations can also work through U.S.-based "Friends" groups or ally with an American charity with 501(c)(3) status. Because Canadian organizations can fairly easily meet the Affadavit of Equivalency requirements, they would probably not need to use these methods, which are more likely to be useful for agencies in developing countries.

Glossary

A-133 audit: A compliance audit required of nonprofit organizations, local governments, Indian tribes, and educational institutions that receive more than $500,000 in federal funds annually. Named for OMB Circular A-133, which required the audit and established standards for it. (*See also* compliance audit, single audit.)

accounting: An information system for conveying financial information about a specific entity. (*See also* financial accounting, management accounting.)

accounts payable: An account that tracks money that an organization owes to its suppliers, vendors, contractors, and other creditors.

accounts receivable: Income already promised or earned but not yet received by an organization. Can be further specified as, for example, grants receivable, contracts receivable, pledges receivable.

accrual accounting: An accounting method in which an organization records revenues and expenses when the actual transaction is completed, rather than when cash is received or paid out. (*Compare with* cash accounting.)

activity: Anything that incurs a cost.

administrative activity: The finance, legal, board-related, and general oversight of a nonprofit organization.

advance ruling: A tentative IRS opinion regarding eligibility to be treated as a 501(c)(3) public charity.

aging accounts receivable: The process of classifying accounts receivable by the time elapsed since the claim came into existence, for the purpose of estimating the amount of uncollectable debts.

allocation: The process of spreading costs to two or more activities.

amortization: Expensing an intangible asset, such as a loan or trademark, over its useful life. (*Compare with* depreciation.)

annuity: A series of equal cash flows received or paid over equal intervals of time.

appropriation: Authorization granted by a legislative body to incur liabilities for purposes specified in an appropriation act.

arms-length transaction: A transaction that involves two parties who can act independently of each other and have no financial relationship to each other.

assets: The properties or resources the agency owns and uses; for example, cash, investments, receivables, buildings, and equipment. Defined as a thing of value, owned by the organization, that has a measurable cost. Assets are found on the Statement of Financial Position.

audit: The process completed by an auditor, involving analysis, tests, and confirmations, that results in an issued opinion on whether year-end financial statements reflect the actual financial activity and condition of the organization for the time period in question.

audit committee: A committee of the board that hires the outside auditor and oversees the audit process. In some smaller nonprofits, this committee may actually perform an internal audit.

audit trail: The link between original source documents or transactions—such as checks, invoices, sales reports—and the balances reported in the accounting records and reports. Also called a "paper trail."

auditor's report: A report included with audited financial statements that expresses an opinion on the fairness of the material presented, according to generally accepted accounting principles. Also called "auditor's opinion" or "auditor's letter."

balance sheet: The Statement of Financial Position.

below-the-line allocation: The process of allocating total common costs proportionately among the activities of the organization. (*See also* allocation, common costs.)

benchmarking: A systematic approach to identifying best practices to help an organization improve performance.

block grant: Large sums that the state or federal government allocates to fund a specific activity.

bond: A certificate to show evidence of debt. Local governments generally issue two types: (1) general obligation bonds, which are backed by their taxing authority and paid back by tax revenues, and (2) revenue bonds, which are paid back from the revenues generated by what the bonds financed.

book value: The carrying value (cost less any depreciation) of an asset or liability, regardless of actual or market value.

bookkeeping: The process of analyzing and recording transactions in the accounting records.

budget: The organization's plan of action expressed in dollars (income and expense). Allows the organization to track actual performance against a board-approved plan.

business-type activity: An activity of local governments that involves exchanging value and is intended to make a profit. Reported separately in government-wide statements.

capital: The resources of an organization that provide the financial base or underpinning for operations; also called "net assets."

capital budget: A budget that projects both cash required to purchase fixed assets and depreciation calculations. Such long-term purchases are not included in the organization's operating budget. Similarly, they are recorded on the Balance Sheet and not on the Statement of Activities.

capitalization: Recording something as a capital asset rather than as an expense when it is purchased. Usually requires a minimum useful life of three to five years and a dollar threshold (with nonprofits, usually $1,000 or more).

capitation grant: A grant based on the number of people served, such as patients or students.

cash accounting: An accounting method in which an organization records revenues and expenses only when the cash is actually received (income) and the bills are actually paid (expense). (*Compare with* accrual accounting.)

cash equivalent: A short-term, highly liquid investment such as a money market account, CD, or bond, which is due to mature in one or two months.

cash flow: The amount and timing of money that moves into and out of an organization.

Catalog of Federal Domestic Assistance (CFDA): A listing of all federal grant programs, available as a book or an on-line database at http://www.cfda.gov.

Catalog of Federal Domestic Assistance (CFDA) Number: The identifying number that a federal program is assigned in the Catalog of Federal Domestic Assistance.

certified public accountant (CPA): An accountant who has satisfied the statutory and administrative licensure requirements of his or her state.

challenge grant: *See* matching grant.

charitable gift annuity; charitable lead trust; charitable remainder trust: *See* split-interest agreement.

charitable trust: A grant-making organization established by a private contract, often established in a will or estate, as opposed to a foundation (which is a corporation). The IRS treats grant-making charitable trusts as private foundations under the law. (Note: This is slightly different in Canada.)

chart of accounts: The numerical system for tracking assets, liabilities, net assets, income, and expenses in an accounting system. Drives the reporting capacity of an organization.

chartered accountant: The Canadian equivalent of a certified public accountant in the United States.

cognizant agency: A federal agency that deals with a grantee or auditee, as a representative of all federal agencies, under the Single Audit Act.

collection: Works of art, books, memorabilia, botanical or animal specimens, and the like used for educational display or study. Collections are sometimes given special treatment in accounting.

common costs: Those costs that benefit more than one activity and that are not easily identifiable with a single activity. (*See also* indirect costs.)

community foundation: A foundation that makes grants to address the needs of a specific community or region. Its funds come from many donors, and its board is chosen to be representative of the community. Community foundations are usually classified under the tax code as public charities and therefore are subject to different rules and regulations than those governing private foundations.

compliance audit: An audit designed to show that a grantee organization has complied with applicable laws and regulations. U.S. nonprofits are governed by OMB A-133.

condition: A requirement that something must happen before funds can be spent; for example, matching funds have to be raised. (*Compare with* restriction.)

consolidated financial statement: A report that combines the assets, liabilities, revenues, and expenses of a parent organization and any subsidiary organizations.

continuation grant: A grant approved for multiple-year funding. Typically the actual funds are committed only one year at a time.

contribution: A gift or donation given to an organization for which the donor receives no direct private benefits in return.

CONUS: The continental United States domestic per diem (amount per day) that the U.S. government will reimburse federal employees for travel expenses, and therefore a good model for figuring travel in a grant budget.

cooperative agreement: An award of financial assistance that is used to enter into the same kind of relationship as a grant. Distinguished from a grant in that it provides for substantial involvement between the federal agency and the recipient in carrying out the activity contemplated by the award.

corporate foundation: A private foundation established by a company to direct its charitable giving. Usually has a board composed of corporate officials and makes grants in fields related to corporate activities and/or in communities where the corporation operates.

cost center: A department whose manager is responsible for managing costs.

cost effective: Yielding a high return in benefits for the resources invested.

cost share or match: The portion of project or program costs not borne by the funding agency.

current assets: Cash, cash equivalents, and assets that can be converted to cash or consumed within one year.

current liabilities: Debts or other obligations that will be paid within one year.

Data Universal Numbering System (DUNS): A unique nine-character identification number provided by the commercial company Dun & Bradstreet (D&B). Required for all federal grants after 2003.

deferred revenue: Revenue received before it is earned, such as income from the sale of season tickets or memberships. Recorded as a liability on the balance sheet.

deficit: Expenses in excess of related income in an accounting period.

depreciation: The process whereby the cost of purchasing a capitalized item, such as a building or major piece of equipment, is allocated across the years of its "useful life." The depreciation of each asset accumulates, and its book value is its cost less "accumulated depreciation." Although businesses often use accelerated depreciation for tax reasons, nonprofits generally use straight-line depreciation, dividing the value by the number of years of useful life. In the United States, *depreciation* refers to physical assets like buildings, and *amortization* refers to intangible assets like trademarks. (*Compare with* amortization; *see also* capitalization.)

designated funds: Assets set aside for a specific use by action of the governing board. These funds are considered unrestricted for accounting purposes. (*Compare with* restricted funds.)

determination letter: An opinion of the IRS concerning a nonprofit organization's tax-exempt and private foundation status. Often called a "501(c)(3) letter."

direct costs: Expenses specifically associated with and identifiable by program, project, or activity. In grant budgeting, these are the costs of actually operating the grant program, such as program staff and supplies. (*Compare with* indirect costs.)

disallowed costs: Charges to an award that the awarding agency determines to be unallowable, in accordance with applicable federal cost principles or other terms and conditions contained in the award.

discretionary grant: A grant (or cooperative agreement) for which the federal awarding agency generally may select the recipient from among all eligible recipients; may decide to make or not make an award based on the programmatic, technical, or scientific content of an application; and may decide the amount of funding to be awarded.

disqualified person: A person or entity in a certain relationship with a nonprofit who is subject to restraints on financial transactions with the organization for federal tax purposes, especially for determining the organization's private foundation status.

diversification: Having a variety of funding types and sources so that the nonprofit organization is not unduly dependent on a handful of sources.

DUNS number: *See* Data Universal Numbering System.

earmarked grant: Congressionally designated funds, often called "pork barrel." Although not a true grant, a proposal still has to be prepared for the congressperson sponsoring it, and the standard forms have to filled out for the federal agency from whose budget it comes.

earned revenue: Income that the organization obtains through exchange transactions such as fees, ticket sales, and certain, but not all, government contracts.

effective date: The date a grant award is formally made.

employee benefits: Noncash employee compensation such as health insurance and retirement plans. These benefits are voluntarily or contractually supplied by an employer, unlike payroll taxes, which are mandatory. Accounted for as personnel costs.

employer identification number (EIN): Also known as a federal tax identification number, every corporation (which includes nonprofits) and partnership must have one and use it for reporting to the IRS.

endowment: A fund whose donated assets are permanently restricted by the donor. Interest or income generated may be unrestricted, temporarily restricted, or permanently restricted.

entity: A person, corporation, government, or other organization.

excise tax: A federal penalty tax that can be assessed for the performance of prohibited activities by private foundations and public charities.

exempt organization: A nonprofit corporation, trust, or association qualified for exemption from federal income tax and most state and local taxes. Not all nonprofit organizations are tax exempt. The Internal Revenue Code lists 26 different categories of tax-exempt organizations in Section 501(c). Only 501(c)(3) organizations are eligible for foundation grants.

external reporting: Reporting to readers outside the organization, such as funders, regulators, donors, and the general public, as opposed to internal reporting for management purposes.

face value: As applied to securities such as bonds, the amount of liability stated on the security document.

fair market value: Amount for which an investment could be sold between willing parties (i.e., not a forced or liquidation sale).

FASB: *See* Financial Accounting Standards Board.

fee/activity supported organization (FASO): An organization that normally receives more than one-third of its support from gifts, grants, and membership fees and less than one-third from investments and unrelated business income. This definition is used by the IRS as part of its complex calculation to determine that a 501(c)(3) organization is "not a private foundation."

FICA: Social Security tax that must be paid by both employer and employee on all earned income. Required by the Federal Insurance Contributions Act.

fiduciary fund: Any fund held by a governmental unit in a fiduciary capacity, usually as an agent or trustee. There are four categories: agency funds, pension trust funds, investment trust funds, and private-purpose trust funds.

financial accounting: The accounting for assets, liabilities, revenues, and expenses of an organization. (*Compare with* management accounting.)

Financial Accounting Standards Board (FASB): The body that sets accounting and reporting standards for both for-profit and nonprofit organizations in the United States, established in 1973.

financial statements: Reports of financial activity that has already occurred, drawn from accounting records. The required statements for GAAP reporting of nonprofit organizations under SFAS 117 are the Statement of Activities, Statement of Financial Position, Statement of Cash Flows, and Notes. A Statement of Functional Expenses is also required of health and welfare organizations. Generally prepared as comparative statements, showing information for two successive years.

fiscal year: A 12-month period selected by an organization for reporting purposes. A nonprofit cannot change its fiscal year without informing the IRS.

501(c)(3): The portion of the Internal Revenue Code that defines tax-exempt organizations which meet certain criteria as "public charities." Contributions to 501(c)(3) organizations can be deducted from donors' income taxes. These organizations are also eligible for foundation grants. Also used to refer to such an organization. (*See also* exempt organization, public charity.)

fixed assets: Assets with a prolonged useful life, such as equipment, land, and buildings.

fixed costs: Costs that are relatively constant over a period of time and not affected as activity increases or decreases—for example, basic telephone service and rent (if you are not adding space).

Form 990: The federal tax information form required to be filed annually with the IRS by most nonprofits.

Form 990-PF: The federal tax information form required to be filed annually with the IRS by private foundations.

full-time equivalent (FTE): A calculation of staffing that equates all positions to full-time employment. For example, two full-time and two half-time staff people equals a total of four employees, but three FTEs.

fully vested: An employee who has rights to all of the pension plan benefits purchased with his or her contributions, whether or not he or she still works for the employer.

functional expense classification: The presentation of expenses by function: program, administration, and fundraising.

fund: A fiscal and accounting entity with a self-balancing set of accounts recording income and expense, assets and liabilities.

fund accounting: An accounting system organized on the basis of funds, each of which is considered a separate accounting entity. Used by local governments and, before SFAS 117, by many nonprofits.

fund balance: Governmental funds representing the difference between assets and liabilities. The equivalent of net assets for nonprofits and equity for businesses.

funding cycle: The range of time during which grant proposals are accepted, reviewed, and awarded.

fungible: Something capable of being used in place of another thing. Money is fungible, thus restricted grants funds can be used to replace other funds, thereby freeing those funds for other purposes. (Note: Government grants call this "supplanting funds" and usually forbid it.)

FUTA: Federal unemployment insurance, required by the Federal Unemployment Tax Act.

future value: The amount a current sum of money earning a stated rate of interest would be worth at the end of a future period.

general operating support: Funds for running an organization that are not restricted to any program.

generally accepted accounting principles (GAAP): The rules for financial reporting that ensure that financial reports are relevant, reliable, consistent, and presented in a way that allows the reader to compare the results to prior years and to other organizations.

generally accepted auditing standards (GAAS): Assumptions and rules set by the American Institute of Certified Public Accountants that govern a CPA's ability to accept an auditing engagement and the procedures that must be undertaken during the course of the audit.

government contract: An agreement to provide a direct service in response for a fee, which is paid by the government. Examples include Medicaid and Medicare reimbursement, where payment is for units of service. Providing a service such as computer maintenance or facility rental to a government is obviously also a contract rather than a grant. Government contracts generally result from a request for proposals, where the government agency pre-sets the conditions for the contract. (*Compare with* grant.)

Governmental Accounting Standards Board (GASB): The body that sets accounting and reporting standards for state and local governments and governmentally related nonprofit organizations, established in 1984.

grant: Generally a cash award from an organizational funder (foundation, corporation, or government agency—the grantor) to a grant-eligible organization (nonprofit or government—the grantee) to accomplish a specific purpose, such as starting a project, serving the needy, or purchasing a piece of equipment. Grants are often funded in response to a proposal from the grantee, although some are awarded through RFPs. Government contributions are grants when their purpose is to provide a service for public benefit, rather than to serve the direct and immediate needs of the grantor. (*Compare with* government contract.)

grants receivable: Grant funds that have been awarded but not yet received.

imprest fund: Petty cash fund; cash kept on hand to pay for minor expenses.

improvement: An expenditure to extend the useful life of an asset or to improve its performance. Capitalized as part of the asset's cost, as opposed to expenses for maintenance or repair, which simply keep it in service.

indirect costs: Costs not readily identifiable with a particular aspect of an organization's operations.

indirect cost rate: A ratio or percentage used to fully cost or allocate program services by calculating the proportionate share of indirect costs. Generally negotiated with a federal agency.

in-kind contribution: Services or goods contributed without charge.

internal audit: An audit conducted by employees to ascertain whether or not internal control procedures are working, as opposed to an external audit conducted by a CPA.

internal controls: A set of policies and procedures created by the organization to prevent deliberate or misguided use of funds for unauthorized purposes.

Internal Revenue Code (IRC): The entire body of U.S. tax laws.

LEA: A local education agency (e.g., a school district).

lease: A contract calling for the lessee (user) to pay the lessor (owner) for the use of an asset (the leasehold).

leasehold improvement: An expenditure that improves leased property, such as carpeting. The value of the improvement transfers to the property owner after the end of the lease.

leverage: Using assets or borrowing against their value to obtain or control greater amounts of money.

liabilities: The debts of the organization, such as accounts payable, unpaid employee salaries and vacation leave, and loans.

line item: A specific item in a budget, such as rent or telephone, that is shown on a single line. Used to denote listing each item separately instead of grouping them in a larger category such as "administration" or "overhead."

line of credit: An agreement with a bank that allows short-term borrowing to meet cash flow challenges. Should be used for income timing problems, not for profitability problems.

liquidity: The capacity of an organization to meet its financial obligations as its debts are due. Refers to having assets that are cash or quickly convertible to cash.

lobbying: Direct contact with members of legislative bodies (and for some purposes, with the executive branch of a government) to urge or oppose the introduction or passage of specific legislation. Tax-exempt organizations are subject to special limitations and reporting requirements regarding lobbying.

long-term debt: Financial obligations (liabilities) that an organization must pay more than 12 months in the future, such as mortgages.

management accounting: Reporting designed to enhance the ability of management to do its job of decision making, planning, and control. (*Compare with* financial accounting.)

management letter: A letter an auditor addresses privately to the board of directors that suggests changes in accounting procedures and identifies potential weaknesses. Different from an auditor's report, which is part of the audit presented to outside parties.

matching funds: Funds that a grantee or other outside party contributes toward a grant-funded project.

matching grant: A grant with a requirement to raise equal or varying amounts from other funding sources. Also called a "challenge grant."

Medicare: Federal health insurance program for people 65 years of age and older and for younger people with certain disabilities. Part A (Hospital Insurance, HI) is financed through taxes on covered wages paid by employers and employees, self-employed people, or individuals through monthly premiums. Part B (Supplemental Medical Insurance, SMI) is financed by individuals' monthly premiums.

minimum distribution: The required 5 percent of investment assets that a private foundation is required to spend or grant for charitable purposes. Also called "minimum investment return" or "qualifying distribution."

minimum investment return: *See* minimum distribution.

modified accrual: The basis of accounting required for government funds in which revenues are recognized when they become "available and measurable" and expenditures are recognized when a liability is incurred.

natural expense classification: The grouping of things by category (total salaries, total rent, and such) rather than assigning them to specific activities or functions (departments).

net assets: The resources ultimately available to the organization after paying all liabilities: assets – liabilities = net assets. Net assets for nonprofits are divided into unrestricted, temporarily restricted, and permanently restricted. Found on the Statement of Financial Position.

NOFA (Notice of Funding Availability): Another name for Request for Proposal.

nonexchange transaction: A transaction, such as charitable contributions and taxes, that is not the result of an arms-length exchange between two parties, and for which nothing is received in return (such as in exchange for goods or services).

nonprofit organization: An entity with the following characteristics: (1) receives significant resources from donors who do not expect equivalent value in return; (2) operates for purposes other than to provide goods or services at a profit; and (3) lacks an identifiable individual or group of individuals who holds a legally enforceable residual claim. Being nonprofit does not automatically confer tax exemption. Also called "not-for-profit organization."

notes to the financial statements: The section of an audit that offers additional detail about the numbers in the statements.

OMB A-133: A publication of the Office of Management and Budget that provides guidance for auditors of states, local governments, and nonprofit organizations as required by the Single Audit Act. The A-133 audit is required of any nonprofit that receives more than $500,000 in federal awards in a year.

operating foundation: A private foundation that funds the programs of a specific institution, such as a hospital or university. Operating foundations rarely give grants to outside organizations.

opportunity cost: The income that could be obtained if the resources committed to one action were used in the most desirable alternative action.

overhead activity: The combination of administrative and fundraising activities.

payroll taxes: Taxes levied on the salaries or wages paid to employees, such as Social Security, Worker's Compensation, or Unemployment. Both taxable and tax-exempt organizations must pay these taxes.

per diem: The market rate or assigned amount per day for costs such as meals, travel, and lodging.

permanent restriction: A donor-imposed restriction on donated assets that stipulates that those resources be maintained permanently, but permits the organization to use up or expend part or all of the income (or other economic benefits) derived from them. (*See also* endowment.)

POV rate: The mileage reimbursement rate the federal government uses when an employee uses a privately owned vehicle (POV) for business travel. A good model for figuring the mileage amount in a federal grant budget.

prepaid expense: An expenditure incurred in one period whose benefits are not immediately realized, such as insurance. Recorded as an asset on the balance sheet.

present value: The value today of an amount to be paid or received later, discounted for inflation or used to figure an interest rate for future payment.

private foundation: A charitable organization whose revenues and assets come from a small group of contributors. Private foundations are subject to special rules governing their activities, such as the distribution of at least 5 percent of assets annually.

profit: The money an organization earned or took in, after paying all associated expenses. Nonprofit organizations can make the equivalent of a profit, but those funds cannot go to any outside individuals; they must remain within the organization to be used for its charitable purpose.

pro forma: Hypothetical financial statements designed to show the financial effect if some event, such as a merger or construction of new facilities, were to occur.

program activity: The mission-related work of a nonprofit organization that is not administration or fundraising activity.

program income: Gross income earned by the grant recipient that is directly generated by a supported activity or earned as a result of the grant award.

project costs: All allowable costs incurred by a grant recipient, as set forth in the applicable federal cost principles of the relevant OMB Circular or the Code of Federal Regulations, and the value of the contributions made by third parties in accomplishing the objectives of the award during the project period.

public charity: Nonprofit organizations that are tax exempt under IRC 501(c)(3) and meet the definitions of IRC 509(a)(1) or 509(a)(2), which distinguish them from private foundations. Churches, schools, and hospitals are treated as public charities without regard to their sources of support. Other charities that receive over one-third of their support from the general public also qualify.

publicly supported organization (PSO): An organization that normally receives a substantial part of its support from a governmental unit or from direct or indirect contributions from the general public. A definition used by the IRS to find that a 501(c)(3) organization is "not a private foundation," under a complex calculation.

qualified opinion: An audit report in which the auditor provides an "except for" opinion. Results from an organization's failure to follow GAAP or from a limitation in scope.

qualifying distribution: *See* minimum distribution.

quasi-endowment: A fund established by a governing board that sets aside unrestricted funds "as if" they were an endowment with the intent never to spend them. According to GAAP, these monies must be reported as unrestricted funds, since the board could lift the conditions at any time.

ratio: The comparison of two numbers to create a financial indicator.

real property: Land, including land improvements, buildings, and structures, but excluding movable machinery and equipment.

recognize: To enter a financial transaction in the accounting books.

releasing funds from restriction: Spending temporarily restricted funds in accordance with an approved work plan or budget and/or in a specified time frame, which satisfies the restrictions put on them by donors. Such funds are moved from temporarily restricted to unrestricted on the Statement of Activities.

rent: The charge for the use of an asset, such as a building.

Request for Proposals (RFP): A funder's solicitation for grant proposals, usually describing the project to be funded, amounts of funds available, timelines, and other criteria. Generally used by governments and sometimes by larger foundations.

Request for Qualifications (RFQ); Request for Programmatic Qualifications (RFPQ): Similar to an RFP, but seeking an applicant organization's qualifications or capacity to carry out a specific project.

research and development (R&D): Research is the activity aimed at discovering new knowledge. Development is the translation of knowledge into a new or improved product or service. R&D costs are expensed, on the grounds that the future benefits are too uncertain to warrant capitalization.

reserve: The accumulated unrestricted net assets available for the organization's use.

restricted funds: Funds with a limitation set by a donor on how they can be spent, usually for a specific program, item, or service. (*Compare with* condition, permanent restriction; *see also* designated funds *and entries at* temporary *and* unrestricted.)

revenue: Strictly speaking, earned income rather than donations; however, many nonprofits include all income as revenue.

single audit: The audit prescribed by federal law for state and local governments, colleges and universities, and nonprofit organizations that receive federal funds above $500,000 annually.

split-interest agreement: An agreement between a donor and a nonprofit organization in which the donor (or named beneficiary) and the organization split the income or principal of the gift. Examples include charitable lead trusts, charitable remainder trusts, and several other investment vehicles.

Statement of Activities: A report that shows the financial activity of the organization by function over a period of time. In the for-profit world, it is also called the Income Statement or Profit and Loss Statement.

Statement of Cash Flows: A report that shows the effect on an organization's cash position of all financial activities (operating, financing, and investing). In effect, it converts accrual accounting to cash accounting for reporting purposes.

Statement of Changes in Net Assets: A report that shows how results of operations have affected net assets, and temporarily and permanently restricted net assets. Often included as part of the Statement of Activities.

Statement of Financial Accounting Standards (SFAS): Official pronouncements of the Financial Accounting Standards Board, which establish standards for GAAP financial statements. SFAS 116 and 117, released in the mid 1990s, required substantial changes in nonprofit accounting.

Statement of Financial Position: A report that summarizes the assets, liabilities, and net assets of the organization as of a specific date. In the for-profit world, it is known as the Balance Sheet.

Statement of Functional Income and Expense: A report that matches income and expense by function, for example, key programs, administration, and fundraising. Used to evaluate the surplus or deficit status of each activity.

subaward: An award of financial assistance in the form of money, or property in lieu of money, made as an award by a recipient to an eligible sub-recipient or by a sub-recipient to a lower-tier sub-recipient.

substantial contributor: A person who contributes the greater of $5,000 or 2 percent of an organization's total contributions. Used to calculate an organization's public support for determining its private foundation status.

sunk costs: Costs incurred in the past that are not affected by, and hence irrelevant for, current decisions.

supplant: To use grant funds to replace other funds. Federal and other government agencies often prohibit their grant funds from supplanting other funds.

supporting organization: A tax-exempt organization created and operated to benefit one or more nonprofits, government agencies, or universities, and controlled by or responsive to the charity it supports. Defined by Section 501(a)(3) of the IRC.

tax: A nonpenal, but compulsory, charge levied by a government on income, consumption, wealth, or other basis, for the benefit of all governed.

tax-exempt: Not required to pay specific taxes, generally in return for some public benefit. Organizations that are tax-exempt under IRC 501(c)(3) are eligible to receive foundation grants.

taxpayer identification number (TIN): The number used to identify an employee (Social Security Number, SSN) or employer (employer identification number, EIN) for tax reporting purposes.

temporary restriction: A donor-imposed restriction that permits the donee organization to expand the donated asset as specified, and is satisfied either by the passage of time or by specified actions of the organization.

temporarily restricted contributions: Grants and contributions that are to be spent for a specific purpose or during a specified period of time.

tipping: The condition when too much of a nonprofit organization's income comes from one source, thus can *tipping* it into being considered a private foundation. (*See also* disqualified person.)

transaction: An exchange between two parties that leads to an accounting entry.

unrealized gains or losses on investments: The amount by which the market value of an asset exceeds or is less than the original cost of that asset.

unrelated business income: Income from business activities that do not promote or advance a nonprofit's charitable or exempt purpose. This income is taxable and must be reported to the IRS on Form 990-T.

unrestricted contributions: Grants and contributions given by a donor without reference to a specific purpose or time period.

unrestricted net assets: The part of net assets of a nonprofit organization that is neither permanently restricted nor temporarily restricted by donor-imposed stipulations. For reporting purposes, this includes board-designated funds. (*See also* designated funds.)

variable costs: Costs that increase proportionally as activity increases; for example, costs for personnel paid by the hour.

working capital: An organization's current assets minus its current liabilities, which yields the funds it has to continue operations. Also called "net current assets."

write down: To reduce the value of an asset, as through depreciation or devaluation.

The author gratefully acknowledges these sources of information for the Glossary definitions:

Accounting: The Language of Business (3rd edition) by Sidney Davidson, James S. Schindler, Clyde P. Stickney, and Roman L. Weil. Thomas Horton and Daughters, Inc., Glen Ridge, New Jersey (1977).

Bookkeeping Basics: What Every Nonprofit Bookkeeper Needs to Know by Debra L. Ruegg and Lisa M. Venkatrathnam. Wilder Foundation, Minneapolis, Minnesota (2003).

Essentials of Accounting for Governmental and Not-for-Profit Organizations by John H. Engstrom and Paul A. Copley. McGraw-Hill/Irwin, New York (2004).

Financial Leadership for Nonprofit Executives by Jeanne Bell Peters and Elizabeth Schaffer. Amherst H. Wilder Foundation, Minneapolis, Minnesota (2005).

Financial Planning for Nonprofit Organizations by Jody Blazek. John Wiley & Sons, New York (1996).

Grants.gov available at http://www.grants.gov/CustomerSupport#glossary.

Management Accounting: A Strategic Approach by Wayne J. Morse, James R. Davis, and Al. L. Hartgraves. South-Western College Publishing, Cincinnati, Ohio (1996).

Nonprofit Law Dictionary by Bruce R. Hopkins. John Wiley & Sons, New York (1994).

Not-for-Profit Accounting Made Easy by Warren Ruppel. John Wiley & Sons, New York (2002).

Not-For-Profit Budgeting and Financial Management by Edward McMillan. John Wiley & Sons, Hoboken, New Jersey (2003).

Webster's New Universal Unabridged Dictionary, Jean L. McKetchnie, editor. Simon & Schuster, New York (1983).

Annotated Bibliography

Books

Bookkeeping Basics: What Every Nonprofit Bookkeeper Needs to Know by Debra L. Ruegg and Lisa M. Venkatrathnam. Wilder Foundation, Minneapolis, Minnesota (2003)—Just what the title says. Grantwriters probably don't need this, but if you're in a small organization, recommend it to whomever does your books.

Essentials of Accounting for Governmental and Not-for-Profit Organizations by John H. Engstrom and Paul A. Copley. McGraw-Hill/Irwin, New York (2004)— A good basic introduction to government accounting, written as a textbook. Despite the title, it is weak on nonprofits.

Financial and Accounting Guide for Not-For-Profit Organizations by Malvern Gross, John McCarthy, and Nancy Shelmon. John Wiley & Sons, Hoboken, New Jersey (2005)—This is *the* textbook for nonprofit accounting.

Financial Leadership for Nonprofit Executives by Jeanne Bell Peters and Elizabeth Schaffer. Amherst H. Wilder Foundation, Minneapolis, Minnesota (2005)—Looking at the big picture, for nonprofit executive directors.

Financial Management Strategies for Arts Organizations by Frederick J. Turk and Robert P. Gallo. American Council of the Arts, New York (1984)— I actually prefer the shorter 1975 edition, which is out of print (but may be in your library).

Fiscal Sponsorship: 6 Ways To Do It Right by Gregory Colvin. Study Center Press, San Francisco (2000)—Fiscal sponsorship is so easy to do wrong, and the IRS isn't as forgiving as it used to be. If you're considering doing it, read this book.

Forming and Managing a Non-Profit Organization in Canada by Flora MacLeod. Self Counsel Press, North Vancouver, British Columbia (1995)—The only book I could find on Canadian nonprofits, and unfortunately out of print.

Handbook of the Canadian Institute of Chartered Accountants. Available through the CICA website at http://www.cica.ca/index.cfm/ci_id/261/la_id/1.htm.

Not-for-Profit Accounting Made Easy by Warren Ruppel. John Wiley & Sons, New York (2002)—A good basic explanation in plain English.

Not-For-Profit Budgeting and Financial Management by Edward McMillan. John Wiley & Sons, Hoboken, New Jersey (2003)—Everything you need to know about financial planning and budgeting.

The Oregon Nonprofit Corporation Handbook: How to Start and Run a Nonprofit Corporation by Cynthia Cumfer and Kay Sohl. Technical Assistance for Community Services, Portland, Oregon (1993)—This is the best basic nonprofit book I know, and the majority of it is not specific to Oregon.

Streetsmart Financial Basics for Nonprofit Managers by Thomas A. McLaughlin. John Wiley & Sons, New York (2002)—Nitty gritty, hands-on finances. Read this in addition to anything else for an opinionated and right-on description of how things really work. Comes with a CD-ROM of forms.

Unified Financial Reporting System for Not-for-Profit Organizations by Russy D. Sumariwalla and Wilson C. Lewis. Jossey Bass, San Francisco (2000)—Pretty technical. You as a grantwriter don't need this, but if you're in a large nonprofit, your CFO might want to read it.

Other Resources

Form 990: A Detailed Examination by Peter Swords. Nonprofit Coordinating Committee of New York, New York (2003)—Available for download as a Word document at www.npccny.org.

The Grantsmanship Center Magazine has excellent articles on many aspects of grantwriting, nonprofit management, and finances. You can read past issues at www.tgci.com/magazine/archives.asp.

Appendix | A

Is This Grant Right for Your Organization?

One of the most important, but least recognized, jobs of the grant professional is deciding when *not* to apply for a particular grant. This can be difficult if there is pressure from management and board members to go after all available grants just to bring funds into the organization.

The best defense against these pressures is to have previously agreed upon criteria for choosing new grant opportunities. If the organization has a strong mission and a strategic plan, every major grant opportunity should be judged against these criteria:

- Does this grant support our mission?

- Does this grant further the goals in our strategic plan?

- Does this grant strengthen the organization as a whole?

From the financial side, agreed upon criteria could include:

- Does this grant pay all of its costs or bring additional revenue to the organization?

- Does this grant increase the organization's ability to raise or earn money?

- Does this grant create or acquire assets for the organization?

Of course, not every nonprofit has the luxury of taking the long-range view on all of its grants. For an organization with a deficit or cash flow problems, sometimes the financial considerations are more immediate, and grant opportunities must be evaluated by their short-term fiscal impact.

My friend Kay Sohl, executive director of Technical Assistance for Community Services (TACS) in Portland, created a three-part tool for making these grant decisions. The "Evaluating the Impact" chart is useful for helping staff choose among several grant opportunities. The "Grant Budget Worksheet" is an internal document for calculating whether a grant helps by paying already budgeted costs or hurts by creating new unfunded expenses. The "Identifying All Costs" sheet helps staff think about the hidden expenses that can be created by a grant program.

These documents are reprinted here by permission of TACS. If you want to use them, contact TACS using the information at the bottom of each page. For more information about TACS, please visit www.tacs.org.

Figure A-1. TACS Charts

TECHNICAL
ASSISTANCE
FOR
COMMUNITY
SERVICES

Evaluating the Impact of Grant Proposals on Budgets

Grant proposals will reduce a deficit (or help the overall financial situation) of the organization only if:
- The funds will be unrestricted and can be used to offset expenses already shown in the organization's budget, OR
- The grantor will permit use of some grant funds to partially offset expenses shown in the organization budget, including shared overhead and/or administrative costs.

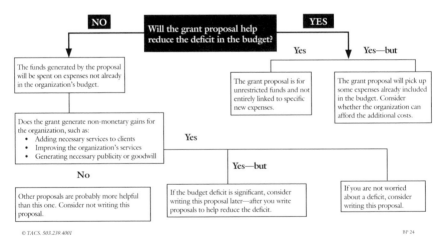

© TACS. 503.239.4001

BP 24

Figure A-1. *Continued*

TECHNICAL
ASSISTANCE
FOR
COMMUNITY
SERVICES

Identifying All the Costs in a Grant Proposal

Checklist of Items Causing Additional Expenses
Above Those Usually Requested in the Grant

1.   How much supervision time (from existing staff) will be required for new persons hired because of the grant?

2.   How much additional administrative expense will there be? (Monthly billings, financial reports, meetings with the funding source, inspections by the funding source, etc.)

3.   How much additional bookkeeping time will be required?

4.   How much unsubsidized cost will be added? Are there unsubsidized benfits or payroll taxes? Will there be additional telephone charges, mileage reimbursements, household supplies, program supplies, and/or occupancy/utilities costs which aren't covered by the grant?

5.   Are the conditions and terms of employment the same in the grant as in your Personnel Policies? Will employees hired under the grant cause any additional personnel costs? Grievances?

6.   Will the agency have to pay a substitute if the employee funded from the grant can't come to work on any day? Are "substitutes" covered in the grant?

7.   Will the new personsl hired under the grant cause staff meetings to be harder or longer?

8.   How will existing staff feel about the new staff? Rate of pay? Work load?

Figure A-1. *Continued*

TECHNICAL
ASSISTANCE
FOR
COMMUNITY
SERVICES

Grant Budget Worksheet

Budget Category	Total Grant Request		Total Donated
	Expenses requested in grant proposal		Expenses of the proposed project *not* requested in the grant proposal
	Expenses already shown in the organization budget	Expenses *not* shown in the organization budget	
Salaries			
Employer Taxes			
Employee Benefits			
Professional Services			
Rent			
Utilities			
Supplies			
Insurance			
Printing			
Postage			
Transportation			
Technology			
Other			

© *TACS. 503.239.4001*

BP 26

Appendix | B

An Insider's Look at Form 990

Jason Orme, a nonprofit and tax accountant, developed this Form 990 markup for use in his presentations on avoiding 990 pitfalls. When I saw him use it in a workshop, I was blown away. I asked if I could include it in this book, and he generously agreed. The latest version is presented here.

This complete walk through the 990 tells you exactly what to look for in every box. If you ever (heaven forbid) have to complete your organization's 990, this supplement to the official instructions will help you avoid common mistakes and get it right the first time. You can be a hero to your finance director by providing her or him with a copy.

Figure B-1. Annotated Form 990

Form **990**

Department of the Treasury
Internal Revenue Service

Return of Organization Exempt From Income Tax

Under section 501(c), 527, or 4947(a)(1) of the Internal Revenue Code (except black lung benefit trust or private foundation)

▶ The organization may have to use a copy of this return to satisfy state reporting requirements.

OMB No. 1545-0047

2004

Open to Public Inspection

A For the 2004 calendar year, or tax year beginning _____, 2004, and ending _____, 20___

B Check if applicable:
☐ Address change
☐ Name change
☐ Initial return
☐ Final return
☐ Amended return
☐ Application pending

Please use IRS label or print or type. See Specific Instructions.

C Name of organization

Number and street (or P.O. box if mail is not delivered to street address) Room/suite

City or town, state or country, and ZIP + 4

D Employer identification number

E T(

F A

This is a public document. Nothing is confidential except donor names and addresses on Schedule B.

● Section 501(c)(3) organizations and 4947(a)(1) nonexempt charitable trusts must attach a completed Schedule A (Form 990 or 990-EZ).

H and I are not app
H(a) Is this a group return for affiliates? ☐ Yes ☐ No
H(b) If "Yes," enter number of affiliates ▶ _____
H(c) Are all affiliates included? ☐ Yes ☐ No
(If "No," attach a list. See instructions.)
H(d) Is this a separate return filed by an organization covered by a group ruling? ☐ Yes ☐ No
I Group Exemption Number ▶

G Website: ▶

J Organization type (check only one) ▶ ☐ 501(c) ( ) ◀ (insert no.) ☐ 4947(a)(1) or ☐ 527

K Check here ▶ ☐ if the organization's gross receipts are normally not more than $25,000. The organization need not file a return with the IRS; but if the organization received a Form 990 Package in the mail, it should file a return without financial data. **Some states require a complete return.**

M Check ▶ ☐ the
to attach Sch

If Schedule B is not required, make sure box is checked.

L Gross receipts: Add lines 6b, 8b, 9b, and 10b to line 12 ▶

Part I Revenue, Expenses, and Changes in Net Assets or Fund Balances (See page 18

Revenue	1 Contributions, gifts, grants, and similar amounts received	
	a Direct public support	1a
	b Indirect public support	1b
	c Government contributions (grants)	1c
	d **Total** (add lines 1a through 1c) (cash $ _____ noncash $ _____)	1d
	2 Program service revenue including government fees and contracts (from Part VII, line 93)	2
	3 Membership dues and assessments	3
	4 Interest on savings and temporary cash investments	4
	5 Dividends and interest from securities	5
	6a Gross rents	6a
	b Less: rental expenses	6b
	c Net rental income or (loss) (subtract line 6b from line 6a)	6c
	7 Other investment income (describe ▶	7
	8a Gross amount from sales of assets other than inventory (A) Securities (B) Other	8a
	b Less: cost or other basis and sales expenses	8b
	c Gain or (loss) (attach schedule)	8c
	d Net gain or (loss) (combine line 8c, columns (A) and (B))	8d
	9 Special events and activities (attach schedule). If any amount is from **gaming**, check here ▶ ☐	
	a Gross revenue (not including $ _____ of contributions reported on line 1a)	9a
	b Less: direct expenses other than fundraising expenses	9b
	c Net income or (loss) from special events (subtract line 9b from line 9a)	9c
	10a Gross sales of inventory, less returns and allowances	10a
	b Less: cost of goods sold	10b
	c Gross profit or (loss) from sales of inventory (attach schedule) (subtract line 10b from line 10a)	10c
	11 Other revenue (from Part VII, line 103)	11
	12 **Total revenue** (add lines 1d, 2, 3, 4, 5, 6c, 7, 8d,	12
Expenses	13 Program services (from line 44, column (B))	13
	14 Management and general (from line 44, column	14
	15 Fundraising (from line 44, column (D))	15
	16 Payments to affiliates (attach schedule)	16
	17 **Total expenses** (add lines 16 and 44, column (	17
Net Assets	18 Excess or (deficit) for the year (subtract line 17 from line 12)	18
	19 Net assets or fund balances at beginning of year (from line 73, column (A))	19
	20 Other changes in net assets or fund balances (attach	20
	21 Net assets or fund balances at end of year (combine lin	21

Mandatory entry. If none, enter N/A.

Qualified sponsorship payments are reported here.

Do not include rental income from exempt purpose. Report this income on Line 2 instead.

Include capital gain dividends here, rather than on Line 5.

Lump sum reporting for publicly traded securities.

Make sure contribution portion of special event revenue is reported here and on Line 1, not on Line 9a.

Unrealized gains/losses on investments reported here.

New check box to disclose gaming activities.

For Privacy Act and Paperwork Reduction Act Notice, see the sep No. 11282Y Form **990** (2004)

© Jason R. Orme. Used with permission.

Figure B-1. *Continued*

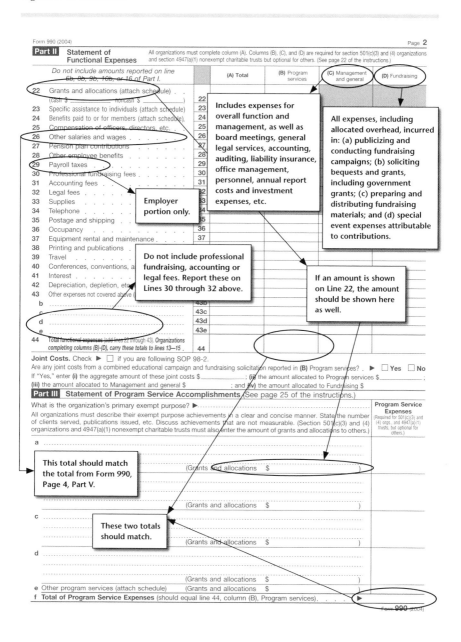

Figure B-1. *Continued*

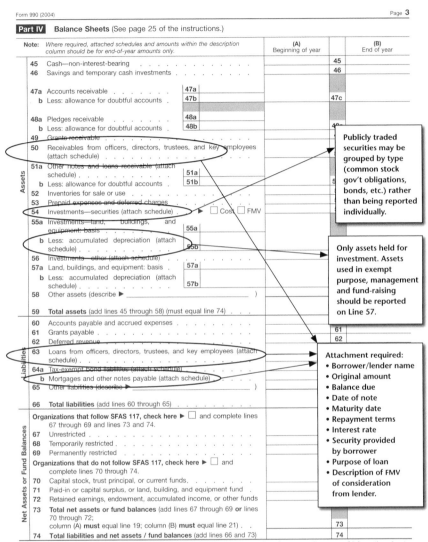

Form 990 (2004)   Page **3**

Part IV **Balance Sheets** (See page 25 of the instructions.)

			(A) Beginning of year	(B) End of year
Note:	*Where required, attached schedules and amounts within the description column should be end-of-year amounts only.*			
45	Cash—non-interest-bearing			45
46	Savings and temporary cash investments			46
47a	Accounts receivable	47a		
b	Less: allowance for doubtful accounts	47b		47c
48a	Pledges receivable	48a		
b	Less: allowance for doubtful accounts	48b		48
49	Grants receivable			
50	Receivables from officers, directors, trustees, and key employees (attach schedule)			
51a	Other notes and loans receivable (attach schedule)	51a		
b	Less: allowance for doubtful accounts	51b		5
52	Inventories for sale or use			
53	Prepaid expenses and deferred charges			
54	Investments—securities (attach schedule) ▶ ☐ Cost ☐ FMV			
55a	Investments—land, buildings, and equipment: basis	55a		
b	Less: accumulated depreciation (attach schedule)	55b		
56	Investments—other (attach schedule)			
57a	Land, buildings, and equipment: basis	57a		
b	Less: accumulated depreciation (attach schedule)	57b		
58	Other assets (describe ▶ _____)			
59	**Total assets** (add lines 45 through 58) (must equal line 74)			
60	Accounts payable and accrued expenses			
61	Grants payable			61
62	Deferred revenue			62
63	Loans from officers, directors, trustees, and key employees (attach schedule)			
64a	Tax-exempt bond liabilities (attach schedule)			
b	Mortgages and other notes payable (attach schedule)			
65	Other liabilities (describe ▶ _____)			
66	**Total liabilities** (add lines 60 through 65)			

(Assets — left margin label)
(Liabilities — left margin label)

Organizations that follow SFAS 117, check here ▶ ☐ and complete lines 67 through 69 and lines 73 and 74.

67	Unrestricted			
68	Temporarily restricted			
69	Permanently restricted			

Organizations that do not follow SFAS 117, check here ▶ ☐ and complete lines 70 through 74.

70	Capital stock, trust principal, or current funds			
71	Paid-in or capital surplus, or land, building, and equipment fund			
72	Retained earnings, endowment, accumulated income, or other funds			
73	**Total net assets or fund balances** (add lines 67 through 69 **or** lines 70 through 72; column (A) **must** equal line 19; column (B) **must** equal line 21)			73
74	**Total liabilities and net assets / fund balances** (add lines 66 and 73)			74

(Net Assets or Fund Balances — left margin label)

Form 990 is available for public inspection and, for some people, serves as the primary or sole source of information about a particular organization. How the public perceives an organization in such cases may be determined by the information presented on its return. Therefore, please make sure the return is complete and accurate and fully describes, in Part III, the organization's programs and accomplishments.

Callout boxes (right side):

Publicly traded securities may be grouped by type (common stock gov't obligations, bonds, etc.) rather than being reported individually.

Only assets held for investment. Assets used in exempt purpose, management and fund-raising should be reported on Line 57.

Attachment required:
• Borrower/lender name
• Original amount
• Balance due
• Date of note
• Maturity date
• Repayment terms
• Interest rate
• Security provided by borrower
• Purpose of loan
• Description of FMV of consideration from lender.

Figure B-1. *Continued*

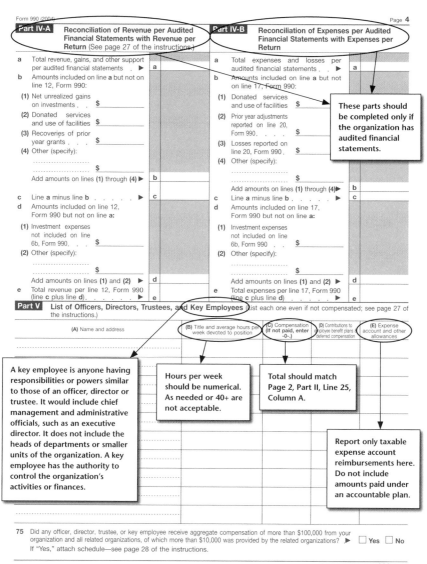

Figure B-1. *Continued*

Form 990 (2004)   Page **5**

Part VI   Other Information (See page 28 of the instructions.) | Yes | No |

76 Did the organization engage in any activity not previously reported to the IRS? If "Yes," attach a detailed description of each activity.   **76**

77 Were any changes made in the organizing or governing documents but not reported to the IRS? . . .   **77**
    If "Yes," attach a conformed copy of the changes.

78a Did the organization have unrelated business gross income of $1,000 or more during the year covered by this return?   **78a**
  b If "Yes," has it filed a tax return on **Form 990-T** for this year? **78b**

79 Was there a liquidation, dissolution, termination, or substantial contraction during the year? If "Yes," attach a statement   **79**

80a Is the organization related (other than by association with a statewide or nationwide organization) through common
    membership, governing bodies, trustees, officers, etc., to any other exempt or nonexempt organization? . .   **80a**
  b If "Yes," enter the name of the organization ▶ ....
    .... and check whether it is ☐ exempt **or** ☐ nonexempt.

81a Enter direct and indirect political expenditures. See line 81 instructions . . | **81a** |
  b Did the organization file **Form 1120-POL** for this year? **81b**

82a Did the organization receive donated services or the use of materials, equipment, or facilities at no charge
    or at substantially less than fair rental value? **82a**
  b If "Yes," you may indicate the value of these items here. Do not include this amount
    as revenue in Part I or as an expense in Part II. (See instructions in Part III.) | **82b** |

83a Did the organization comply with the public inspection requirements for returns and exemption applications?   **83a**
  b Did the organization comply with the disclosure requirements relating to quid pro quo contributions? . .   **83b**

84a Did the organization solicit any contributions or gifts that were not tax deductible? **84a**
  b If "Yes," did the organization include with every solicitation an express statement that such contributions
    or gifts were not tax deductible? **84b**

85 *501(c)(4), (5), or (6) organizations.* **a** Were substantially all dues nondeductible by members? **85a**
  b Did the organization make only in-house lobbying expenditures of $2,000 or less? . . . .
    If "Yes" was answered to either 85a or 85b, **do not** complete 85c through 85h below unless
    received a waiver for proxy tax owed for the prior year.
  c Dues, assessments, and similar amounts from members . . . . | **85c** |
  d Section 162(e) lobbying and political expenditures . . . . | **85d** |
  e Aggregate nondeductible amount of section 6033(e)(1)(A) dues notices . . . | **85e** |
  f Taxable amount of lobbying and political expenditures (line 85d less 85e) . . | **85f** |
  g Does the organization elect to pay the section 6033(e) tax on the amount on line 85f? . . .   **85g**
  h If section 6033(e)(1)(A) dues notices were sent, does the organization agree to add the amount on line 85f to its
    reasonable estimate of dues allocable to nondeductible lobbying and political expenditures for the following tax
    year? **85h**

86 *501(c)(7) orgs.* Enter: **a** Initiation fees and capital contributions included on line 12 . | **86a** |
  b Gross receipts, included on line 12, for public use of club facilities . . . . | **86b** |
87 *501(c)(12) orgs.* Enter: **a** Gross income from members or shareholders . . . | **87a** |
  b Gross income from other sources. (Do not net amounts due or paid to other
    sources against amounts due or received from them.) . . . . | **87b** |

88 At any time during the year, did the organization own a 50% or greater interest in a taxable corporation or
    partnership, or an entity disregarded as separate from the organization under Regulations sections
    301.7701-2 and 301.7701-3? If "Yes," complete Part IX **88**

89a *501(c)(3) organizations.* Enter: Amount of tax imposed on the organization during the year under:
    section 4911 ▶ _____ ; section 4912 ▶ _____ ; section 4955 ▶ _____
  b *501(c)(3) and 501(c)(4) orgs.* Did the organization engage in any section 4958 excess benefit transaction
    during the year or did it become aware of an excess benefit transaction from a prior year? If "Yes," attach
    a statement explaining each transaction **89b**
  c Enter: Amount of tax imposed on the organization managers or disqualified persons during the year under
    sections 4912, 4955, and 4958 . . . . ▶ _____
  d Enter: Amount of tax on line 89c, above, reimbursed by the organization . . . . ▶ _____
90a List the states with which a copy of this return is filed ▶ ....
  b Number of employees employed in the pay period that includes March 12, 2004 (See instructions.) | **90b** |
91 The books are in care of ▶ .... Telephone no. ▶ (......) ....
    Located at ▶ .... ZIP + 4 ▶ ....
92 *Section 4947(a)(1) nonexempt charitable trusts* filing Form 990 in lieu of **Form 1041**—Check here . . . . . . ▶ ☐
    .... tax-exempt inte...

Form **990** (2004)

> **For organizations eligible to receive deductible contributions under §170(c), this question should be answered "N/A".**

> **Answer all questions. If something is not applicable, enter "N/A".**

> **The value of donated services or the use of materials, equipment or facilities at no charge should not be included in revenue or expense on pages 1 and 2 of Form 990. Include in reconciliation on Parts IV-A and IV-B if required.**

Figure B-1. *Continued*

Form 990 (2004) — Page 6

Part VII Analysis of Income-Producing Activities (See page 33 of the instructions.)

Note: Enter gross amounts unless otherwise indicated.

	Unrelated business income		Excluded by section 512, 513, or 514		(E) Related or exempt function income
	(A) Business code	**(B)** Amount	**(C)** Exclusion code	**(D)** Amount	

93 Program service revenue:
a
b
c
d
e
f Medicare/Medicaid payments
g Fees and contracts from government agencies
94 Membership dues and assessments
95 Interest on savings and temporary cash investments
96 Dividends and interest from securities
97 Net rental income or (loss) from real estate:
a debt-financed property
b not debt-financed property
98 Net rental income or (loss) from personal property
99 Other investment income
100 Gain or (loss) from sales of assets other than inventory
101 Net income or (loss) from special events
102 Gross profit or (loss) from sales of inventory
103 Other revenue: a
b
c
d
e
104 Subtotal (add columns (B), (D), and (E))
105 Total (add line 104, columns (B), (D), and (E))
Note: Line 105 plus line 1d, Part I, should equal the amount on line 12, Part I.

Callout: Select the most appropriate exclusion code from the instructions.

Callout: Only income from activities related to the organization's exempt purpose should be listed in this column. Activities which generate income used for exempt purposes should not be included here.

Part VIII Relationship of Activities to the Accomplishment of Exempt Purposes (See page 34 of the instructions.)

Line No. ▼ Explain how each activity for which income is reported in column (E) of Part VII contributed importantly to the accomplishment of the organization's exempt purposes (other than by providing funds for such purposes).

Callout: Explanation should describe how the activity is related to the organization's exempt purpose. Simply stating that the activity provides funds for exempt purpose is insufficient.

Part IX Information Regarding Taxable Subsidi...

(A) Name, address, and EIN of corporation, partnership, or disregarded entity
%
%
%
%

Part X Information Regarding Transfers Associated with Personal Benefit Contracts (See page 34 of the instructions.)

(a) Did the organization, during the year, receive any funds, directly or indirectly, to pay premiums on a personal benefit contract? ☐ Yes ☐ No
(b) Did the organization, during the year, pay premiums, directly or indirectly, on a personal benefit contract? ☐ Yes ☐ No
Note: If "Yes" to (b), file Form 8870 and Form 4720 (see instructions).

Please Sign Here — Under penalties of perjury, I declare that I have examined this return, including accompanying schedules and statements, and to the best of my knowledge and belief, it is true, correct, and complete. Declaration of preparer (other than officer) is based on all information of which preparer has any knowledge.
Signature of officer   Date
Type or print name and title.

Paid Preparer's Use Only
Preparer's signature   Date   Check if self-employed ▶ ☐   Preparer's SSN or PTIN (See Gen. Inst. W)
Firm's name (or yours if self-employed), address, and ZIP + 4   EIN ▶   Phone no. ▶ ( )

Form **990** (2004)

Figure B-2. Annotated Form 990, Schedule A

SCHEDULE A
(Form 990 or 990-EZ)

Department of the Treasury
Internal Revenue Service

Organization Exempt Under Section 501(c)(3)

(Except Private Foundation) and Section 501(e), 501(f), 501(k), 501(n), or Section 4947(a)(1) Nonexempt Charitable Trust

Supplementary Information—(See separate instructions.)

▶ **MUST be completed by the above organizations and attached to their Form 990 or 990-EZ**

OMB No. 1545-0047

2004

Name of the organization | **Employer identification number**

Part I **Compensation of the Five Highest Paid Employees Other Than Officers, Directors, and Trustees**
(See page 1 of the instructions. List each one. If there are none, enter "None.")

(a) Name and address of each employee paid more than $50,000	**(b)** Title and average hours per week devoted to position	**(c)** Compensation	**(d)** Contributions to employee benefit plans & deferred compensation	**(e)** Expense account and other allowances
Total number of other employees paid over $50,000 . . . . ▶				

Do not include anyone listed on Form 990, Page 4, Part V.

Part II **Compensation of the Five Highest Paid Independent Contractors for Professional Services**
(See page 2 of the instructions. List each one (whether individuals or firms). If there are none, enter "None.")

(a) Name and address of each independent contractor paid more than $50,000	**(b)** Type of service	**(c)** Compensation
Total number of others receiving over $50,000 for professional services . . . . ▶		

Report professional service providers only, i.e., attorneys, accountants, doctors and professional fundraisers.

For Paperwork Reduction Act Notice, see the Instructions for Form 990 and Form 990-EZ. Cat. No. 11285F **Schedule A (Form 990 or 990-EZ) 2004**

Figure B-2. *Continued*

Schedule A (Form 990 or 990-EZ) 2004   Page **2**

Part III Statements About Activities (See page 2 of the instructions.)		Yes	No

1 During the year, has the organization attempted to influence national, state, or local legislation, including any attempt to influence public opinion on a legislative matter or referendum? If "Yes," enter the total expenses paid or incurred in connection with the lobbying activities ▶ $ _____ (Must equal amounts on line 38, Part VI-A, or line i of Part VI-B.) . . . . | **1** | |

Organizations that made an election under section 501(h) by filing Form 5768 must complete Part VI-A. Other organizations checking "Yes" must complete Part VI-B AND attach a statement giving a detailed description of the lobbying activities.

2 During the year, has the organiza[...] substantial contributors, trustees, [...] with any taxable organization wit[...] owner, or principal beneficiary? *(I[...]* *transactions.)*

> If any compensation was paid to officers, directors, trustees or key employees (Form 990, Page 2, Part II, Line 25), this question should be answered "yes". If this is the only reason for answering "yes", write "See Part V, Form 990" on the dotted line to the left.

a Sale, exchange, or leasing of prop[...] | **2a** | |
b Lending of money or other extens[...] | **2b** | |
c Furnishing of goods, services, or facilities? . . . . | **2c** | |
d Payment of compensation (or payment or reimbursement of expenses if more than $1,000)? . . . . | **2d** | |
e Transfer of any part of its income or assets? . . . . | **2e** | |
3a Do you make grants for scholarships, fellowships, student loans, etc.? (If "Yes," attach an explanation of how you determine that recipients qualify to receive payments.) . . . . | **3a** | |
b Do you have a section 403(b) annuity plan for your employees? . . . . | **3b** | |
4a Did you maintain any separate account for participating donors where donors have the right to provide advice on the use or distribution of funds? . . . . | **4a** | |
b Do you provide credit counseling, debt management, credit repair, or debt negotiation services? . . . . . | **4b** | |

Part IV Reason for Non-Private Foundation Status (See pages 3 through 6 of the instructions.)

The organization is not a private foundation because it is: (Please check only **ONE** applicable box.)

5 ☐ A church, convention of churches, or association of churches. Section 170(b)(1)(A)(i).

6 ☐ A school. Section 170(b)(1)(A)(ii). (Also complete Part V.)

7 ☐ A hospital or a cooperative hospital service organization. Section 170(b)(1)(A)(iii).

8 ☐ A Federal, state, or local government or governmental unit. Section 170(b)(1)(A)(v).

9 ☐ A medical research organization operated in conjunction with a hospital. Section 170(b)(1)(A)(iii). **Enter the hospital's name, city, and state** ▶ ....

10 ☐ An organization operated for the benefit of a college or university owned or operated by a governmental unit. Section 170(b)(1)(A)(iv). (Also complete the **Support Schedule** in Part IV-A.)

11a ☐ An organization that normally receives a substantial part of its support from a governmental unit or from the general public. Section 170(b)(1)(A)(vi). (Also complete the **Support Schedule** in Part IV-A.)

11b ☐ A community trust. Section 170(b)(1)(A)(vi). (Also complete the **Support Schedule** in Part IV-A.)

12 ☐ An organization that normally receives: **(1)** more than 33⅓% of its support from contributions, membership fees, and gross receipts from activities related to its charitable, etc., functions—subject to certain exceptions, and **(2) no more than 33⅓%** of its support from gross investment income and unrelated business taxable income (less section 511 tax) from businesses acquired by the organization after June 30, 1975. See section 509(a)(2). (Also complete the **Support Schedule** in Part IV-A.)

13 ☐ An organization that is not controlled by any disqualified persons (other than foundation managers) and supports organizations described in: **(1)** lines 5 through 12 above; or **(2)** section 501(c)(4), (5), or (6), if they meet the test of section 509(a)(2). (See section 509(a)(3).)

Provide the following information about the supported organizations. (See page 5 of the instructions.)

(a) Name(s) of supported organization(s)	**(b)** Line number from above

> Selection here should match the reason for non-private foundation status in the organization's exemption letter.

14 ☐ An organization organized and operated to test for public safety. Section 509(a)(4). (See page 5 of the instructions.)

Schedule A (Form 990 or 990-EZ) 2004

Figure B-2. *Continued*

Schedule A (Form 990 or 990-EZ) 2004 — Page **3**

Part IV-A **Support Schedule** (Complete only if you checked a box on line 10, 11, or 12.) *Use cash method of accounting.*
Note: *You may use the worksheet in the instructions for converting from the accrual to the cash method of accounting.*

Calendar year (or fiscal year beginning in) ▶	(a) 2003	(b) 2002	(c) 2001	(d) 2000	(e) Total
15 Gifts, grants, and contributions received. (Do not include unusual grants. See line 28.)					
16 Membership fees received					
17 Gross receipts from admissions, merchandise sold or services performed, or furnishing of facilities in any activity that is related to the organization's charitable, etc., purpose					
18 Gross income from interest, dividends, amounts received from payments on securities loans (section 512(a)(5)), rents, royalties, and unrelated business taxable income (less section 511 taxes) from businesses acquired by the organization after June 30, 1975					
19 Net income from unrelated business activities not included in line 18					
20 Tax revenues levied for the organization's benefit and either paid to it or expended on its behalf					
21 The value of services or facilities furnished to the organization by a governmental unit without charge. Do not include the value of services or facilities generally furnished to the public without charge					
22 Other income. Attach a schedule. Do not include gain or (loss) from sale of capital assets					
23 Total of lines 15 through 22					
24 Line 23 minus line 17					
25 Enter 1% of line 23					

This means what it says. All amounts should be cash basis.

Note that these lines are gross receipts, not net amounts that are reported on Form 990 Page 6.

26 **Organizations described on lines 10 or 11:** a Enter 2% of amount in column (e), line 24 ▶ **26a**
b Prepare a list for your records to show the name of and amount contributed by each person (other than a governmental unit or publicly supported organization) whose total gifts for 2000 through 2003 exceeded the amount shown in line 26a. **Do not file this list with your return.** Enter the total of all these excess amounts ▶ **26b**
c Total support for section 509(a)(1) test: Enter line 24, column (e) ▶ **26c**
d Add: Amounts from column (e) for lines: 18 ___ 19 ___ 22 ___ 26b ___ ▶ **26d**
e Public support (line 26c minus line 26d total) ▶ **26e**
f **Public support percentage (line 26e (numerator) divided by line 26c (denominator))** ▶ **26f** %

27 **Organizations described on line 12:** a For amounts included in lines 15, 16, and 17 that were received from a "disqualified person," prepare a list for your records to show the name of, and total amounts received in each year from, each "disqualified person." **Do not file this list with your return.** Enter the sum of such amounts for each year:
(2003) ___ (2002) ___ (2001) ___ (2000) ___
b For any amount included in line 17 that was received from each person (other than "disqualified persons"), prepare a list for your records to show the name of, and amount received for each year, that was more than the **larger** of **(1)** the amount on line 25 for the year or **(2)** $5,000. (Include in the list organizations described in lines 5 through 11, as well as individuals.) **Do not file this list with your return.** After computing the difference between the amount received and the larger amount described in **(1)** or **(2)**, enter the sum of these differences (the excess amounts) for each year:
(2003) ___ (2002) ___ (2001) ___ (2000) ___
c Add: Amounts from column (e) for lines: 15 ___ 16 ___ 17 ___ 20 ___ 21 ___ ▶ **27c**
d Add: Line 27a total, ___ and line 27b total ___ ▶ **27d**
e Public support (line 27c total minus line 27d total) ▶ **27e**
f Total support for section 509(a)(2) test: Enter amount from line 23, column (e) ▶ **27f**
g Public support percentage (line 27e (numerator) divided by line 27f (denominator)) ▶ **27g** %
h **Investment income percentage (line 18, column (e) (numerator) divided by line 27f (denominator)).** ▶ **27h** %

28 **Unusual Grants:** For an organization described in line 10, 11, or 12 that received any unusual grants during 2000 through 2003, prepare a list for your records to show, for each year, the name of the contributor, the date and amount of the grant, and a brief description of the nature of the grant. **Do not file this list with your return.** Do not include these grants in line 15.

Form 990 or 990-EZ 2004

Unusual grants are generally substantial contributions and bequests from disinterested persons and are: (a) attracted because of the organization's publicly supported nature; (b) unusual and unexpected because of the amount; and (c) large enough to endanger the organization's status as normally meeting the support test.

Figure B-2. *Continued*

Part V — Private School Questionnaire (See page 7 of the instructions.)
(To be completed ONLY by schools that checked the box on line 6 in Part IV)

		Yes	No
29	Does the organization have a racially nondiscriminatory policy toward students by statement in its charter, bylaws, other governing instrument, or in a resolution of its governing body?		
30	Does the organization include a statement of its racially nondiscriminatory policy toward students in all its brochures, catalogues, and other written communications with the public dealing with student admissions, programs, and scholarships?		
31	Has the organization publicized its racially nondiscriminatory policy through newspaper or broadcast media during the period of solicitation for students, or during the registration period if it has no solicitation program, in a way that makes the policy known to all parts of the general community it serves?		

If "Yes," please describe; if "No," please explain. (If you need more space, attach a separate statement.)

_____

32 Does the organization maintain the following:
a Records indicating the racial composition of the student body, faculty, and administrative staff? — 32a
b Records documenting that scholarships and other financial assistance are awarded on a racially nondiscriminatory basis? — 32b
c Copies of all catalogues, brochures, announcements, and other written communications to the public dealing with student admissions, programs, and scholarships? — 32c
d Copies of all material used by the organization or on its behalf to solicit contributions? — 32d

If you answered "No" to any of the above, please explain. (If you need more space, attach a separate statement.)

_____

33 Does the organization discriminate by race in any way with respect to:
a Students' rights or privileges? — 33a
b Admissions policies? — 33b
c Employment of faculty or administrative staff? — 33c
d Scholarships or other financial assistance? — 33d
e Educational policies? — 33e
f Use of facilities? — 33f
g Athletic programs? — 33g
h Other extracurricular activities? — 33h

If you answered "Yes" to any of the above, please explain. (If you need more space, attach a separate statement.)

_____

34a Does the organization receive any financial aid or assistance from a governmental agency? — 34a
b Has the organization's right to such aid ever been revoked or suspended? — 34b
If you answered "Yes" to either 34a or b, please explain using an attached statement.

35 Does the organization certify that it has complied with the applicable requirements of sections 4.01 through 4.05 of Rev. Proc. 75-50, 1975-2 C.B. 587, covering racial nondiscrimination? If "No," attach an explanation — 35

Figure B-2. *Continued*

Schedule A (Form 990 or 990-EZ) 2004

Part VI-A Lobbying Expenditures by Electing Public Charities (See page 9 of the instructions.)
(To be completed **ONLY** by an eligible organization that filed Form 5768)

Check ▶ **a** ☐ if the organization belongs to an affiliated group. Check ▶ **b** ☐ if you checked "a" and "limited control" provisions apply.

Limits on Lobbying Expenditures (The term "expenditures" means amounts paid or incurred.)		(a) Affiliated group totals	(b) To be completed for ALL electing organizations
36	Total lobbying expenditures to influence public opinion (grassroots lobbying)	36	
37	Total lobbying expenditures to influence a legislative body (direct lobbying).	37	
38	Total lobbying expenditures (add lines 36 and 37)	38	
39	Other exempt purpose expenditures	39	
40	Total exempt purpose expenditures (add lines 38 and 39)		
41	Lobbying nontaxable amount. Enter the amount from the following table—		

41 Lobbying nontaxable amount. Enter the amount from the following table—

If the amount on line 40 is—	**The lobbying nontaxable amount is—**
Not over $500,000	20% of the amount on line 40 . .
Over $500,000 but not over $1,000,000 .	$100,000 plus 15% of the excess over $500,000
Over $1,000,000 but not over $1,500,000 .	$175,000 plus 10% of the excess over $1,000,000
Over $1,500,000 but not over $17,000,000.	$225,000 plus 5% of the excess over $1,500,000
Over $17,000,000	$1,000,000 . . . .

42	Grassroots nontaxable amount (enter 25% of line 41). . . . . .
43	Subtract line 42 from line 36. Enter -0- if line 42 is more than line 36. . .
44	Subtract line 41 from line 38. Enter -0- if line 41 is more than line 38. . . .

> Complete Part VI-A if the organization has made the §501(h) election. Other organizations should complete Part VI-B. Mark the inapplicable part "N/A".
>
> If lobbying activities are reported in Part VI-B, attach an explanation of each activity.

Caution: *If there is an amount on either line 43 or line 44, you must file Form 4720.*

4-Year Averaging Period Under Section 501(h)
(Some organizations that made a section 501(h) election do not have to complete all of the five columns below.
See the instructions for lines 45 through 50 on page 11 of the instructions.)

		Lobbying Expenditures During 4-Year Averaging Period				
Calendar year (or fiscal year beginning in) ▶		(a) 2004	(b) 2003	(c) 2002	(d) 2001	(e) Total
45	Lobbying nontaxable amount					
46	Lobbying ceiling amount (150% of line 45(e))					
47	Total lobbying expenditures					
48	Grassroots nontaxable amount					
49	Grassroots ceiling amount (150% of line 48(e))					
50	Grassroots lobbying expenditures					

Part VI-B Lobbying Activity by Nonelecting Public Charities
(For reporting only by organizations that did not complete Part VI-A) (See page 11 of the instructions.)

During the year, did the organization attempt to influence national, state or local legislation, including any attempt to influence public opinion on a legislative matter or referendum, through the use of:

		Yes	No	Amount
a	Volunteers			
b	Paid staff or management (Include compensation in expenses reported on lines **c** through **h.**) . . .			
c	Media advertisements.			
d	Mailings to members, legislators, or the public			
e	Publications, or published or broadcast statements			
f	Grants to other organizations for lobbying purposes			
g	Direct contact with legislators, their staffs, government officials, or a legislative body. . . .			
h	Rallies, demonstrations, seminars, conventions, speeches, lectures, or any other means . . .			
i	Total lobbying expenditures (Add lines **c** through **h.**)			

If "Yes" to any of the above, also attach a statement giving a detailed description of the lobbying activities.

Schedule A (Form 990 or 990-EZ) 2004

Figure B-2. *Continued*

| **Part VII** | **Information Regarding Transfers To and Transactions and Relationships With Noncharitable Exempt Organizations** (See page 11 of the instructions.) |

51 Did the reporting organization directly or indirectly engage in any of the following with any other organization described in section 501(c) of the Code (other than section 501(c)(3) organizations) or in section 527, relating to political organizations?

		Yes	No
a	Transfers from the reporting organization to a noncharitable exempt organization of:		
(i)	Cash . . . . **51a(i)**		
(ii)	Other assets . . . . **a(ii)**		
b	Other transactions:		
(i)	Sales or exchanges of assets with a noncharitable exempt organization . . . . **b(i)**		
(ii)	Purchases of assets from a noncharitable exempt organization . . . . **b(ii)**		
(iii)	Rental of facilities, equipment, or other assets . . . . **b(iii)**		
(iv)	Reimbursement arrangements . . . . **b(iv)**		
(v)	Loans or loan guarantees . . . . **b(v)**		
(vi)	Performance of services or membership or fundraising solicitations . . . . **b(vi)**		
c	Sharing of facilities, equipment, mailing lists, other assets, or paid employees . . . . **c**		

d If the answer to any of the above is "Yes," complete the following schedule. Column (b) should always show the fair market value of the goods, other assets, or services given by the reporting organization. If the organization received less than fair market value in any transaction or sharing arrangement, show in column (d) the value of the goods, other assets, or services received:

(a) Line no.	(b) Amount involved	(c) Name of noncharitable exempt organization	(d) Description of transfers, transactions, and sharing arrangements

52a Is the organization directly or indirectly affiliated with, or related to, one or more tax-exempt organizations described in section 501(c) of the Code (other than section 501(c)(3)) or in section 527? . . . . ▶ ☐ Yes ☐ No

b If "Yes," complete the following schedule:

(a) Name of organization	(b) Type of organization	(c) Description of relationship

Schedule A (Form 990 or 990-EZ) 2004

Figure B-3. Annotated Form 990, Schedule B

Schedule B
(Form 990, 990-EZ, or 990-PF)
Department of the Treasury
Internal Revenue Service

Schedule of Contributors

Supplementary Information for line 1 of Form 990, 990-EZ, and 990-PF (see instructions)

OMB No. 1545-0047

2004

Name of organization | **Employer identification number**

Organization type (check one):

Filers of:	**Section:**
Form 990 or 990-EZ	☐ 501(c)( ) (enter number) organization
	☐ 4947(a)(1) nonexempt charitable trust **not** treated as a private fo
	☐ 527 political organization
Form 990-PF	☐ 501(c)(3) exempt private foundation
	☐ 4947(a)(1) nonexempt charitable trust treated as a private founda
	☐ 501(c)(3) taxable private foundation

Note special rule for organizations that meet 33 1/3% support test. Only persons who contributed the greater of $5,000 or 2% of total contributions need to be reported.

Check if your organization is covered by the **General Rule** or a **Special Rule.** (**Note:** *Only a section 501(c)(7), (8), or (10) organization can check boxes for both the General Rule and a Special Rule—see instructions.*)

General Rule—

☐ For organizations filing Form 990, 990-EZ, or 990-PF that received, during the year, $5,000 or more (in money or property) from any one contributor. (Complete Parts I and II.)

Special Rules—

☐ For a section 501(c)(3) organization filing Form 990, or Form 990-EZ, that met the 33⅓% support test of the regulations under sections 509(a)(1)/170(b)(1)(A)(vi) and received from any one contributor, during the year, a contribution of the greater of $5,000 or 2% of the amount on line 1 of these forms. (Complete Parts I and II.)

☐ For a section 501(c)(7), (8), or (10) organization filing Form 990, or Form 990-EZ, that received from any one contributor, during the year, aggregate contributions or bequests of more than $1,000 for use *exclusively* for religious, charitable, scientific, literary, or educational purposes, or the prevention of cruelty to children or animals. (Complete Parts I, II, and III.)

☐ For a section 501(c)(7), (8), or (10) organization filing Form 990, or Form 990-EZ, that received from any one contributor, during the year, some contributions for use *exclusively* for religious, charitable, etc., purposes, but these contributions did not aggregate to more than $1,000. (If this box is checked, enter here the total contributions that were received during the year for an *exclusively* religious, charitable, etc., purpose. Do not complete any of the Parts unless the **General Rule** applies to this organization because it received nonexclusively religious, charitable, etc., contributions of $5,000 or more during the year.) . . . . ▶ $ ________

Caution: *Organizations that are not covered by the General Rule and/or the Special Rules do not file Schedule B (Form 990, 990-EZ, or 990-PF), but they* ***must*** *check the box in the heading of their Form 990, Form 990-EZ, or on line 2 of their Form 990-PF, to certify that they do not meet the filing requirements of Schedule B (Form 990, 990-EZ, or 990-PF).*

For Paperwork Reduction Act Notice, see the Instructions for Form 990, Form 990-EZ, and Form 990-PF. Cat. No. 30613X **Schedule B (Form 990, 990-EZ, or 990-PF) (2004)**

Figure B-3. *Continued*

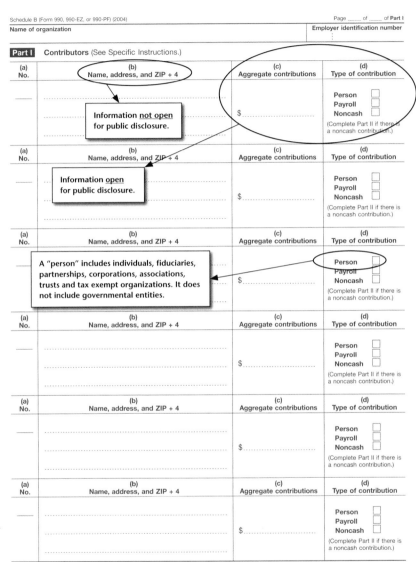

Figure B-3. *Continued*

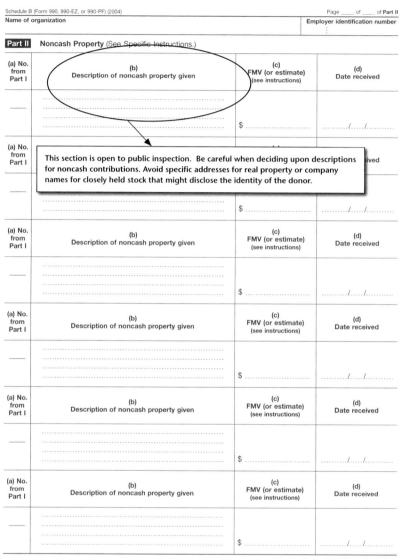

Schedule B (Form 990, 990-EZ, or 990-PF) (2004) Page ____ of ____ of **Part II**

Name of organization	Employer identification number

Part II **Noncash Property** (See ~~Specific Instructions~~.)

(a) No. from Part I	(b) Description of noncash property given	(c) FMV (or estimate) (see instructions)	(d) Date received
____		$	/ /

This section is open to public inspection. Be careful when deciding upon descriptions for noncash contributions. Avoid specific addresses for real property or company names for closely held stock that might disclose the identity of the donor.

(a) No. from Part I			ived
____		$	/ /

(a) No. from Part I	(b) Description of noncash property given	(c) FMV (or estimate) (see instructions)	(d) Date received
____		$	/ /

(a) No. from Part I	(b) Description of noncash property given	(c) FMV (or estimate) (see instructions)	(d) Date received
____		$	/ /

(a) No. from Part I	(b) Description of noncash property given	(c) FMV (or estimate) (see instructions)	(d) Date received
____		$	/ /

(a) No. from Part I	(b) Description of noncash property given	(c) FMV (or estimate) (see instructions)	(d) Date received
____		$	/ /

Schedule B (Form 990, 990-EZ, or 990-PF) (2004)

Figure B-3. *Continued*

Schedule B (Form 990, 990-EZ, or 990-PF) (2004)   Page ____ of ____ of **Part III**

Name of organization | Employer identification number

Part III | *Exclusively* religious, charitable, etc., individual contributions to section 501(c)(7), (8), or (10) organizations aggregating more than $1,000 for the year. (Complete columns **(a)** through **(e)** and the following line entry.)

For organizations completing Part III, enter the total of *exclusively* religious, charitable, etc., contributions of **$1,000 or less** for the year. (Enter this information once—see instructions.) ▶ $

(a) No. from Part I	(b) Purpose of gift	(c) Use of gift	(d) Description of how gift is held

(e) Transfer of gift

Transferee's name, address, and ZIP + 4	Relationship of transferor to transferee

Schedule B (Form 990, 990-EZ, or 990-PF) (2004)

Appendix | C

Changes to Nonprofit Accounting Rules

When the FASB assumed responsibility for setting accounting rules from the AICPA Accounting Principles Board in 1973, there were no formal accounting principles for nonprofit organizations. In 1977, the FASB announced it was considering a "conceptual framework policy statement" for nonprofit organizations. That statement was published in 1985. However, until 1993, nonprofits operated under fairly loose definitions and used many of the same accounting practices as local governments.

SFAS 116 and 117

In 1993, the FASB released two bombshells, SFAS 116 and 117. These had the net effect of making nonprofit financial statements more uniform and accurate, but at the same time harder for the non-accountant to read and understand. Three changes in particular have been difficult for many nonfinancial, nonprofit managers and board members, and have created extra work for financial staff.

1. SFAS Statement 116 required that pledges be recorded as income and that multiyear pledges and grants be reported as income in the year the pledge was made, even if the cash is received in later years.[31] This requirement can make an organization look like it has lots of net assets, when in fact it has only pledges—a situation that can be confusing for potential donors and for board members.

2. SFAS 117 ended the practice of fund accounting, thereby requiring entirely new formats that readers of nonprofit financial statements must learn.

---

[31] This was a response to some large institutions, such as hospitals and universities, that did not show pledges received when they were conducting capital campaigns, thus making it look like they still needed large gifts, when in fact they had already met their goals in pledges.

3. SFAS 117 codified reporting of restricted income and created the principle that restricted income or assets become unrestricted once the restrictions have been met, so that no restrictions are shown in expenses. This makes it difficult to show the connection between restricted funding and the programs it pays for.

SFAS 136, 124, and 93

There are several other changes, also shown in Figure C-1. Note that these are for formal GAAP financial statements and may be handled differently for internal reporting, where some nonprofits still use fund accounting and show future years' pledges separately from the current year's income. Figure C-1 shows all these changes in the order of their impact on nonprofit accounting practices.

Figure C-1. SFAS Statements Before and After Rule Changes

SFAS 117 (Took effect 1995)	
BEFORE	**AFTER**
Terminology: • Balance Sheet • Statement of Support, Revenue and Expense • Fund Balance	*Terminology:* • Statement of Financial Position • Statement of Activities • Net Assets
Required Statements: • Balance Sheet • Statement of Support, Revenue and Expense	*Required Statements:* • Statement of Financial Position • Statement of Activities • Statement of Cash Flows • Statement of Functional Expenses (for health and welfare organizations)
Fund Accounting: • Many nonprofits maintained complete sets of accounts for several funds (unrestricted, one or more restricted funds, capital, plant and equipment, and endowment). Governments still use this method.	*Functional Expenses:* • Reporting is for "entity as a whole" rather than separate fund groups. • Requires functional categories: Program Services, Management, Fundraising, Membership (if applicable).

Reporting Restrictions:
• Reporting of donor restrictions was not required, and was handled differently by different organizations.
	Reporting Restrictions:
	• Requires classification of contributions, revenues, and net assets based on donor-imposed restrictions:
	  – Permanently restricted
	  – Temporarily restricted
	  – Unrestricted.
	• Board-imposed restrictions are classified as unrestricted, disclosed in notes.

Reporting Expenses: • Expenses were reported by "natural" categories (i.e., salaries, rent, etc.). • Expenses of restricted funds were sometimes shown under expenses.	*Reporting Expenses:* • Expenses are reported by functional categories (programs, management and general, and fundraising) rather than by natural categories. • Expenses are reported in the unrestricted column even though the source of the funds may have been restricted. Restricted funds become unrestricted income when restrictions are met, and there are no restricted expenses.

Figure C-1. *Continued*

SFAS 117 (Took effect 1995)	
BEFORE	**AFTER**
Reporting Capital Gains: • Capital gains were handled differently, often kept on books at cost.	*Reporting Capital Gains:* • All capital gains and losses on investments and other assets are reported in the unrestricted category (unless donor or state law requires otherwise).

SFAS 116 (Took effect 1995)	
BEFORE	**AFTER**
Recording Pledges: • Many nonprofits only recorded pledges when cash was received.	*Recording Pledges:* • Requires that contributions, including promises to give (pledges), be recognized as revenues in the period received at fair market value.
Contributions with Conditions: • There were no specific rules for contributions with conditions.	*Contributions with Conditions:* • Contributions with a donor-imposed *condition*, such as a matching requirement, are not recognized until the condition has been met.
Contributions with Restrictions: • Many nonprofits listed restricted contributions of multiyear grants as "deferred revenue" on the Statement of Financial Position.	*Contributions with Restrictions:* • Contributions with a donor-imposed *restriction*, such as being restricted for a specific operating purpose or a future period, are recorded immediately as income even though the donor restrictions may have not been met.
Multiyear Grants: • Many nonprofits listed future years of multiyear grants as "deferred revenue" on the Statement of Financial Position.	*Multiyear Grants:* • Grants are treated the same as restricted contributions (above) and the entire amount recorded as income in the year the grant is awarded. • There is no liability to the future grant, so they are not listed as deferred revenue.
Contributions Defined: • Contributions were loosely defined, so that (for example) tickets to a fundraising dinner were sometimes treated as totally tax deductible, rather than subtracting the cost of the meal.	*Contributions Defined:* • Contributions are defined as being an "unconditional, nonreciprocal transfer of assets." This means the donor should not be receiving anything of value back; otherwise, the contribution is either only part contribution and part fee for service or possibly not a contribution at all.

In-Kind Contributions:
• The criteria for recognizing contributed services were less defined and restrictive.
	In-Kind Contributions:
	• Contributed services are only recognized if they:
	  1. Create or enhance nonfinancial assets
	  2. Require specialized skills (generally a "professional"), and
	  3. Would typically be purchased if not donated.

Art Collections: • There were no specific rules for capitalizing collections.	*Art Collections:* • Contributions of works of art, historical treasures, and similar assets need not be recognized as revenues and capitalized if the donated items are added to collections held for public exhibition, education, or research.

Figure C-1. *Continued*

Other FASB Statements Affecting Nonprofits

| SFAS 136 (Took effect 1999) ||
BEFORE	AFTER
• There were no specific reporting standards for transactions when one nonprofit accepts donations on behalf of another entity.	• This statement establishes reporting standards for transactions when one nonprofit accepts donations on behalf of another entity. Unless your organization is involved in such an arrangement, you don't have to know about this.

| SFAS 124 (Took effect 1995) ||
BEFORE	AFTER
• Many nonprofits previously didn't report capital gains and losses, but carried assets at cost. • In late 1960s, many nonprofits started moving their endowment from fixed-income bonds into the more profitable but more volatile stock market.	• This statement requires that investments in equity securities (stocks) with readily determinable fair values and all investments in debt securities (bonds) be reported at fair value with gains and losses included in the Statement of Activities.

| SFAS 93 (Took effect 1988) ||
BEFORE	AFTER
• Many nonprofits did not recognize depreciation, regarding it as tax-related accounting that didn't apply to tax-exempt organizations.	• This statement requires nonprofit organizations to show depreciation of "long-term physical assets" such as buildings or equipment. • It makes an exception for collections of works of art, for example.

Consolidated Internal Revenue Code for 501(c)(3) Tax Exemption

Nonprofit organizations operate under the rules of the Internal Revenue Code, which determine their tax-exempt status, allowable activities, and grant eligibility. Yet most nonprofit managers and grant professionals don't know exactly what the code actually says. This is understandable, because the rules aren't laid out in one single place and are often defined by omission or comparison with other entities. Congress didn't set out to create nonprofit tax exemption; it just emerged as the tax laws were being written.

What does the Internal Revenue Code actually say about tax-exempt status? For reference purposes, here are all of the major sections of the IRC governing nonprofit organizations that are tax exempt under section 501(c)(3).

501(c)(3): Tax exemption

U.S. Code; Title 26 (Internal Revenue Code), Subtitle A (Income taxes), Chapter 1 (Normal taxes), Subchapter F (Exempt organizations), Part I (General Rule), § 501 (Exemption from taxation), c (list of exempt organizations).

§ 501. Exemption from tax on corporations, certain trusts, etc.

(a) Exemption from taxation. An organization described in subsection (c) or (d) or section 401 (a) shall be exempt from taxation under this subtitle unless such exemption is denied under section 502 or 503.

(b) Tax on unrelated business income and certain other activities. An organization exempt from taxation under subsection (a) shall be subject to tax to the extent provided in parts II, III, and VI of this subchapter, but (notwithstanding parts II, III, and VI of this subchapter) shall be considered an organization exempt from income taxes for the purpose of any law which refers to organizations exempt from income taxes.

(c) List of exempt organizations. The following organizations are referred to in subsection (a):

(3) Corporations, and any community chest, fund, or foundation, organized and operated exclusively for religious, charitable, scientific, testing for public safety, literary, or educational purposes, or to foster national or international amateur sports competition (but only if no part of its activities involve the provision of athletic facilities or equipment), or for the prevention of cruelty to children or animals, no part of the net earnings of which inures to the benefit of any private shareholder or individual, no substantial part of the activities of which is carrying on propaganda, or otherwise attempting, to influence legislation (except as otherwise provided in subsection (h)), and which does not participate in, or intervene in (including the publishing or distributing of statements), any political campaign on behalf of (or in opposition to) any candidate for public office.

170. (b) More definitions of tax exempt organizations:
U.S. Code; Title 26 (Internal Revenue Code), Subtitle A (Income taxes), Chapter 1 (Normal taxes), Subchapter B (Computation of Taxable income), Part VI (Itemized deductions for individual and corporations), § 170 (Charitable, etc. contributions and gifts), a (General rule)

§ 170. Charitable, etc., contributions and gifts
(b) Percentage limitations
(1) Individuals
In the case of an individual, the deduction provided in subsection (a) shall be limited as provided in the succeeding subparagraphs.

(A) **General rule** Any charitable contribution to—

(i) a church or a convention or association of churches,

(ii) an educational organization which normally maintains a regular faculty and curriculum and normally has a regularly enrolled body of pupils or students in attendance at the place where its educational activities are regularly carried on,

(iii) an organization the principal purpose or functions of which are the providing of medical or hospital care or medical education or medical research, if the organization is a hospital, or if the organization is a medical research organization directly engaged in the continuous active conduct of medical research in conjunction with a hospital, and during the calendar year in which the contribution is made such organization is committed to spend such contributions for such research before January 1 of the fifth calendar year which begins after the date such contribution is made,

(iv) an organization which normally receives a substantial part of its support (exclusive of income received in the exercise or performance by such organization of its charitable, educational, or other purpose or function constituting the basis for its exemption under section 501 (a)) from the United States or any State or political subdivision thereof or from direct or indirect contributions from the general public, and which is organized and operated exclusively to receive, hold, invest, and administer property and to make expenditures to or for the benefit of a college or university which is an organization referred to in clause (ii) of this subparagraph and which is an agency or instrumentality of a State or political subdivision thereof, or which is owned or operated by a State or political subdivision thereof or by an agency or instrumentality of one or more States or political subdivisions,

(v) a governmental unit referred to in subsection (c)(1),

(vi) an organization referred to in subsection (c)(2) which normally receives a substantial part of its support (exclusive of income received in the exercise or performance by such organization of its charitable, educational, or other purpose or function constituting the basis for its exemption under section 501 (a)) from a governmental unit referred to in subsection (c)(1) or from direct or indirect contributions from the general public,

(c) Charitable contribution defined

For purposes of this section, the term "charitable contribution" means a contribution or gift to or for the use of—

(1) A State, a possession of the United States, or any political subdivision of any of the foregoing, or the United States or the District of Columbia, but only if the contribution or gift is made for exclusively public purposes.

(2) A corporation, trust, or community chest, fund, or foundation—

(A) created or organized in the United States or in any possession thereof, or under the law of the United States, any State, the District of Columbia, or any possession of the United States;

(B) organized and operated exclusively for religious, charitable, scientific, literary, or educational purposes, or to foster national or international amateur sports competition (but only if no part of its activities involve the provision of athletic facilities or equipment), or for the prevention of cruelty to children or animals;

(C) no part of the net earnings of which inures to the benefit of any private shareholder or individual; and

(D) which is not disqualified for tax exemption under section 501 (c)(3) by reason of attempting to influence legislation, and which does not participate in, or intervene in (including the publishing or distributing of statements), any political campaign on behalf of (or in opposition to) any candidate for public office.

509 (a) "Not a private foundation" and definitions of Publicly Supported Organizations (PSOs) and Fee/Activity Supported Organizations (FASOs)

U.S. Code; Title 26 (Internal Revenue Code), Subtitle A (Income taxes), Chapter 1 (Normal taxes), Subchapter F (Exempt organizations), Part II (Private Foundations), § 509 (Private Foundation defined), a (General rule)

§ 509. Private foundation defined

(a) General rule For purposes of this title, the term "private foundation" means a domestic or foreign organization described in section 501 (c)(3) other than—

(1) an organization described in section 170(b)(1)(A) (other than in clauses (vii) and (viii));

(2) an organization which—

(A) normally receives more than one-third of its support in each taxable year from any combination of—

(i) gifts, grants, contributions, or membership fees, and
(ii) gross receipts from admissions, sales of merchandise, performance of services, or furnishing of facilities, in an activity which is not an unrelated trade or business (within the meaning of section 513), not including such receipts from any person, or from any bureau or similar agency of a governmental unit (as described in section 170(c)(1)), in any taxable year to the extent such receipts exceed the greater of $5,000 or 1 percent of the organization's support in such taxable year, from persons other than disqualified persons (as defined in section 4946) with respect to the organization, from governmental units described in section 170(c)(1), or from organizations described in section 170(b)(1)(A) (other than in clauses (vii) and (viii)), and

(B) normally receives not more than one-third of its support in each taxable year from the sum of—

(i) gross investment income (as defined in subsection (e)) and
(ii) the excess (if any) of the amount of the unrelated business taxable income (as defined in section 512) over the amount of the tax imposed by section 511;

(3) an organization which—

(A) is organized, and at all times thereafter is operated, exclusively for the benefit of, to perform the functions of, or to carry out the purposes of one or more specified organizations described in paragraph (1) or (2),
(B) is operated, supervised, or controlled by or in connection with one or more organizations described in paragraph (1) or (2), and
(C) is not controlled directly or indirectly by one or more disqualified persons (as defined in section 4946) other than foundation managers and other than one or more organizations described in paragraph (1) or (2);

(NOTE: This last section 3 defines "supporting organizations.")

Index

About the Author

Michael Wells has been working with nonprofits for over 30 years as staff, volunteer, board member, and consultant. In the early 1980s, he realized that he "had been working with all of these people in nonprofits who wanted to do good in the world and not spend all of their time thinking about money. But they spent all of their time thinking about money." He got a job as a development director to learn how to raise funds, and after a couple of development staff positions, began consulting on grants in 1987.

Michael has worked with dozens of nonprofit agencies, health clinics, Native American tribes, school districts, and local governments, and has helped them raise over $50 million. His background in all aspects of nonprofit management gives him a broad perspective of organizational needs. His stints in the business world as a journalist and salesman help him recognize differences and similarities in the sectors. He likes grantwriting because it combines the opportunity to do good in the world with the chance to learn about a wide variety of subjects: "I get to develop all of these wonderful projects and get them funded, but I don't have to run them."

Michael is a partner in the consulting firm Grants Northwest. He is a Certified Fund Raising Executive (CFRE) and has a master's degree in humanities. He is a faculty member at Portland State University, where he teaches grantwriting. He is editor of the online Charity Channel *Grants and Foundation Review* and a national board member of the Grant Professionals Certification Institute (GPCI). He lives with his wonderful wife Julie in Portland, Oregon. He has three grown daughters and three grandchildren.

Coming in Spring 2007

Evaluation for Grantwriters

Evaluation for Grantwriters, the next book in the Grantwriting Beyond the Basics series, is due in Spring 2007. Most funders today ask for some sort of evaluation of your grant project, and government agencies and national foundations are requiring increasingly sophisticated evaluation techniques. This book will cover the field from the most basic small grant evaluation to full-blown research projects. Areas covered will include:

- The benefits to your organization of good evaluation.

- Determining the right kind of evaluation for your grant.

- The tension between direct service staff and evaluators.

- Writing evaluate-able goals and objectives.

- Effective presentation of charts and tables in your grant proposals.

- Understanding best practices, evidence-based practices, and promising practices.

- Establishing baselines for evaluation.

- Evaluation, continuous quality improvement (CQI), and quality assurance (QA).

- Using logic models in grants and for evaluation.

- Quantitative vs. qualitative methods in evaluation.

- When to use outside evaluators, how to choose them, and when to involve them.

- What you need to know about statistics.

- Using control groups or comparison groups in direct service organizations.

- Data collection: agency records, field data, focus groups and surveys, trained observers, pre- and post-testing, and more.